Searching the Ruins

A memoir

I.B. Hunger

I. B. Hunger 10-19-2015

Authors Note: Some names in this work have been changed. Any resemblance to living persons is purely coincidental.

Searching the Ruins: Growing up in WWII Germany/I.B. Hunger – 1st edition

Summary: I.B. Hunger lived with her family less than 30 miles from Dresden, Germany when WWII changed their lives forever. Fleeing East Germany in a cattle car, surviving a refugee camp, and discovering a strange country led to her heartache as her family broke under the stress of war-torn Germany. Her memoir catches a rarely told story – how a child discovers her own path in pre- and post-war Germany.

Copyright © 2014 Manuela I.B. Hunger
Cover Design: Barbara Fletcher-Brink O'Connor
Photo by: Manuela Hunger Stafford

Krone Publishing Company – New Braunfels, Texas
All Rights Reserved

ISBN - 13:9781484949702
ISBN - 10:1484949706
Library of Congress Control Number – 2014900391

[1. WWII – Memoir. 2. German families – Memoir.]

TO MY OMI

**THIS MAP IS AN APPROXIMATION WITH THE
BORDERS OF POST WORLD WAR II GERMANY**

The German map seen on the opposite page is an approximation with towns and cities added to help the reader. The map shown represents Germany's size after 1945 and Silesia as now being Poland.

Germany is in the center of Europe, facing the North Sea, Denmark and the Baltic Sea to the north; Poland and the Czech Republic to the east; Austria and Switzerland to the south and France, Luxembourg, Belgium and the Netherlands to the west. Germany borders more European countries than any other country. From the end of WWII until 1990 Germany was divided into West and East Germany. The West was allied with NATO and was a part of the European Union. East Germany was dominated by the Soviet Union and was a part of the Warsaw Pact. Germany has the largest economy and second largest population in Europe.

Because I used many words from my language of origin, I have included a Glossary at the end of the book for the reader's convenience.

Growing up in Germany

Welcome to a different world, WWII Germany, where I grew up. As an ordinary girl, I lived during unusual times with unusual people.

My first name, Manuela, was deemed un-German in the thirties and raised concerns. My parents insisted on Manuela as a Christian name for their firstborn. They wanted to honor a friend in Spain. My name includes two initials I. B. My father, Vati, named Joachim, my mother, Mutti, named Hedi, decided to name me after two beloved elders; one was my paternal grandmother, My Omi Ilse which you will meet. The other one was Bettina, my mother's grandmother who died before 1938.

My early life's story will start by introducing my extended family. It will tell you about various little trips Mutti and Vati took to avoid the war and at the same time live close to my paternal grandparents, Omi and Opa. You may be surprised to learn that the German upper class still enjoyed a late nineteen century life style which was to crumble within a few years. In the end, all privileges were lost and possessions stolen. I saw my family ripped apart, struggling not to lose hope. My parents forged their niche in a new world order. As a little girl I could not relate to the unfolding history of the time. I felt that I needed to remind the reader of events during those years in order to bring my story to life. The reader can judge how a youngster could make sense of much chaos and instability.

Sincerely yours,
Manuela I.B. Hunger

Forbidden Marriage

Dresden before WWII was an exciting city with theatres, concerts, dress shops, and the latest French fashion. Marie Teichmann, a well-to-do relative of my father, lived there. Everybody remotely related to her was welcome to stay in the widow's large house.

Mutti worked for Frau Teichmann. She did light household duties and accompanied Mrs. Teichmann on outings. In fact, she was like the daughter Marie never had.

Mutti's father, my grandfather Körber, objected when his daughter left her home in Magdeburg. After high school graduation, she packed a few belongings and went to Dresden, partially to avoid her disagreeable stepmother and what she believed were unreasonable household duties, such as scrubbing kitchen floors and cleaning toilets. Through personal recommendations, Mutti found work with Mrs. Teichmann.

Heinrich Körber never forgave his daughter for leaving. He could have agreed with her decision to earn money for a home economics teachers' program. However, Heinrich was offended, because she never consulted him. Apparently, Mutti left abruptly and Heinrich couldn't find it in his heart to reconsider his decision. He told his daughter that marrying into money would not bring happiness. But Heinrich was a self-centered and hard-headed man who would not forgive easily. In fact, he waited close to twenty years before he longed for contact with me and my brother.

My mother and father met while she worked for Marie Teichmann. Marie was the aunt of the dashing man who became my father. Marie encouraged the young couple's friendship. But for my father to feel love for a woman of low family standing was difficult. His parents didn't believe that Marie's companion was the right girl for their son. However, Marie loved young Hedi, appreciated her intelligence and ability to easily learn and adopt a new lifestyle. She made it possible for her nephew to see Hedi against the wishes of Opa and Omi. The young couple's courtship was short, less than one year, when they decided to get married.

Vati fell in disfavor when he announced his intentions to marry my mother even though she was outside their social circle. The fact alone that Mutti worked as a maid in the Teichmann household raised suspicion. No girl from the upper classes, either money or aristocracy, would ever work as a domestic help. What distinguished people was usually their different level of education. Mutti was a high school graduate (Gymnasium in Germany) and had a broad education including the arts and one foreign language. She was well-spoken and expressed her opinion about current events discussed in national newspapers or popular books. In the 1930s, people in Germany still held on to a class thinking that discouraged breaking rules. My father's upper class family opposed their son's involvement with a girl whose father ultimately was unwilling to give his daughter a dowry or make some conciliatory gestures. Why bother with unknown folks from Magdeburg which wasn't even located in their home state of Saxony but in Brandenburg. My grandparents couldn't handle these unknown and suspicious factors. What was wrong with a local girl whose parents had their own business or factory?

Before meeting Mutti, Vati had left his stepfather's factory where he had been groomed to be a textile engineer. The outside world looked far more enticing. He studied languages in Paris and was confident he could find a suitable job anywhere. The idea of working for his provincial stepfather didn't hold much interest for him and above all, he didn't want to be controlled by an old-fashioned father. After Vati's western Parisian exposure, he felt disillusioned in following old fashioned ideas of class-thinking and modern business practices that pertained to his family's textile mill.

The young couple made a conciliatory attempt to appease Mutti's father. They went to see him in Magdeburg, but he pouted like an obstinate child. My father followed traditional customs and asked my grandfather, Heinrich Körber, for Mutti's hand. But Heinrich thought his future son-in-law appeared snobbish and self-assured. It was easier for Heinrich to remain stubborn and offended. Needless to say, the young couple's visit lacked happy embraces and well-wishes.

As I grew up, Opa Körber didn't exist and I never heard mention about him other than he married an evil woman after his wife's death and made Mutti's life a living hell while growing up. Whatever transpired while the couple visited in Magdeburg was documented with family photos. Mutti and Vati were shown with other of her relatives in the country which included aunts, uncles, and a few cousins. Everybody smiled; however, Opa was nowhere to be seen.

Spanish Bliss 1936-1938

In June 1936, my parents married at the German consulate in Barcelona. Vati worked for an import-export company, and Mutti was employed as a governess by the same people. Their stay was brief, because my father had to register with the Draft Board in Germany. The Spanish Civil War escalated, and Spain became an unsafe place for foreigners. At the same time Germany, under Hitler's leadership, sent shock waves across the globe. Central Europe, including Italy, became a hornet's nest, and citizens felt powerless so they caused trouble through civil disobedience, such as voicing an opposing opinion and associating with Jews.

Through letters, cards and photos Omi kept and gave me important details. I learned that Mutti and Vati spent happy years in Spain. They enjoyed marital bliss away from their families' initial opposition. They made many friends, and their two salaries afforded them a decent living. One photo I especially cherished showed them, all dressed up sitting at the beach of the Costa Brava.

Mutti had one special girlfriend named Manuela. When my parents had to return to Germany, they lost contact. Mutti thought that Manuela possibly died during the Spanish Civil War. As a tribute, my mother named her first child after her cherished friend, Manuela. I wished I could have learned more about Mutti's friend for I wondered all my life what attributes made Manuela dear to Mutti.

Back to Germany – 1938

The approaching war had the power to force my parents move back to Germany. Several surprises awaited them. Hitler's speeches degrading German Jews upset the couple. My father found new employment in Gelsenkirchen, leading him back to the textile business. Recommendations from his former boss in Barcelona, gave him the opportunity to temporarily take over his brother's fabric shop. Most of their friends had been Jewish, since the textile industry had about 50 percent Jewish ownership. My grandparents always

6

maintained cordial relationships with their competitors, and the specialized industry with many diverse products neither interfered nor cut into their profits.

The main benefit of living in Spain was that my father's family missed him and wanted the couple to come home, regardless of the fact that they initially disapproved of his marriage to my mother. Ilse Wagner, my Omi, wrote letters to her son and new daughter-in-law with encouraging words and repeated invitations. Her communications mended old hurts and the previous hurdles of class differences faded into the past. At least for the Wagner and Hunger families social class distinctions were suddenly perceived as antiquated. But my parents' time in Spain and away from the Wagners had had a positive effect.

When my parents arrived back in Germany, all the family members forged an immediate bond with Mutti. Naturally, it helped that she was a beautiful, poised woman, who moved among the upper class like she was born into it. Omi was especially impressed that her daughter-in-law spoke French, which traditionally was considered chic in the nineteenth century.

In later years, my grandmother called Mutti her special daughter. Neither Omi's daughter Annemarie, nor her step-daughter, Elisabeth had children. Mutti never forgot to thank her mother-in-law for whatever she did for her and her children. Omi appreciated her gratefulness and respectful ways.

Mutti kept her status for a lifetime; nothing would ever break her connection with the Hunger-Wagner family.

Living in Gelsenkirchen – 1938

In September 1938, my parents, Hedi and Joachim

Hunger, arrived at Gelsenkirchen's train station from Barcelona, each carrying two suitcases. The couple was too preoccupied to notice black smokestacks and gray skies, grayer than a normal autumn day in central Germany. Rumbling trains rushed and created a draft that played havoc with Hedi's skirt. She put down her suitcases, and clasped the collar of her jacket.

She breathed in rapid intervals as her husband raced down the platform. She collapsed on a bench nearby and waited for her husband to notice her not following him. He did, and promptly returned to her with a confused look on his face.

"I thought Mr. Lehman would be here to pick us up." She motioned for him to sit down. "I'm sorry, but I'm exhausted already. Do we wait here? I need some help with those suitcases."

"Sorry, darling, I'm not very considerate. I have too many things on my mind. But being pregnant gives you special rights." Joachim stood in front of Hedi watching the platform for Mr. Lehmann.

"He should look exactly like our friend, David, in Barcelona." Joachim smiled at Hedi, "Of course they are twins, remember?"

Hedi nodded. She held her linen jacket close. Its light weight was not suited for fall in Germany. "Not like Spain, Jochen. I don't even remember Germany being so drab and sad." She turned her head toward the overcast sky, her eyes tearing up. Jochen was short for Joachim, and most of the family preferred Jochen.

"Hedi, relax. Things will be all right," her husband consoled. "We are only here in Gelsenkirchen for a short spell." He sighed. "I'm so grateful that David referred me to handle Max's liquidation of his business." Out loud he said, "God knows what we will be faced here, Hedi. "We didn't choose to leave Spain. It's wrong, wrong, wrong… but what's a man to do when he runs away from a civil war in Spain to enter another one in the making." Again, Joachim stretched his neck, noticing that most passengers had left and he could see that the exit was in clear view.

Hedi slowly found her composure and her voice calmed down.

"Darling, I'm thinking about baby furniture your father ordered for us." Mutti's letters sounded so sweet and inviting. Nobody would believe it if we told them how I was once rejected by your family."

"Yes, my parents will go crazy over the first grandchild." With this, Joachim's attention was diverted; he jumped up and down, waving with both his arms. "It's him, Hedi – just like his brother David, the same swaying gait." Joachim helped his wife off the bench and placed a kiss on her forehead, "Come on, sweetheart. All is good now, I promise."

Max Lehman waved in return and rushed closer to greet the Hungers. "Mrs. Hunger, welcome to Gelsenkirchen, the asshole of Germany. Ha, ha," he snickered. "You and Joachim will find your little habitation quite cozy."

"Danke vielmals (thanks a lot)." Hedi was overwhelmed and could say no more.

"Young lady, I arranged a car for you not too many automobiles are available these days. We will be there within fifteen minutes." Then Max turned to Jochen and gave him a hearty handshake, "Willkommen, Mr. Hunger. It seems that we have known each other a long time. My brother mentioned you many times."

Jochen gave Max a broad smile, "Thank you, my

friend, you're so helpful."

Within minutes they reached the street; suitcases lined up and ready to take the ride to the apartment. Hedi fell into the back seat of an old Horch – model 1931. The seat springs pinched her and she uttered, "Oha."

"Ooops, sorry for the antiquity of this vehicle," Max choked. It's time to live in Switzerland, right, Hunger?" He slapped Joachim jovially on his back and pushed him to the other sagging back seat.

After Max and the young couple were seated in the car, there was no space for their luggage. Max noticed the predicament. He hadn't thought out the logistics of this. The chauffeur who drove Max to the station looked frustrated.

Max stepped outside the Horch and suggested, "Would you take their luggage into the station. You will have to drive back later. That would be workable, right?"

Max settled into the front seat, turned and said, "My friends, your luggage will be safe at the station. The driver will fetch it later.

"Fine with us." Joachim said. Hedi attempted a hopeful smile.

Max twisted in his seat. "My brother told me about your circles of friends in Spain and how well you did business with David. He spoke highly of you, Joachim. And you, Mrs. Hedi, took such good care of the youngsters." With a nervous glance out of the car, but windows closed, Max continued. "We have to be careful. Jews are being targeted these days. It's getting worse. I changed my apartment and presently live with my cousin, a Lutheran pastor, believe it or not. All Jews are not practicing their faith. And as far as I'm concerned, I am German first, regardless what religion we believe in."

The driver returned, and the engine started with a roar.

"Where to, Mr. Lehman?" The driver asked as he tipped his chauffeur's cap.

"Toward Stadtgarten…"

"Danke." Anton spoke with a nod toward the rear mirror. "Are you, *Herrschaften* (Ladies and gentlemen) new to Gelsenkirchen?"

"Yes," They echoed from the back. "New it is, and hopefully we'll not be old when we leave this city." Joachim replied sarcastically as his emotions looked for expression.

"Sorry, Joachim, I didn't hear what you said."

"Never mind, Max, it was a slip of the tongue. I'll tell you later after my wife is comfortably settled so we can have our Cognac."

"I accept. We need to catch up on the happenings in Spain." Max straightened the collar of his brown Gabardine jacket.

Joachim admired the fabric. It was the type his father used to make in his factory. He wondered what the remnants in Max's store would look like. Good materials were flying off the shelves. People knew quality, now that everything produced went to the war effort. He hoped the job with Max would hold him over until he braced himself for the unknown.

Both Hedi and Joachim liked their apartment. It was furnished with older but comfortable furniture. A small extra guestroom remained unfurnished, but yellow and white polka dotted curtains suggested a potential nursery.

Jochen and Max sat down holding their glasses of Cognac. Max had also placed a few bottles of Rhein wine and a basket of fragrant apples on the kitchen counter. Three white chrysanthemums adorned a round table where the men sipped their Cognac. Hedi pulled off her linen jacket and retired to the bedroom to freshen up and leave the men to talk.

11

"Listen, Hunger, I'll have my cousin, Pastor Franz, be our go-between. He can handle some of the finances, you understand. Reliable sources warned us about Hitler's next move. We have to run, before it's too late."

"Max, God bless you," My father said sadly. "Please, be assured, we are on your side. I'll take care of your business. Nobody can predict what this Austrian bully is plotting next." My father got up from the couch to hide his tears. After an hour of visiting and planning, Max left.

The men trusted each other. Vati and Mutti had no prejudice and kept mainly Jewish friends while living in Spain. Because they worked in the textile industry, their difficulty was to be accepted by the predominately Catholic society. German Jews and German Protestants became close friends.

Gelsenkirchen had other problems. Over the black and smoky horizon lurked more darkness to come. Time was clicking away, and war was less than one year away. My father had barely taken over the Lehman Company, when Max bid them goodbye.

"Listen, Hunger, I'll have our Pastor Franz as a go-between to handle business matters. He will be in contact, and we will talk through him. Reliable sources tell us about Hitler's next nasty move. We've to run, before it's too late." Max hugged my father, which wasn't too common among stoic German men.

"Max, God bless you." My father repeated. "I'll look after things. Meanwhile, Hedi and I are stuck here. Nobody knows what this Hitler is planning next."

Fortunately, the legal transfer of Lehman's business into an *Aryan* name was timely. On the ninth and tenth of November that year, *Kristallnacht* surprised Germany and the world. SA (*Sturmabteilung*), the assault division of the military and designated civilians, implemented a series of coordinated attacks on Jewish-owned stores, buildings and synagogues. Jewish homes, hospitals, and schools were ransacked as terrified Germans stood behind curtains watching attacks on defenseless, innocent people. There was no declared war yet; however, the burning buildings and broken glass foretold disaster yet to come.

German and Austrian authorities organized these attacks. They claimed it was politically justified by Poland's extradition of 17,000 German-born Jews to Germany. Originally, this was one of the reasons for the escalation of Jewish persecution. But Hitler's regime swiftly took another approach and focused more on improving their financial strength, and so Jewish property was systematically confiscated. More discriminatory laws forbade Jews to work in certain professions or government positions to make way for non-Jews to assume the jobs. Jewish doctors could only treat Jews, and only Aryans were allowed to marry other Aryans.

My father was relieved, yet always on edge concerning the legal transfer of this business. No longer Lehman Bros, it became Hunger GmbH (compared to Inc.) My father feared becoming a suspect of perpetrating a crime against the *Reich*. *Kristallnacht* had changed the atmosphere in doing business in Germany.

The year 1938 was not normal. My parents felt they embarked on a game of Russian roulette when they moved to Gelsenkirchen. My mother was in her last trimester of pregnancy with me when they accepted the new job with Max. It was disconcerting to both of my parents to expect a child in times that teetered between madness and chaos. My mother at

13

twenty-seven was considered old for a first time mother. Vati was not thrilled about having a family, but he reasoned, now or never.

Max Lehman fled to Switzerland six weeks later and entrusted my father with the liquidation of his textile business. Pastor Franz Lehman took his cousin's apartment. Nobody paid attention to the change. When Franz married a Gentile, both went against a new law. As a Lutheran pastor working in the school system, nobody suspected Franz's Jewish heritage. For the moment he was safe; Pastor Lehman looked like any Gentile German.

Young Mrs. Lehman, clever and assertive, was protective of her husband. She urged him to join his relatives in Switzerland as soon as possible. Originally from Mannheim, she had taught elementary school at the same school where she met her husband. They were respected and well liked.

It was December 1938, and another happy season rolled around. The first Advent of the traditional Christmas celebrations began. Paradoxically, this happy season came with candle lighting on fresh pine wreaths on every household's dining table, while Hitler commenced his saber rattling. The citizens continued preparing in their familiar ways and added an additional red candle every Sunday until the fourth was lit, on the Sunday before December 24th. They awaited the birth of Christ, and every German Protestant or Catholic prepared for Christmas in the same manner.

However, Pastor Lehman and wife didn't join in any Christmas joy that year. Instead, they took advantage of the school's Christmas vacation and disappeared via Mannheim to Switzerland. Mrs. Lehman had prudently prepared to store all her household goods with relatives in Mannheim. They came by to bid my parents farewell and exchanged important addresses. The Lehmans and the Hungers hugged, wished each other God's speed. The pastor gave his farewell blessings. In parting they expressed their hope to meet again someday, somewhere.

About Gelsenkirchen

Gelsenkirchen was located east of Düsseldorf in western Germany and in the middle of the so-called Ruhr-Pot. This region of the state of Westphalia was rich in coal reserves and thus developed a heavy industry. Since about 1840, with the Industrial Revolution sweeping through Europe, energy demands increased. During this era, Gelsenkirchen grew from an insignificant village into one of the most important industrial cities in Germany. *The Reich's* hunger for more energy and more steel production kept the city on the map.

Especially then, months before the war broke out, Gelsenkirchen's industrial production increased. More energy was needed to forge iron, build tanks and guns, and mine more of this German "Black Gold," which became an essential part of cranking up the war machine even further. Gray skies daily, winter had reached the northern part of Westphalia with plenty of chilly moisture in the air that was mixed with toxic pollution of many unpronounceable chemicals. In spite of this unhealthy environment in the *Ruhr-Pot*, people flocked there, for it offered plenty of commerce and employment. The newcomers to Gelsenkirchen unwittingly contributed to an approaching war. They were just relieved to have new employment after the lean years of post-WWI. The irony was that the intent of the Versailles Treaty of 1918 was to end all wars, but instead it created hardships with insurmountable war reparation payments that Germany failed to make.

This was my parents' world. They settled into their small apartment in Gelsenkirchen, prepared for the arrival of their first child and waited for things to come. All of their friends were gone, they fled the Hitler regime. In addition to his worries, Vati also expected to hear from the Draft Board soon, and was naturally concerned how he would be able to continue the new business, if he were drafted. One day at a time, he thought.

But in the end, Vati got his wish of not growing old in Gelsenkirchen after all.

Gelsenkirchen proved to be an ugly city in many ways. The place was chosen to become another site for a sub camp to Buchenwald. Many such lower security concentration camps were scattered all over the industrialized area housing prisoners for forced labor. Gelsenkirchen, I learned, was used for female prisoners in munitions factories, and when the Allies bombed the city, all these women lost their lives. Not only Jews, but also other political and religious dissidents, which included "undesirable" foreigners of Slavic backgrounds that had been locked away.

The Birth of a Girl: December 1938

Regardless of uncertain times, my grandparents still observed family events in style. Such was the case on December 4, 1938 when their daughter, Elisabeth celebrated her engagement to Karl Goerner. Two prominent families joined their children in matrimony. Maids rushed about with dessert and Champagne glasses as people talked all at the same time, wishing the young couple the very best.

Is everything fine, Mutti?" Opa always called his wife, Mutti. Omi had answered the phone outside the dining room and returned to the gathering of guests. Everyone wanted to know why she was so excited.

"We have our first grandchild, a little girl, Manuela." Omi announced. "Let us drink to the child and all the happiness ahead." Aunt Elisabeth told me many times that my birth announcement had changed the focus of her engagement party. She was my favorite aunt, and for a long time I didn't comprehend our relationship was by marriage only. I couldn't have loved her more if we'd shared the same lineage.

And so I, Manuela, was born into this ugly city of Gelsenkirchen on the first Advent Sunday in December. All I knew about the city was its name in my birth certificate and passport and how much Vati and Mutti hated that place. It must have transferred over to me, because I never felt the urge to go back and see Gelsenkirchen for myself.

How lucky for me that I was born at all, but God allowed me to see the gloomy sky of Gelsenkirchen without leaving any memory. He delivered me into a rapidly changing world. Peace one day, war the next, privileged today and adrift tomorrow. My family life would turn into a wild rollercoaster ride.

Before my name could be registered, it needed to be researched by the authorities. Germany's rules determined that if an uncommon name wasn't listed in the birth register, the parents had to choose a different one. Amazingly enough, Manuela was listed as an acceptable derivative of the male name Emanuel. Emanuel meant "God be with you," so by logic, it carried over to Manuela.

1939 - A Rapidly Changing World

It didn't take long for my grandmother Ilse to come to Gelsenkirchen to see her first grandchild. It was also timely, since soon after my birth I developed a severe milk allergy.

Mutti was unable to nurse, and I couldn't gain weight and fell seriously ill. Omi rushed to the scene and intervened with money and connections to help the pitiful-looking girl stay alive.

Although medicines and alternative methods were disappearing to support an imminent war and doctors wrung their hands and shook their heads, Omi was able to move the bureaucratic system and found an alternative milk product. I never found out what was the lifesaving product.

"But I am going to find some baby food. Don't you worry, Hedi," Omi said. She must have found the appropriate baby food, because I'm here to write about my life.

Mutti told me more than once. "With your Omi around, I couldn't do anything right. Nothing was ever good enough for Mani. You were spoiled beyond words." It was a rare criticism.

As a toddler, I became Mani. I walked and talked early. Whatever couldn't be pronounced, I shortened it by adding the letter "I." German grandmother, Oma, turned into Omi, *Nuni* were noodles. My four syllable name naturally was cut short. Manuela evolved into Mani.

My brother's name Achim was shortened to Aschi. He was only thirteen-months younger than I. It seemed that I had corrupted his name, for he disliked being called Aschi. Omi continued with these earlier coined names and called her second grandchild, Aschi. For years, he protested in vain. When I realized how much he hated this, I switched back to calling him Achim. In fact, I felt bad to have started this controversy. I was sympathetic, since I was unhappy with my given name. I simply hated the name Manuela, because I was frequently asked about my un-German name. "Why not Ursula, Helga, or Sigrid?" With time I responded smiling and repeated my story about Spain and accepted the apparent anomaly to be different.

Interlude Mannheim 1939-1940

My parents moved away from Gelsenkirchen to Mannheim. I never quite understood why, but I surmise my father resold the business to a non-Jew and transferred the funds to Pastor Lehman. My brother was born there in February of 1940, and by then I was already an active toddler, keeping adults breathless-chasing after me. We lived in an apartment building in the Wespinstraße on Mannheim's *Oststadt* (Eastside).

I don't remember much about our home there. But I was able to study several black and white photos from that time. Omi came to visit, and she was shown walking in a park, hanging on to her fashionable hat while chasing after me. My baby harness dragged next to me on the ground, and I ran a good distance. At the time, Omi was trying to maneuver a baby carriage with my little baby brother and an untamed toddler, me. I was expected to walk like a trained puppy next to Omi. Wrong idea. This old picture revealed important early attributes about me: I wanted to be free and explore, both things the war made challenging, and personal traits I possess even today.

Most pictures depicted me with Omi alone. I was her first grandchild, the spoiled one, who loved anything Omi did or said. This perception never changed, and I often sought her guidance. She harnessed me with love. She inspired and encouraged me to reach for higher goals in life.

Our stay in Mannheim was short. My father had only been working for a few months in a large department store when he was called to serve in the *Wehrmacht*. Judging from photos, our apartment living must have been comfortable, and its location was close to the *Hauptbahnhof* in the center of downtown. Mannheim's impressive landmark, the water tower, was visible from there and divided the main shopping area from a residential part of town.

At the turn of the century, unique Art Nouveau structures stood in the middle of town. There was the water tower, the Civic Center and rows of five-storied apartment buildings that stretched for at least one city block. Behind the water tower, facing away from downtown, was a lovely pond with a cascading waterfall. A fountain on the lowest level filled a pond with water. The pond's circumference had grassy boundaries and was manicured with flowerbed patches and blooms of the season.

I saw pictures of Mutti with me in a stroller. In later years when I came to Mannheim for the second time, I was able to fill in what black and white pictures couldn't. The colorful carpets created by plants, relaxed the senses. A wonderful respite. Winding gravel paths went through shady arbors, overgrown by pale purple wisteria vine. It called for a moment's rest and an escape into a romantic corner. Couples took advantage by sneaking kisses and embraces, and mothers fed babies and exchanged ideas with other moms. It was 1940, frozen in time.

Strangely enough, life would return me to this very city around 1952. As a teenager I learned about Mannheim. I saw its smoke stacks and chemical fumes that blew eastwards over the Rhein River. The city Ludwigshafen, west from Mannheim, sent nasty fumes across the river to its sister city. At the junction of the rivers Neckar and Rhein, Mannheim was vibrant with art, theatre and trade that gave opportunities for making a good living. Mannheim invested in its citizens' broader education and culture, offering subsidized tickets to most cultural events. It was not unusual for blue collar workers to change work clothes for a suit and attend an evening performance of *Aida*, or a classical play like *Die Räuber* (The Robber) by Schiller which was premiered at the Mannheimer National Theater in 1782. No class distinction in the arts.

Pastor and Mrs. Lehman were still in Mannheim when Achim was born. Paperwork for their asylum in Switzerland had been delayed. They were in hiding, and moved back and forth between friends and family. They had left Gelsenkirchen unreported, not giving the required change of address and hadn't shown up for work either, making them immediately suspicious to the police.

My paternal grandparents visited Mannheim at least once. I wasn't baptized yet when Achim was born, so my parents decided to christen both children at home. This seemed unusual; but the Nazi regime increasingly harassed churches; therefore, my father visited Franz Lehman and asked him to baptize a baby and a toddler at home in our apartment. Vati found the Lehmans since he knew their relatives' whereabouts. Franz Lehman was delighted to baptize us two Hunger children in the privacy of our home and under clandestine conditions. I am grateful to the faithful photographer, Vati, who captured the sacred moment.

Vati took several family pictures that day. Pastor Lehman wasn't shown in any of them. Maybe he was in a hurry to leave. The Lehmans and the Hungers spent the ensuing war years over 600 kilometers away from each other, not knowing if they would see each other again. In 1940 we couldn't foretell our future. But in 1951 we met again in Mannheim. No Holocaust for the Lehmans; and for us a new and very different life. When we met again, I was fourteen, had my first box camera, and took a picture of Pastor Lehman, which has remained crisp and clear through half a century.

The war started September 1, 1939. City living became unsafe. What would be the next move? My father was already in basic training while we lived in Mannheim which would have made his earlier business transactions with the Lehmans more believable.

These were dangerous times. We escaped the first bombing of Mannheim and our apartment on Wespinstraße. We had barely left, when the building burned to the ground. I searched for the building later in 1952, and all I found was an empty lot.

In fact, Mannheim had been an early target for the British Wellingtons. They bombed Mannheim's industry, all downtown, and locations around the *Bahnhof* which was in walking distance from Wespinstraße. Blocks of precious Art Nouveau buildings lay in ruins, including the water tower with its ornate copper roof, Mannheim citizen's pride, and the historic theatre and opera house were nothing but rubble.

I was told that Gelsenkirchen, my birth place was also bombed. The third near-death-experience came through the mere fact that we moved close to Dresden, less than 30 miles away where the worst devastation would take place in February of 1945.

Döbeln, Saxony 1940 – 1946

With threads of another war brewing, the German people were urged to evacuate major cities. Vati was drafted into the military and looked for a new home for his young family away from Mannheim. He wanted them closer to his parents in Saxony and the estate in Schosdorf in Silesia.

Döbeln in Saxony, close to Dresden, was chosen. It was a quaint place of 20,000 people compared to Mannheim's 385,000 people. Mannheim was the eighth largest industrial German city in the 1940s and a predictably prime target.

Omi and Opa lived further east from Döbeln. It was a two-hour train ride on slow, local transportation. I surmised Mutti's initial desire was to have some space between her in-laws since her acceptance of the family had evolved slowly. In fact, Omi and Opa became our lifeline. While Vati was serving in the *Wehrmacht*, Mutti and we children lived safely and happily in our safe cocoon, another sizable and comfortable apartment in this lovely and peaceful town of Döbeln. That's how it looked in 1940.

Actually, my early childhood was as normal as any child could have wished for. I was oblivious of the war and civil unrest and content to push around my first doll carriage in Döbeln's city park. Another little girl looked longingly at my brown baby doll. "Why a brown doll?"

Vati had brought it from France as a Christmas present. I named her Marianne. Vati suggested the more French-sounding name Babbette, befitting a dark-skinned, foreign-looking doll. But to me she was Marianne. I learned later that Vati worked for the commander in chief of the Naval Group West in Paris. That must have been after the German troops had marched into France. I didn't understand at the time where that exactly was, but I loved it when he came home for Christmas carrying presents from France, seemingly from very far away.

While we lived in Döbeln, Vati served the military. He was lucky and relatively safe with his special assignment. During most of the war, good fortune hid him from bullets and placed him in convenient hide-away locations. He had refused

23

to become an officer and found many excuses why he couldn't be a weapon-carrying soldier. He showed proof of a hereditary defect, so-called multiple "exostoses" on his knees, which were extra bones interfering with his tendons. The x-rays proved it and his arguments sounded plausible to the military doctors; he succeeded somewhat, for he never fought at the front.

Joining the Nazi Party wasn't in Vati's plan either. His lack of party membership fortunately went undetected. His years in Spain allowed him not to be involved with home politics. When he returned to Germany, he had changed residencies twice, moved his family to an out-of-the-way town and slipped through red tape. Later, he announced proudly to whoever cared to listen that war was the biggest waste of time in his life. The *Wehrmacht* held on to whoever, young or old, fit for service or not. No excuses. Luckily, Vati knew important languages, was far above average intelligence, and proved to be useful somewhere behind a desk at the Western Command Center in Paris.

My brother and I saw Vati maybe twice a year while he was in the *Wehrmacht*. Vati's uniform confused me. In early 1941, he wore an infantry recruit's uniform and in December of this year he came home wearing an impressive navy uniform. Mutti told us that Vati was not high ranking, which confused me even further. He looked handsome to me and brought lovely gifts. With time, however, Vati gradually faded from my memory since life revolved around our little town of Döbeln, our new neighbors, and many vacations at the grandparents' house and their estate in Schosdorf.

We lived in Döbeln for over five years, from late 1940 until 1946. I was two years old when we arrived and over seven when we left. What I remember from this time compares to a kaleidoscope of bright, moving objects, hints of images that linger, sometimes running together like blended watercolors.

Our four-story corner-apartment building stood at the intersection of Hauptstraße and Moltkestraße. We lived on the third floor, a spacious apartment with about 3,200 square feet that wrapped around facing both streets. The master bedroom was like an observatory with a perfect panoramic view. A sweep of about six or eight large side-by-side windows helped me witness historical events in snippets.

Opa Wagner provided the apartment's furniture, since my parents hadn't accumulated much with their previous moves. At least, we felt safe in this calm region that most likely would not see air attacks. Achim and I shared the children's room, not luxurious by modern standards. The furniture was built from solid wood and painted glossy white. It had a large chest of drawers, a children's settee with a square table, and a low table with two matching chairs. An authentic Steiff elephant on four little wheels stood two foot high. We had plenty of space to ride the toy animal back and forth.

The windows faced out to Hauptstraße, a welcoming spot for watching marching German soldiers singing electrifying songs. We heard them often. Practice parades to celebrate Adolf Hitler's birthday on April, 20 was an exciting spectacle. Mutti ignored most of the commotion, only following orders to hang the mandatory red flags. The little settee in the Kinderzimmer converted into a perch. Mutti or our young maid, or *Pflichtsjahrmädchen*, held us tight, so we wouldn't reach too far or by chance pull on the fluttering flag. Windows swung open, double paned without screens. I never heard of children falling out of windows, but we lived with many looming dangers without noticing them. Besides, screens represented a modern American invention that never impressed Germans up to this date. Too ugly for them.

"Just don't lean too far," Mutti warned.

Living in the corner apartment building had great benefits. Overlooking this intersection was entertaining, but also informed us about new social trends. If nothing else, we observed the *Capitol* movie house to our left on Moltkestraße, and the old, ornate civic center from the late nineteenth century to our right across Hauptstraße. Exclusively children's movies like fairytales were shown for Sunday matinees. We peeked over from our upstairs window to check when the Capitol's doors opened, to get ready in plenty of time.

Mandated by Hitler, our young maid belonged to MDM (*Bund Deutscher Mädchen*), a girl's organization. These girls were obligated to serve for one year. Parents could negotiate to which organization a fourteen-year-old boy or girl should belong. Young men in their khaki colored uniforms, belonged to the Hitler *Jugend* (Hitler youth). Youngsters, depending on their education, joined either the basic *Volksschule* (school for the folks) or Gymnasium (secondary tract), according to their age. For the most part, the German youth was organized and trained to focus on their *Führer* and *Vaterland*. Nationalistic thinking was designed to inspire and push forward a new generation with lectures on how to regain former German lands with German speaking people who were split off from the homeland as a result of WWI's decrees.

Most youngsters lacked the historical understanding of those previous hostile engagements. Years of high inflation their parents and grandparents suffered through, as well as reparation payments to foreign countries dictated by the Versailles Treaties of 1918 following WWI, wasn't relevant to them any longer. After 1918, rampant unemployment and civil unrest, and a young democracy with too many intellectuals and idealists tried to impress each other with high-sounding speeches. Most politicians lacked political savvy, couldn't find compromises, and opened the door to the rise of a bully group that systematically took over the powers of a broken Germany.

Our life in Döbeln for the most part was ordinary. The majority of mothers stayed at home and raised their children. The more children the better. At least that's what Hitler proclaimed.

Mothers who bore four children or more received a *Mutterverdienstkreuz*, a medal to honor German motherhood. Mutti was satisfied with two children, had household help and built-in babysitters with young girls, the *Plichtjahrmädchen*, who fulfilled their year-long household duties. I don't remember inconvenient intrusions into our personal life by politics. German civilian were complacent and followed orders and Mutti obeyed displaying our apartment's flags on special days and listened like all her neighbors to the latest radio reports and speeches of politicians. I learned to block out their unpleasant screaming voices.

Around Town

Our daily routine included walking several times a day. We went to the center of town, about four or five blocks away for grocery shopping and picked up a few items every time from mostly family-owned stores. Flour and sugar, if available, sold in bulk and was weighed on old scales by pounds and grams. In exchange, we used different colored ration stamps. Every month another color was issued for milk, butter, eggs, sugar, coffee, and cigarettes when at all available.

Cutting off individual stamps was a tedious procedure. Women waited in line with impatient little kids in tow. But in order to stay afloat, we repeated our shopping trips twice a day. We couldn't accomplish much with long lines and little obtainable amount of food. When we saw our house doctor, Dr. Otto, the tailor, shoe repair shop, stationery shop, and miniature department store, the owners greeted us personally. Even though all the services were within a two mile circle, it was a lot of walking for short legs and small feet. Living in Döbeln meant crossing also a total of seven bridges over the Mulde River which seemed fascinating each time we walked over them. The rushing water held a magic spell for me. I wanted to climb down the embankment and watch the fish and take off my shoes and test the current. But I wasn't allowed to get off the bridge for Mutti told me, we had a nice swimming pool in town, and the Mulde River was muddy and would swallow up little curious children.

After our obligatory afternoon nap, the walking resumed. Life without cars and streetcars seemed normal. The war had restricted gas consumption, and private cars were parked out of sight. In those days, I remembered empty streets, only horse-drawn carriages that delivered the basics.

The railroad was a faster mode of transportation. We walked to the train station, way out of town, to receive packages that had arrived from the grandparents' farm to supplement our food. Or when lucky, we rode the train to see Omi and Opa. Traveling meant we had to carry suitcases to the station and use a little wooden cart, called *Leiterwagen*. We left it at the station with name attached, and retrieved it on our way back home. In the early forties, this cart was a

28

necessity. Occasionally, I could get a ride in such a *Leiterwagen*. Usually, Achim preempted my attempts. So I trudged along, obediently tolerating such tiresome outings. Such was life.

I loved to explore the buildings we passed. Mutti had things to do and didn't care to waste time looking around inside the courthouse or the theatre to indulge a child. One time while walking to downtown, Mutti and I passed the courthouse with neo gothic embellishment which I mistakenly took for a church. The building was four stories high, not including the gable which had extra windows and a centrally located bell tower and belfry. How would I have known otherwise? Erected in 1910, and the tower counted 160 steps. On our daily strolls, we also passed the theatre, dated 1872, in its eclectic style as were most of the houses of Döbeln. They reflected a neo classic architectural style and were the typical representation of middle class houses. Handed over from one generation to the next, they received their occasional face-lifts. Most of them needed a fresh coat of paint, but during an ongoing war people concentrated on basic needs.

Right in the middle of ancient cobblestones were ugly train tracks that collected nothing but dirt and horse poop.

"Mutti, where's the train?" I pointed to the tracks.

"Child, that was long ago." Mutti answered me and grabbed my hand in order to avoid the tied up Clydesdale horses in front of the butcher shop.

"Long time ago? For what?" I wondered.

"Mani, that's when they had streetcars drawn by horses."

I must have had a blank stare on my face. It was a hard concept for a four-year old.

"A streetcar…hum…a train in the middle of town?"

Mutti redirected my attention to enter the butcher shop. She was focused on one thing at a time, and dawdling around wasn't planned for in the morning routine. But I stood there obsessed with the idea of a so-called streetcar that was no longer in operation.

"Can we ride a train instead of walking all the time?" I asked.

"Let's go inside and see what Butcher Maier has today." Mutti tried to distract me, so she tempted me, "What about a hot broth with dumplings?"

"When can we ride this town car again?" I didn't give up easily.

"Come on now, probably after the war," Mutti answered, adding, "It's a streetcar, Mani, not a town car."

I heard the word 'war' so much, but I neither could see nor touch it. Maybe a hot broth was better than wondering about iron tracks and horse manure. I was happy to enter the shop where three round bistro tables and chairs invited customers to sit and enjoy Mr. Mayer's *Schlachtsuppe* (referring to slaughter and soup). It was Friday, because I heard our neighbor, Mrs. Dietz mention it earlier and that Maier's soup would warm up hungry bellies any time of the day, not only on Fridays. These recommendations went from tenants to tenants and from one apartment to another. The idea offering snacks and soups in a butcher shop was a new idea in 1942.

Mutti motioned for me to sit at one of the tables. She placed her leather gloves on the empty chair next to mine. The place was buzzing with women trying to buy their week's meat ration. Mutti carried over two cups with steaming broth. It didn't take long for her to devour her soup. She watched as I took my time and said, "Blow a bit, Mani, so the soup doesn't burn you." She demonstrated with her empty spoon. I was supposed to follow her example and not to spill on the front of my hand-knitted beige sweater. It was my lucky day, all alone with Mutti and Achim at home with the maid. Running errands with two small children wasn't easy, and I could carry at least a bag and make myself helpful.

Markklösse tasted heavenly. Made from beef bone marrow, one would scoop the raw marrow; add an egg, seasoning and parsley including breadcrumbs to form it into truffle-size balls which would be gently boiled in the broth, minutes before serving. I was glad about my earlier ignorance; otherwise I might have opened a tirade about animal cruelty. For the most, I managed without spilling too much at least not on the new sweater.

Suddenly, I stopped when I discovered glossy circles of *something* on the surface. "What's that swimming on top?" I asked.

"Child, eat now. These are *Fettaugen* (fatty eyes), and they'll make you strong."

My spoon fell out of my hand. "But I do not want fat eyes," I complained.

"Shhh, shhh, people are looking, everybody loves Mr. Mayer's broth with dumplings."

I searched for the mentioned dumplings. "But they are so small, Mutti." Strange foods couldn't be trusted.

At home, my eating habits were usually corrected by the maid. But at the butcher's, Mutti was suddenly exposed and observed by town's people witnessing a contrary little girl. I was naughty; fussing about food during war time was inexcusable. With Mutti's stern look at me, I finished my soup, fatty eyes, chives, miniature dumplings, tiny pieces of carrots, and all.

On the Corner of Hauptstraße

On the ground floor of our apartment building was a department store with rows of sparkling windows. One day, I noticed that all the store's windows were covered up with brown paper. The Schwertfegers, the owners of the business, had left for America in 1943. I couldn't comprehend the sudden transformation into this ugly butcher paper look.

Kristallnacht and its ripple effects came late to the provinces. The world's outside changes sneaked into Döbeln like a thief climbing through a window in the middle of the night. It happened in a deceptive, hidden way. No bangs, no shootings, no shouting, and no arrested people or anybody dragged out of their beds in the night.

While Vati was away at war, we had close contact with our immediate neighbors who lived on the same floor. They had a son, Walter, who was like my older brother and first love. He was a precious, handsome, well-spoken young man who was about to graduate from high school. Walter spent a lot of time at our place, as our apartments joined. We had separate front doors and bells with polished brass shields which read "Dietz and "Hunger." Mutti established an open-door policy between us, which Walter frequently used. He was a hungry teenager, and Mutti was a good cook and had far more groceries available than any of our neighbors. Opa's farm fed more people than just our family.

Achim and I spent many hours with the Dietzes. First, I visited alone. Older and more out-going, I wasn't shy with strangers and was curious how other people lived. Ever since his sickness and spending weeks exclusively with Mutti, Achim was close to her and remained in the background when visiting with Omi and Opa. I wasn't sure if I was Omi's little girl, and he exclusively Mutti's boy.

Onkel and Tante Dietz were of modest means. They dressed in nondescript beige with beige or grayish-black with gray or black. Tante Dietz's mother passed away not long before, and I figured that she kept her mourning wardrobe, finding more reasons why not to return to regular clothes.

I was not too familiar with electrical appliances. But I noticed that Tante Dietz kept strange looking irons on her coal-fired stove and pressed her clothes with them. They spewed steam, which made it look like a bad witch was cooking stew. How Tante Dietz transferred red-burning coal into one iron while using the other one was a bit scary. We had an electric iron with a long cord, and Mutti fussed at us not to touch or tangle with it. "Causes bad accidents," I heard frequently. Ironically, the hot coal and spewing iron of Tante Dietz never caused danger warnings.

Onkel Dietz was first a school teacher and couldn't make enough money to support a family, so he became a barrister. As far as I knew, Tante Dietz never worked outside her home. Both seemed very old in relationship to their young and good-looking son.

Walter was their only beloved off-spring. But soon they opened their hearts and included us as younger adopted kids. In fact, they doted on me and my brother. What a blessing it was to gain pseudo-grandparents next door. Mutti also acquired trustworthy friends to lean on. But it wasn't long before Walter, short of high school graduation, was drafted into the military. Walter was a gifted student and was given an emergency baccalaureate.

We all missed him and awaited anxiously his letters. But now the lonely Dietzes embraced Achim and me even more. I believe we distracted them from their anguish, and in turn we gained a great substitute teacher when all schools were mandated to be closed because of frequent air raids.

I absolutely adored Walter Jr's wooden desk. In his absence, his father kept it like a shrine. It took up a special space in the overcrowded living room with inherited old furniture crammed everywhere. The desk stood next to a large window opening up to a view of an old narrow alley way. A row of one-storied houses stood there, attached to one another. They had been there for over 200 years, I was told.

Moreover, the Dietzes allowed me the honor of studying and learning at Walter's inspiring desk. I loved him as much as I loved his desk. Learning new skills was as easy for me as saying the Lord's Prayer.

At the Dietzes, no harsh word was either spoken, nor any disturbing war news heard. I could sit at Walter's desk and dream about learning to read and write. It wasn't long before I'd enter school.

This magic desk influenced somewhat my adult life. I understood there was valuable learning away from the schoolhouse. Up to the end of WWII, in our family and others, women ruled the roost in the home but didn't venture out much. Some called it "the good old days of the 19th-century women." I was born at the end of this era. Girls needed to be better educated.

Getting Ready for School

In spring of 1943, I was five and one half years old and stood about four feet tall against a green door, the entrance of the building, measuring at least ten feet in height. I remember that aside from our spacious apartment and the broad view from its windows, I loved the staircase. The clomp-clomp, percussive sound of my wooden shoes against the stone floors was fun. I ran three flights up and down creating delightful echoing sounds. Mutti worried and called down the hallway, "Don't stomp. We don't want the neighbors to complain!"

Here, I felt at home, and strangers became friends. I didn't believe any of our neighbors would complain about me. I reasoned that a few more clunking sounds wouldn't bother anybody. So I went once more clomp, clomp, clomp as if to say goodbye to my shoes. Soon I'd be in first grade, and Omi promised to give me a pair of leather shoes. I wasn't sure if Mutti would allow me to keep my old wooden shoes.

On the ground floor of our corner apartment house were businesses, on Moltkestraße as well as on Hauptstraße. One was the barber shop that also gave children's haircuts. Achim and I had the privilege of sitting in a higher chair for kids. He was a short, stubby man with a moon-face, so I named the barber Mr. Roundface, but mumbled it only under my breath.

"Mani, you are a naughty child." Mutti reprimanded me. "Call him by his proper name, Mr. Kowalski, "she said.

"If I can say his name, I will." But I never could. Thus, he remained Mr. Roundface, which truly fit him, as he had full black hair surrounding a moon-shaped face and a black mustache that reminded me of another man's picture I saw everywhere we turned. Mr. Barber Roundface wore his white starched coat reaching down to his hips, tied around the waist. He looked like our pediatrician, *Doktor* Otto whose white coat went straight down to his ankles but without a belt.

I felt very important when sitting propped up high and covered by the stiff black barber's cape. However, Mr. K's scissors spelled danger. I dared to speak up.

"Please, Mr. K...do not cut all my hair...I'm a girl, and I like my hair long."

35

Mutti interrupted. "Never mind her, you go ahead and do like always and allow enough hair on top to do the *Hahnenkamm* (rooster's comb). Mutti referred to a twist formed by a small comb that held strands of longer hair neatly tucked under. This simple procedure, bunched up hair on top, was called a rooster's comb. Therefore, this hairdo was commonly used as a compromise for girls with fine, wispy hair. My little girlfriend, Katharina who lived one flight above us had even thinner strands, and hers were blond. And her mama, Mrs. Wüstefeld, managed also to create this *Hahnenkamm* for her. Two proud little girls: One blond and I with brown strings slightly twisted, curly.

The former Schwarz & Schwertfeger department store was two flights below our apartment. The brown paper was eventually removed from its windows. I watched busy hands wash window fronts with an extended ladder on the side walk, splashing water out of a metal pail. I smelled vinegar. The old window cleaner in his blue cotton suit, a typical German worker's uniform, had stacks of newspaper handy. He bunched the newsprint into balls and polished the glass panes with a vengeance until the windows shone like a frozen pond in winter.

A time or so, I sneaked out of the stairwell to pay the department store a short visit. With my hands all over the display cases, I admired notions, buckles and colorful buttons made of glass and metal. It was a nineteenth century set-up and still gave personalized attention to its customers. The sales lady knew me there, and apparently my mother was told about my visits.

One day, she held me by my arms bent down to my face and told me with a more stern than usual voice, "Mani, I don't know the new manager at Schwarz & Schwertfeger anymore. Something changed here, and Mr. Schwertfeger went to America. Therefore, I want you to stay in the courtyard. No more wandering off. Understood? The new owners of the store are no longer our old friends."

I nodded when Mutti warned me to stay away. But I didn't really understand. "What changed?" I wondered.

The store had reopened under new Gentile ownership. Inside the store everything looked exactly the same. Döbeln proved over and over it was safer than other larger city in the *Reich*. Jews left quietly, and only a few folks knew about it.

As a child, I didn't know the difference between Jews and Gentiles. It took me almost two decades to find out what politicians termed German and un-German. Here was my friend, *Doktor* Otto, our beloved doctor in town. Supposedly, he was Jewish. He treated my brother's asthma; he looked after us when we were afflicted with measles, and had us sit under ultraviolet lamps to assure an acquired healthy look. Sitting regularly under the sunlight didn't help Achim's asthma which he developed after a bout with whooping cough. Dr. Otto didn't think that brother and sister should sleep in separate rooms to avoid contagion. He was correct in his diagnosis, for I never got sick, but he suggested to Mutti taking him to a spa in Bad Salzbrunn for inhalation and drinking of mineral waters. That happened in early summer of 1942, while I stayed on the farm in Silesia. When after three weeks Mutti and Achim joined us there, he was improved and his horrible coughs had stopped for good.

Kindergarten – 1943

Doktor Otto declared me healthy and mentally fit at the tender age of five and one half to enter first grade. He called me a good German specimen. This was deceiving, because most children around my age were underweight because of food deprivation. I hadn't learned hunger yet with Omi and Opa's farm providing food throughout the war.

Even though the good doctor believed that I was fit, I felt unprepared, and I was right. Voluntary kindergarten had lasted one day the year before because of Achim's "childish" behavior.

Mutti had walked us to the kindergarten schoolhouse and Achim began screaming in protest when she tried to leave. "Watch over him and remember, he had asthma," she reminded me as she forced the door closed.

Sure, I would watch, he was my brother. But soon, I was sidetracked by new friends. I joined a group of girls playing at a table and started stringing beads and cutting newspaper. Soon I had black, nasty looking hands from the newsprint, and Achim had escaped to the girls' bathroom. He wailed there until I found him.

At noon, when Mutti came for us, she melted over his red, tear-stained face. She couldn't bear to see him struggle with the stress of Kindergarten, so both of our enrollments were forfeited. I got ugly looks and was made to feel like a traitor, because I had failed to hold little brother's hand all the time. It would be another eleven months before I saw the inside of a classroom. Nothing made sense to me, but I knew Mutti wanted to have both of us gone at the same time to have some peace and quiet. Our German Kindergarten was not mandatory, separate from the school system, and represented a daycare center.

First Grade

My first day at school arrived. Omi gave me a *Zuckertüte*, a two foot tall pointed paper bag filled with sweet candy and delicious *Goldparmänen* apples with a perfumed aroma. Similar to piñatas, *Zuckertüte* came into usage around 1810. Traditionally, grandparents gave their grandchildren this present on their first official day in school.

It was pure luxury, given the stores were bare and food rationed. Most German children had never heard of chocolate, much less tasted it. But my Zuckertüte was full of goodies. Omi bartered whatever materials were left over from the factory to buy me the sweets.

She also bought me clothes for my actual first day of school. I wore a baby-doll white linen dress embroidered elaborately across the chest, white socks, and buckled new leather shoes. My short brown hair strained to hold up the giant white bow on top of my head. Not a *Hahnenkamm* today.

The enrollment two weeks earlier stands out more in my memory than my very first day in school. The walk to the school house that enrollment day was my first encounter with the principal. It remains embedded in my brain.

It was a mild, sunny spring day, and the finches whistled happy tunes. I felt so grown up and looked proudly down on my new shiny leather shoes. I was allowed to wear them that day to get a feel for the real day in school. Mutti and I walked one mile over cobblestones, then crossed the river Mulde. The streets were eerily silent from the lack of traffic. We climbed the endless steep stairs of a three-story brick building, the school house.

Seeing the principal seemed important. I remember Mutti wearing a tailored two-piece brown suit, belying war times. During the war German women tended to wear drab looking clothing. Mutti believed in fashion, not exactly realistic in war times.

School standardized tests and official records were non-existent. Everything was done in person in front of the school official. No nurse, no secretary - the principal did it all.

Herr Principal sat behind a huge fortress-like desk, ready to evaluate each child and parent.

My mother peeked into the room. "Good Morning, I am here to enroll my daughter for school."

Herr Principal walked around his fortress and, to my surprise, was shorter than Mutti. Looking up his beaky nose, I fell graciously into a curtsy. *"Guten Morgen."*

He backed away with disgust and turned to my mother. "Haven't you taught your child *den Deutschen Gruß?"* He was inquiring about the then customary salute and clicking of heels to hail the Führer.

My mother gasped, "Pardon me?"

Herr Principal glowed at the possibility teaching an impressionable mind. "Come here, I will show you what your mother has obviously overlooked, the primary lesson of the *Third Reich's* etiquette."

He motioned for us to walk to the opposite side of the room. I dragged my feet a bit which would have been naughty in our household, because good leather shoes had to be preserved for the next little kid like one of my younger cousins in Magdeburg. *What was this all about? The principal didn't like me, but why?*

"Don't you know how a well-bred German lady greets properly," he asked.

Mutti stiffened, but said nothing. What was I suppose to do? Her icy silence filled me with fear.

The principal pointed to a portrait of a mustached general. His brown army boots appeared at eye-level, ready to kick me in the chin, I thought. I raised my head to get the full

40

length view of a man in Nazi uniform with a wide black belt and brass buttons. His black hair swooped across his forehead shadowing his fierce eyes. *Was this a general?*

The principal stood stiff in front of this portrait, awe-stricken, full of respect. "Do you know who this is?"

The gloves in my mother's hand quivered. I remained a silent statue.

"Dear child, do you *not* recognize the Führer?" He rolled his eyes upward, clicked his heels together, and threw up his right arm in a sharp angle to touch his temple.

He looked out of the corner of his eye to see if I was taking the lesson in. With his right arm outstretched and his hand at an unnatural extension he cried, "Heil Hitler!"

I jumped back, nearly falling over my mother, but she pushed me back towards the principal.

He peered down at me. "This is the proper German greeting. Everybody should, at all times, salute in this manner. Is this understood, dear child?"

Mutti's quaking hands pinched me. "Yes, Sir," I whispered.

The principal nodded smugly and swung himself behind the *Great Wall* of his desk. Demurely looking down, I noticed the principal's black shoes, oddly too long and I thought of a clown with flapping oversized shoes. I sat in the chair wondering when Herr Principal would stop asking questions so I could go to a classroom and learn to read.

Herr Principal stood up from his chair. "We are finished here, Manuela." Turning to Mutti he said, "Mrs. Hunger, your daughter's room will be room number four, and her teacher will be Mr. Möller." After a short pause, the principal nodded at me with an apparent expectation. I was supposed to have learned a lesson. I didn't pick up the clue.

41

"Auf Wiedersehen," I said with another curtsy, rendering the principal's lecture erased. With a quick thank you, my mother grabbed my left hand firmer than normal and rushed us out of the room. It felt as if we were running down the hallway, as her pumps click, click, clicked in the stone corridor and all the way down the building's steep steps.

Lucky for us, the *Gestapo* wasn't bearing witness to our civic failures.

We scurried home in silence. I dreaded the moment the giant green door would slam shut and my scolding would begin. I was convinced I had flunked school before I even begun.

As we entered, I braced for the sharp slap.

Mutti exhaled as if all of her energy was seeping onto the floor. I stared at her with wide eyes, waiting for the reprimand about my performance.

"Go change your clothes so they are fresh for the first day of school. You will wear the same dress," she said with her eyes closed.

"I'm allowed to go?" I whispered, completely confused.

"We will never mention this again. For now, go and play in your room. I have things to do."

I was curious about Mutti's "important work," so I came out of my room to discover what this job was all about. She had finished hanging long red flags with the black *Swastika* outside our windows. Of course, a Swastika was unknown to me in 1943 other than as a weird black cross on white, sewn on flags. Our apartment was large, with about eight windows facing Moltkestraße and three more facing Hauptstraße. I lost count of how many flags Mutti posted, but I knew rules existed as to how many flags were required by the size of the dwelling.

Catching her breath, Mutti stretched her back and sighed in relief. "Now, come with me to the front door. Here's another lesson you need to learn today." She pointed to the peephole. "You are not allowed to open the door unless I look through it first." Her voice sounded eerily calm.

"Why?" I asked.

Mutti smiled reassuringly. "When you have a peephole, you should use it all the time, Führer or no Führer."

"No, I meant why can't I open the door?"

Mutti pointed to a grimy frame facing the wall on the table near the apartment door. She turned it around.

"Every household is required to show a portrait of *this man*. I have to see who is outside before I turn the picture around," Mutti tried to explain without frightening me.

It was the very same man from the principal's office, except our image was a flat black and white photo no larger than postcard size.

"He is to face the wall unless I turn him around. Now, let's go practice."

"Practice what?" I asked.

"The salute. You need to have it perfected before you go to school after Easter, or we both are in trouble."

"Do I do it at home too?"

"For goodness sake, no! Eventually, you'll learn when to do it and when not. When it's us, *he* doesn't exist. Only a man's picture facing the wall. Understood?"

I nodded, but comprehended very little.

None of this lesson mattered after all. I failed to do the greeting once when Mr. Möller entered the classroom. I tripped, got hung up on my desk and fell to the floor while trying to imitate the *Deutsche Gruß* (same as *Hitler Gruß*).

The kids all laughed. Fortunately, this never happened again, and I never created another unacceptable scene.

Within weeks, schools were closed and I found one of the best teachers in our next-door-neighbor. Uncle Dietz taught me the basic three R's while Walter was fighting in Russia. I was always eager to follow my beloved Onkel and Tante Dietz's instructions.

Mutti had created the best relationship with the Dietzes. We were war family. Mutti taught me to be as polite as possible, to say *Guten Tag* and *Aufwiedersehen*, because most *other stuff,* mainly war propaganda, would be obsolete soon. She said the war wouldn't last forever. Onkel Dietz predicted Germany's defeat long before most people. Germans couldn't accept the raw reality that Germany was losing the war.

Estate Summers

My grandfather's father had purchased a large estate in Schosdorf during the turn of the 19th century. Manufacturing, specifically textile weaving, had brought good fortune to many families in *der Lausitz*, the region around Zittau und Olbersdorf. The original *Rittergut* was bought as an investment and close vacation spot, easily accessible by car or railroad. During my time, however, private cars stood unused in garages because of fuel shortages, but I saw photos of relatives unloading from Opa's fancy old car, a Horch, following WWI.

Frederick II of Prussia claimed and conquered *Schlesien* from Maria Teresa of Austria. This fertile land had become German. History reported the *Kaiserin* (empress) mourned and cried over the loss of this beloved piece of earth her whole life. Equally, German people cried when they lost this precious jewel after WWII.

My family enjoyed upper middle class status; which came to a screeching halt *in a twinkling of an eye.* I remembered especially the years 1943 and 1944. The summer of 1944 was the very last privileged excursion. Dresden hadn't been bombed yet. But the war was raging all around us while we were vacationing in *Schlesien.* What irony, but we went on believing in another good harvest and a lifestyle which would go forever.

My grandfather still operated and managed his textile factory. I never knew the amount of monetary support Mutti received, but Opa kept us in luxury compared to the general population's conditions. Vati's military pay as a soldier wouldn't have supported our lifestyle. I grew up thinking that families helped each other. I never heard our family discuss money matters during those years. Opa produced sheets for the barracks and artificial silk for the parachutes. The government required him to do so, but he also enjoyed some freedom in producing his pre-war specialty fabrics.

Summer vacation on the estate brought the whole family together. My grandparents lived most of the year close to the factory in Olbersdorf, only a few kilometers out of downtown Zittau. But during the summer months, the farm and estate in Silesia was the whole family's vacation spot. Omi was usually the first one to come and prepare for Mutti and us children's arrival from Döbeln. Annemarie and Suse, housekeeper and cook, lived permanently on the farm and received instructions from Omi on how to get ready for her daughter-in-law and grandchildren's visit. Aunt Annemarie indulged her mother, even though she was quite capable in handling such preparations herself.

Opa joined us later and brought Omi's mother along.

45

We called her Urmi, a derivative of the German word for great-grandmother (*Ur-großmutter*). My grandparents left from Zittau's *Bahnhof.* We traveled from Döbeln and stayed at least eight weeks. I remembered the train stops after Dresden: Bautzen, Löbau, Goerlitz, Laubahn and then Hirschberg and Schosdorf. It seemed so far away. Yet for a modern person, Zittau, where my grandparents lived, was only around the corner. Distances were deceiving for we couldn't travel by cars anymore, and train rides took much longer.

Only three people got off the train. The conductor helped my mother with our extensive luggage. Achim and I climbed out and walked several steps along the tracks and stopped waiting for Mutti. The train made its repeated puffing noises and blew out curly smoke. This would be our destination until the end of August.

Coachman Jan was awaiting us at the station of Schosdorf. Jan couldn't see us right away. The tracks ran on top of a dam, considerably higher than the land around. In fact, the tiny town of Schosdorf lay down a steep hill from the railroad. The coach with its two horses waited on the other side. As far as the eyes could see, the fields were awash with golden wheat.

Jan jumped off the coach to assist us. Below on the dirt road Achim and I kicked some small rocks along. Mutti cut a disapproving look which immediately stopped our kicking. She pointed at Jan's horses resting obediently; one of them neighed as if to welcome us. Jan pulled his flat black cap off, waved and gave us a broad grin with two missing teeth. Mutti acknowledged his greetings with an engaging smile, before she smiled showing her pearly white teeth. The coachman appreciated the attention of the pretty daughter-in-law of Mr. and Mrs. Wagner.

Mutti's clothes were fancy and mostly custom-made thanks to Opa's generosity. Her straw hat was a creation that Omi also could have worn, since both women were fashion-minded. The straw hat was dyed a plum color and sported a wide black ribbon. Mutti held and pressed down its brim with her fingers, while two long feathers stuck out as if misplaced. In spite of her black and brown striped feathers and the breezy air, she succeeded in keeping this piece of art from taking on flight. Her summer dress, simply a shirtdress with narrow belt and short inset sleeves swung with her strides, displaying some delicate little flowers in subdued blues and purples. It was sewn from Opa's pre-war textile collection sold earlier all over Germany.

"Hey, you kids! Not so fast!" Mutti called from behind us.

My brother and I rushed down the stairs, the railroad's dam towering above us. At springtime, this area was fed by several brooks that eventually found their way to the Neisse River. The ground could become swampy very fast. The surrounding landscape appeared luscious with dark, rich soil. Nobody in this area remembered droughts or worried about not having a good annual harvest.

Achim and I greeted the two horses by name. Mutti looked concerned. "Misses," Jan assured her, "Don't worry; the horses remember the children from last year." He patted the sturdy brown animals, one after another and rubbed their foreheads saying, "Right, Hansi und Peter?"

Then Jan attended to our luggage. Bags and suitcases were stowed away, and we arranged ourselves on black leather seats, and my brother crawled onto Mutti's lap. He took the end of his checkered red and white pillow, rubbed it with thumb and index finger, and sucked on his thumb to make up for his missed nap.

I wasn't in need of naps, although the adults would have appreciated it if I did. I was a live-wire, in motion most of the time.

"Jan, can I ride the horses tomorrow?" I wanted to know.

"Yes, girlie, if your *Frau Mutter* will allow you, Frau Wagner would not object either."

Looking in my direction, Mutti placed her index finger over her mouth, indicating to me to be quiet. "Adults need to talk without children interrupting, *verstanden!*"

I leaned back, turning my eyes to the passing landscape. I smelled the wet soil and saw in the distance my grandparents' farmhouse peeking from behind a walled fence. Tall shade trees stood scattered as witnesses from hundred years ago. I recalled from the previous year how soothing their shade felt, and how they provided comfortable respite on hot summer days. How well I knew this ride. As we drove closer, the trees waved a *Willkommen* to me. I loved this vacation spot, its security and possibilities of exploring.

Jan, Mutti, Achim and I rattled down on the bumpy dirt road through healthy looking crops of wheat, barley, sugar beets, potatoes, and fields of bright yellow rape which was a source of oil. A few field workers, black dots on the wide landscape, spotted the productive lowland. The land shone green, and the wheat rolled like ocean waves. Our elevated view from the coach was as entertaining as the Sunday's matinee which we enjoyed back in Döbeln.

I looked around, trying to spot more familiar sites. Our welcome gift was freedom from etiquette, special clothing, and freedom from the city. War raged somewhere else, and the revved up public didn't shout those hateful *Heil*

Hitler greetings here. Propaganda Minister Joseph Goebbels, as I was told later, didn't poison our radio. We made our own music, happy family conversations, laughing, and playing.

I wondered who was going to welcome us at the house. I definitely had my favorite people such as Tante Suse, Frau Seidel, Aunt Annemarie, the Polish Anna, the forest master, and Mr. Schweitzer, the stable master. Omi waved with her white handkerchief.

We circled the property, since the iron wrought back gate was chained close. During peace times, the family rode in a car, which was now in storage. The horses needed to go into their stables. Therefore, the broad front entrance was handier. The barns stood opposite the manor house.

You could hear the horses, flaring sparks of their shoes upon contact with the stones. What a sight, and what an experience! Excited clattering and the rattling of hooves pounded rhythmically on the cobblestones, which were the manor house's announcement: they are here!

The whole courtyard, flanked by large stables and century-old utility buildings built of solid brick and stucco, looked neat and clean. The yard was comparable in size to a football field. The noise woke my brother from his nap. He jumped up and looked with big grey eyes.

"See Mommy, the horses are throwing sparkles!"

"Now dry your wet thumb and put your pillow away. Your auntie is waiting over there. Can you see her? You wouldn't like Aunt see you sucking your thumb, would you?"

Annemarie greeted us, "Hallo, *meine Lieb*en."

"Hello, my dear." Mutti responded.

"Did you have a pleasant trip?" Aunt Annemarie asked us politely.

I did not act politely, but jumped from the carriage and

said, "We did, but I am starving."

"Our girl may yet break a leg before vacation has even started," Aunt Annemarie said.

Fortunately, the circular drive in front of the house was sandy soil and soft enough to absorb the impact when I landed on the ground. No jolted ankle. I rushed into the house and headed straight to the kitchen, dropping my shoes and sweater behind me. "This is where my home is," I thought, "and it will never end."

Where was Vati? It hadn't quite sunk in yet that he was a soldier now and wouldn't spend vacation with us.

I didn't see my father for a long time. I had no idea where he fought or what he did. In two pictures I saw him in two distinctly different uniforms. One photo existed with Vati posing, flat navy cap with two ribbons hanging from its side, proudly next to Mutti. My mother's seating arrangement blocked the view of my father's whole uniform. It must have been an oversight of the photographer, for Vati looked quite handsome.

But for the most part I didn't miss him. He was in and out of the house; never to be counted on to read us a book to us or to take us to the park. One year while on leave, he joined us on the farm, but that last year he was far, far away at war.

With most men gone, females did all the handling of children. Our family had plenty women: aunts, maids, grandmother and great-grandmother, and Mutti. Among them all, my Omi was always my favorite person.

Omi and Opa Wagner's house was always ready for me to visit. Of course, they lived mostly in Olbersdorf outside Zittau on the very southeastern corner of the state of Saxony. The other house was in Schosdorf in Silesia.

After my father was drafted into the Wehrmacht and we had moved to a safer area close to Zittau, we were close to the grandparents and enjoyed years of vacations and luxuries a textile mill owner could provide for his family.

Opa's factory was on the same grounds, surrounded by a sizable English-type park, with century-old oaks, birches and huge willow trees. It had romantic paths with benches and figurines such as a copper flute-player on a pedestal. As a child, I'd stopped and admired him many times and wondered where he had come from. Through decades of exposure to all kinds of weather, he acquired a greenish patina. An asphalt road wound to the house, factory and two entrances with wrought-iron gates leading to the Wagner property.

Happy Activities

My aunt Annemarie managed the country estate in Schosdorf with the help of a few Polish farmhands. They spoke in broken German. We also had two French-men who lived there and with whom we communicated with little difficulties. Achim and I played with them, without any language problems, which surprised our elders.

The *Reich* controlled agriculture in order to procure food for the nation. Foreign workers helped on German farms by government mandate, and it required tedious recordkeeping. Everybody was trained to support the war effort to feed as many people as possible. Farm owner's families set extra food aside to provide for their own needs secretly. Wild animals on Opa's land couldn't easily be estimated. The government had no say on what game, such as deer, rabbits, wild boars, doves, and fish, were used to feed the family. Needless to say, we ate plenty of those, especially since beef was hard to come by. We weren't allowed to

51

slaughter our cows. The Holsteins were strictly dairy cows, and Germans paid exorbitant high prices for milk and butter.

I don't know how Tante Annemarie accounted for all the farm products, or how she filled her expected quota. She was an intelligent and clever woman who could circumvent rules without looking suspicious. I remember, she had to control her tongue during those Hitler years, and as I learned later, she didn't always succeed. Omi told me that governmental spies threatened Annemarie on more than one occasion with a concentration camp when her smart mouth referred to the Nazi Brown shirts as wild boars who trample Germany's culture and to Hitler as the unforgivable Austrian mistake. She confused more than threatened regime-friendly listeners.

My aunt was ahead of her times. She was an agricultural administrator and wore pants all the time. She rode horses and tractors and knew everything about crops and domesticated animals. No doubt in anybody's mind, she was qualified to give orders. She was respected by everybody, and farm-hands and visitors obeyed her. And as far as I knew, no one tried to cross her. Sometimes, her humor turned raucous compared to Omi's and my mother's more subtle ways.

"*Na, na, na,*" Urmi corrected my aunt one day. "How can you speak like this in front of these sweet little children?"

I was honored that Urmi thought we were sweet *kleine Kinder.*

But Tante Annemarie had an effective way of making little children mind her. Repeatedly we were told to keep our shoes on our feet when inside the house. Going barefoot was considered uncouth. When she caught me, she didn't say a word, but took me by the hand to go outside and check on the chickens down the path. When I whimpered while stepping barefoot over the piercing little rocks, she remarked, "You are a little *Zimttüte*." She called me a little bag of cinnamon, or better said, a wimpy kid.

The insult smarted for many years. The expression *Zimttüte* entered our family's dictionary as an effective insult. In fact, she coined many funny words and expressions. But the pain of little sharp stones piercing my bare feet, taught me to keep my shoes on in most places.

Every day at Schosdorf was an adventure and heaven on earth for a child. We could be turned loose in the courtyard, in the park area behind the main house or in the produce garden; we were safe and had the run of the place. I don't remember having any supervision, as Achim and I played unencumbered for hours on end. Sometimes, a farm-hand's son was allowed to join us. I suspect that workers and their families grew up believing that they shouldn't mix with the boss's family unless specifically invited.

Both Achim and I had no fear of little garden creatures. We entertained ourselves by pulling earthworms from the asparagus flat and collecting them in our buckets. My brother usually hesitated, but quickly followed me around and became increasingly more courageous. I was fearless, while he stepped cautiously right behind me. Our last summer in Schosdorf, I gained the reputation as the older, bossy sister.

My early fascination with water and swimming was developing. But repeated warnings about the pond's slimy bottom and its ability to swallow up little children impressed me to keep from entering. I still believed that only adults and very good swimmers could overcome the fear of drowning in this murky water.

We never had an accident while vacationing. A stubbed toe, maybe. I was chased repeatedly by a hen with her chicks and an ugly turkey parading around. They scared me and caused some distress. I liked all the other animals, domestic or wild, big or small and was thrilled when Opa took me to the deer blind. We sat there for hours observing while Opa explained about the foxes and how he used his dachshunds for hunting as they blocked the multiple fox holes of their den.

In Schosdorf, I lived in a safe and whole world. Animals and nature were in harmony and people cooperating and friendly. Considering the world around us, heavy fighting in Russia and people dying daily by the thousands, I existed in an unnatural cocoon. My childhood during the last years of WWII was glorious.

The Premonition Woman

Vera, Tante Annemarie's friend, was also present when we spent summer vacations on the farm. She had a sick husband who underwent treatments at a sanatorium for tuberculosis. Unfortunately, the man never recovered and died before the war's end. I called her Tante, Male Male. The German word *malen* meant drawing or painting, and that's how I formed a new name for Vera. Omi loved my newly coined names and words, and the other family members adopted them too.

Annemarie gave Vera the opportunity to make money while vacationing with us. She was an artist, and an accomplished painter of portraits and landscapes. Painting gorgeous flowers, wide and relaxing landscapes, and handsome little children and their elders, filled Vera's leisure time and the sales of her paintings filled her purse.

She also did pastels of which I inherited a couple of remarkable depictions: We all had our portraits done. My mother's turned out sad-looking. Perhaps Tante Male Male captured a part of her soul? I, on the other hand, looked disgruntled because the sitting took too long. The other problem I remember was the endless smiling and holding my hands motionless in my lap. While posing, my little brother would sneak around and make funny faces. He hid below the artist's easel and I worried about the contraption collapsing any minute. In the end, my picture turned out fine, but the child definitely wasn't me. I looked upset, which didn't reflect my disposition at all.

During Tante Male Male's visit I learned about the ghost who lived in the old manor house. However, the adults didn't give me too much information. The previous owners noted that a ghost occupied the room above the attic. They advised my grandparents to leave it undisturbed. At times, too many guests came to spend weeks at the farm, and we needed all the rooms. Annemarie kept silent and didn't mention the ghost. She also didn't believe the story. Since Tante Male Male was on the farm that summer, quarters were getting tight. Tante Suse, our cook and housekeeper, prepared the attic room for Miss Vera. "Well, Miss Vera, this room has the best view over the courtyard," said Tante Suse with a sly smile. She added, "And you are away from the sweet little children. I'm thinking the view from this attic window should be an idyllic setting for your artistic eye."

Vera was grateful, and she arranged her luggage and easel to her liking. It was comfortable, even without blinds or curtains. The slanted walls didn't bother her. She had a chest of drawers, a bed under the slanted wall, a large nightstand, and a small table with two chairs. A massive antique wardrobe accommodated all her extras, especially her artist supplies. Vera was looking forward to a pleasant vacation.

Helping to support her sick husband must have warmed her heart.

During the first night, Vera woke up frightened. Chilly air whooshed from the wall without cease. With a thump, she jumped out of her bed, and scurried terrified down the stairs in total darkness. Her jet-black hair, with straight thick bangs across the forehead and her pronounced white skin would have in turn scared anybody passing her in the stairwell.

All alone, in the middle of the night, Vera went straight for Annemarie's room, and rushed in, causing a disturbing commotion. My aunt shot up in her bed and turned on the light.

"What on earth is going on with you? Are you sick, Vera? You are as pale as a linen sheet."

Vera trembled and could hardly speak. "No, there's something going on. It's spooky in the attic," she whimpered.

Aunt Annemarie jumped out of her bed saying, "Now, come on, Vera, your imagination overwhelms you. She put her arm around Vera's and tried to comfort her. "You probably had a bad dream. I understand. Let's go upstairs together, and I will stay with you for a while to prove all that's fine."

The two friends climbed up the stairs, quietly tiptoeing so as not to wake anybody. Annemarie made another of her robust jokes, to change the mood, they both laughed, somewhat subdued, and the lightheartedness of my aunt calmed Vera down.

"Vera, go to bed and move over a bit. I'll sleep here on the edge, and we'll test the whole ridiculous situation. I show you, we do not have a ghost. Only children believe this."

Both women settled in. The room became quiet, no

more talking or quiet laughter. Suddenly, both of them sat straight up in bed as if bitten by a tarantula.

"Lord, have mercy, what is blowing the cool air? I cannot believe it," Vera shuttered.

"Let's go downstairs, Vera. It's too scary," Annemarie conceded. She was baffled and admittedly shook up.

During the next weeks all kinds of searches were done to find the ghost. Opa ordered branches from the old acacia tree to be cut away, so limbs couldn't rub against the house. Workers crawled into the attic space behind the slanted wall and examined all rafters and the general structure of the house. Nothing unusual could be found, so the matter of the ghost was temporarily abandoned.

Ignorance was bliss. Mutti, Achim and I remained on the farm in Schosdorf during the summer of 1944 until the end of August. My mother's birthday was the twenty-fourth of August, and all the family was assembled to celebrate. The Polish Anna was my special friend and she knew how to create beautiful wreaths. She adorned my head with one heavy wreath with blue cornflowers. Proudly, I wore it, dancing around like a little ballerina.

We enjoyed the party atmosphere. With the table's extension, hidden behind the buffet, we could to seat extra family and friends. Birthday meals were special, but Sunday gatherings during vacation time also represented memorable events. Opa's hunting friends loved his land and were often invited for dinner. The more, the better, since cooks and female kitchen helpers attended to us like nobility.

Since my grandfather hunted on his land, we had plenty of game to eat. The trick was for us children not to know what kind of meat was being served. So the adults would talk in a hidden language when complimenting the cook. Germans make a big to-do about the food and how good it tastes. It's almost like burping when around Chinese people to acknowledge a fine meal. We children ate pheasant, rabbit, venison, and so forth without suspecting. Who would want to eat wild animals that lived freely in the woods and looked so darling?

I had a silly child's reasons to eat chicken, beef, and pork. Somehow, I had them in different categories. I didn't mention it to Tante Annemarie, but once I was chased by a hen that was protecting her little chicks. We happened to cross path, when the hen chased me the length of the courtyard. I was afraid to be called a Zimttüte. Cows, I reasoned, were impersonal beasts that gave people milk and butter and when old and useless were slaughtered. No excuses for pigs, they had to be slaughtered, because we had to eat sausages.

One time, I raised a fuss during dinner over a sweet little deer. "I will not eat it," I said and stomped my foot. Omi took my hand and excused us for a moment. Mutti would have slapped me across the face, but Omi's approach was a mild form of time-out. As a result of my acting out that one time, all meat was now termed pork or beef. I believed that my family would speak the truth.

Eating at the adult table was always a sign we were "educated" children who knew how to eat properly. My mother drilled us how to handle fork and knife simultaneously. Holding the fork on the left and pushing little peas with the knife onto the fork seemed to me almost acrobatic. Achim still used his little silver "pusher" or *Schieber* to assist the veggies and potatoes onto the fork.

It made it easier for everybody when children sat at a separate little table, called *Katzentisch*. Mistakes could happen there, but not at the grownups-table.

When my great-grandmother, Urmi, was present, we had some additional ground rules. The backrest of a chair was not for resting. It was strictly for good looks and construction. I was supposed to sit straight as a candle. Ur-Omi sat like a bean pole all the time. I was mesmerized when I watched her. Why did she wear a wide black velvet band around her neck? I thought it was to keep her old neck straight and wrinkle free. Her white hair was combed up and rolled into many little curls pinned next to each other and covered by a white net. It was a piece of art and I understood why Omi had her mother's talent for similar coiffeurs.

Looking back, I think my great-grandmother was subjected to her father's overly militaristic and strict discipline with the notion of making her strong and durable for life. Since Urmi's mother died during childhood, her father hired a governess to give his daughter a caring yet restricted life, because she had no playmates her age.

Tante Annemarie had no difficulty analyzing her grandmother. Annemarie was convinced Urmi was stifled by her father's fear. He lost a wife and another daughter. Thanks to Annemarie, I always felt close to my great-great-grandparents Teichmann I'd never met. Annemarie's many stories over the years, plus the letters and pictures she gave me, made my great-great-grandparents very familiar to me. But interesting enough, my aunt refrained from ever correcting her mother, my beloved Omi. She could be very sarcastic as it related to politics and outsiders. Honoring father and mother was a command in our family nobody dared to break. We made excuses, teased each other, but in the end accepted all. Arguments were not condoned by Omi, our peacemaker.

Children went along on errands, quietly keeping up

59

with mothers' strides. When women conversed with each other meeting in the street during daily grocery shopping trips, kids stopped too and extended their right hand to greet the adults. We didn't recognize gossip, because we accepted the ladies' agitated whispering as simply grown up stuff. I saw us like sheep standing in one place and nodding: life's in order, everything's fine and there's nothing to worry about.

Dinners didn't last forever; we were excused early from the table. The maids changed our clothes or let us run naked in the garden. When we played outside, we didn't get much direction. It was a free and unencumbered existence.

Mutti's birthday party signaled the end of our stay at Schosdorf. While there, Achim and I were told very little about spooky things such as the *Ahnfrau*. Nobody wanted to scare us, and Halloween hadn't been introduced to German kids yet. So we lived oblivious of the knowledge that we had shared our space with a real ghost. I definitely wanted to know more about her. Would I ever be able to? Leaving the farm that summer, I thought we would have many more lovely vacations at Schosdorf's estate. Maybe sometime in the future I could even live there with my own family and do Aunt Annemarie's job. But I couldn't have been more wrong.

Other Caretakers and Workers

The female Polish workers looked after us when we spent time in the fields. Summers were moderate, and sun block unheard. Central Europe had mild temperatures, and summers were considered hot when the mercury suddenly hit ninety degrees. I never remembered being sunburned. Sometimes we helped pick blueberries in the woods. We picked buckets and buckets full of them, tiny little berries nobody would buy in the supermarket and ate so much that by the time we returned home, with horse and buggy and servants, we looked like little chimney sweeps. The stains couldn't be removed without bleaching our clothes in the sun. In Germany, Clorox was not used for laundering. We had *Kernseife*, a natural soap without enhancing byproducts such as scent or color and wetted and pretreated the spots over night.

The next day, all kitchen helpers would be summoned to make blueberry preserves. Our richly set breakfast table always had a spread of various preserves, fresh butter, eggs and unpasteurized milk straight from the bucket and directly out of the cow. Omi always said, "We live like God in France." This old German proverb was used regularly. All my life I appreciated a substantial, healthy breakfast.

Other times I remembered the homemade bread. On the farm we savored round crusty breads made by Suse. She placed dough in earthen bowls, and I carried them to the end of the courtyard to the open oven where our breads were baked. Two French men living in a small house close by were in charge of watching the breads in the oven, to take the breads out when perfectly baked.

The two men, Jean and Louis from France, became Achim's and my friends. It surprises me that I never questioned why they lived with us. It didn't matter to us children, because the farm employed many Polish workers who spoke broken German as well. We addressed them also as uncle, and apparently had no language problems with either French or German. They demonstrated to us how to make rings out of pennies, which we wore proudly on our pinkies. With anvil, hammer, flying sparks and plenty of time, these pennies slowly changed shapes, and we had to wait for the rings to cool before we ran off to show everybody in the house what Jean and Louis had made for us.

"Nice, nice," I heard Tante Annemarie say, "But do stay closer to the house. The men have plenty of other work to do."

The Polish Anna was my special friend. Of all the foreigners, she spoke the best German and according to Annemarie was the smartest of the bunch. I adored her. She took me to the fields to make hay, forming pyramids with wooden beanpoles, piled up and covered with cut grass. We created a little teepee, in which we crawled or hid. Anna was very playful herself, probably not older than nineteen. Supervising us kids gave her special privileges at the manor which she used to the fullest extent. She ironed for Omi, carried dirty clothes to the washhouse, straightened out our bedrooms and made sure cut flowers were freshened up daily. I remember Phlox, Shasta Daisies and Canterbury Bells in different vases around living and dining rooms and smaller arrangements in the guestrooms. I didn't realize then how many trips Anna made into the flower garden to cut and arrange the flowers to please the visitors.

My grandmother enlisted her at the house for special occasions to serve at the table. Omi trusted her implicitly. I still have one picture with her, me and her friend, Maria. I specifically remembered her saying, "When the war is over, I will send you a suitcase full of chocolate and raisins."

One of my childhood disappointments was that the promised suitcase never arrived. Omi reported on one occasion that Anna had stolen a diamond broche from her. She mentioned it several times in her old age. She could never understand how Anna could break her trust.

Polish workers never felt free. Germany had created a terrible war where friends turned into enemies overnight. The

Poles we knew took what they could when the winds of war turned in their favor. I couldn't fathom such thoughts, but as I got older I accepted the fact that Anna probably took the brooch as reward for services to the enemy.

Predictably, the war intruded our family paradise as well. The war in Russia was closer than we thought. We enjoyed our privileged country living in Schosdorf to the very end. I remembered those summer days in Schosdorf as true happiness. Unfortunately, I had the very last look at "the good old days" as they moved away like the receding tide. It was the end of August 1944, and we made it back home to Döbeln. There, we hunkered down and waited for the last bombings of Germany. However, we never expected the total devastation of Dresden, too close for comfort, followed by the occupation of Germany.

Surrender 1945

The *Ahnfrau* had warned Annemarie and Suse in Schosdorf about the approaching Russian troops. Mutti, Achim, and I returned to Döbeln, Omi, Opa, and Urmi went back to their houses in Olbersdorf and Zittau. We all waited for the war to end.

Low flying foreign airplanes were approaching in our region to intimidate German resistance. As a child I didn't know about the *Ahnfrau's* warning. She apparently gave warnings to Tante Annemarie still in Silesia, encouraging her to leave and go back to Olbersdorf. I was told that the ghost rumbled, blew cold air, or pulled drawers open, day and night.

What we saw in Döbeln were streams of Germans fleeing from their homeland which was now anything east of the Oder-Neiße-Line and included East Prussia, Pomerania and Silesia not to mention previous territory lost after WWI and repopulated by Germans during the Hitler years. These refugees, expelled from east-central Europe was the largest number in modern European history and in 1950's its number was estimated between million 2.0 to 2.5 million people. Roads were crowded for weeks on end. Coming from the east, the Russians pushed westwards behind the fleeing people and collided with them around Thorgau, southeast of Dresden.

According to historical accounts, three overlapping phases of German refugees moved into western Germany. The first wave of people came spontaneous, and then followed expulsion, and lastly deserting soldiers who had fought in Russia and the Ukraine. We saw many of them, and different phases, coming through Saxony. It was on a straight line west and thus passing through our state and Döbeln.

Not hesitating, the Russians drove their tanks over human bodies. This was documented by American soldiers and a German pilot who was part of the last German resistance. I learned this fact much later and was surprised to learn that WWII was still going on less than thirty miles from Döbeln.

Americans troops under General Courtney H. Hodges, 1st Infantry Division, approached fast. They had fought months earlier in the Normandy, covered 700 miles between France and eastern Germany, and met with their Russian ally on the Elbe River. The war was decided on the western front in June 1944 whereas the eastern front was still defended by sporadic German units in spite of lost battles in Russia. It was April 27, 1945 when Russian Marshall Iwan S. Konew and his American military ally met. One of their American soldiers, Joe Polowsky, kept a war diary in which he described what he saw that day in Thorgau, Saxony. Dead bodies were piled up like fire wood along the Elbe's bank. Refugees, mixed with deserting German soldiers, found their cruel death.

Marshall Konew wrote in his later memoir about his meeting with American General Omar M. Bradley. This famous American Field Commander was in charge of the invasion of Germany from the West and directed its troops over the Rhein River and far eastwards into the Elbe region. He commanded 1.3 million soldiers, the largest body of American soldiers ever to serve. So, he and his Russian counterpart had a friendly meeting and discussed further actions to end the war. That finally happened on May 5th, 1945, forty miles north of Thorgau.

General Bradley was persuaded to move his troops south-westward and leave Prague and its surroundings to the Russians. Thus, by default, American forces withdrew from this eastern area and made room for a later emerging Communist East Germany. As the west and south of Germany became American, English, and French administrative zones, the newly created eastern bloc would soon be encircled by an "Iron Curtain."

All this time, from January through April 1945, we spent many nights in our apartment's air raid shelter. Our basement was one flight underground and qualified as a bunker. We didn't realize either how close the ground fighting of the last resistance had come to Döbeln. North of us in Leipzig, Saxony and east of us around the Elbe and Neisse Rivers, the war raged on. Every night, the sirens blared and we heard the droning of planes approaching. We rushed down into the basement with gas masks in hand. At night, rather than putting on pajamas, we slipped into *Trainingsanzüge* (sweats) to be ready for possible night attacks. Time was precious between the sounding of the air raid sirens, jumping out of bed, finding shoes and coats, and running to the shelter.

Preparedness was drilled into my generation. Children obeyed and followed any repetitive actions without grumbling. Like little soldiers we ran when told, hushed when demanded. I felt no fear as long as familiar, caring adults were present. I hoped nobody would make me wear a gas mask. The first time Mutti pulled one out of a box, checking for size, I cried for fear. This rubbery black mask with goggled eyes and detachable mouthpiece reminded me of a pig's snout. I was told not to worry for chances were slim if it would come to this. Mutti put the masks back in boxes, but had them handy at all times.

Our apartment building was on the intersection of Hauptstraße and Moltkestraße. It had eight apartments on each street with separate entrances. But underground the space was accessible from both houses. The underground space of this corner building had a number of separate stalls for every occupant's storage, and a generous common area. In fact, more people from our neighborhood without secure basements had extra space assigned to them in our underground dwellings.

Our basement was converted into real living quarters. Shelves with canned foods, bins of potatoes, crocks with homemade sauerkraut, bottles of wines and cognac, all neatly stacked. The potatoes sat in the corner almost adjacent to the coal briquettes. They would be hand-carried in sturdy buckets as needed to heat up our upstairs apartment. The food was carried up or down the stairs all the time, because we didn't have refrigeration. Basements stayed cool and kept the perishables cool.

We also had a living room and bedroom. Three *Militär Lazarett Betten* (military *hospital* cots) stood in the middle of our stall. Scratchy, drab olive blankets, kept us warm at night. They probably were also military surplus, because our family was used to finer qualities.

The cellar's stalls hadn't been planned for privacy. One hundred people congregating in one basement wasn't unusual. But living in the same apartment building, we had privileges with our own storage stalls, separated from other tenants and secured with padlocks. We avoided strangers by hovering in our own 9x9 ft private space. In addition, Mutti hung several old sheets to block the view, a fence-like front with widely spaced slats. The view of extra foods could tempt an envious neighbor to break in.

An emergency communal kitchen was also provided with various thermos bottles filled with hot tea, buckets of water placed on the earthen floor or on small tables. All kinds of picnic utensils, made from tin and china pieces, were stacked in wicker laundry baskets. Jars with crackers and cookies, stored in metal boxes, along with canned pickles, dried fruits such as apples and pears kept kids and adults calm during hours of interrupted sleep and stirring of strange people. I didn't know all the neighborhood folk, but learned quickly that one of them, Frau Kellermann. She sat on a chair, had a blanket wrapped around her body, only exposing her legs and feet. Suddenly she led out a blood-curdling sound.

"A Rraaattt."

In the dim light, I saw people jump up from their cots and chairs, stumbling all over each other.

"Did we get hit?" Somebody yelled.

"No, not yet. If Frau Kellermann wouldn't make such a racket, we all could be safer around here."

Mr. Dietz raised his bass voice, "Underground living is for our safety, neighbors. But people need to be disciplined without hysterical outbreaks. We also need to keep our children calm."

From that day on, I knew who Mrs. Kellermann was and found out where she lived. Onkel Dietz was right, how could she scare everybody because the rat ran up her leg. Maybe I didn't see the distinct difference between a mouse and a rat.

Running to the shelter had become a routine that soon became the norm. While in our apartment, we rolled down black, plastic curtains during darkness and used light sparingly, sometimes only candle light. I don't remember much commotion when Mutti went through her routine of getting us to safety. Then the warning sirens blared, folks came running from a few blocks away to reach our bunker. Houses with bomb shelters were marked with a white fat horizontal line, ending with a diagonal line and arrow pointing downward. It was a prominent sign people recognized.

How to use gas masks had been mastered early on. Mutti followed the block warden's instructions regardless of my frightened reactions. The family's gas masks remained out of sight. Mutti didn't care for my screaming.

By the end of the war, our basement was very crowded. Mutti decided to retire into our stall was like hiding in a playhouse, but we also witnessed increased altercations when strangers mingled in the tighter than normal spaces.

February 13 and 14, 1945 remained in my mind forever. Night had come, when we heard the roaring of what seemed like hundreds of bombers. Somehow the block warden knew that Döbeln wasn't in danger, so he allowed the people from the bunker go up into the courtyard and watch. The sky was lit like day light, converging in one area right above us. Hundreds of blinking lights and sounds of angry, swarming bees droned and passed Döbeln, apparently on their eastward flight to Dresden. The sky's illumination was spooky for I had never seen such a spectacle before. I shivered in spite of our cozy sweats and Mutti held us close to her side.

"They are headed toward the big city," one of the bystanders remarked. "We don't get it here, because we are an insignificant town."

Mutti seemed to trust the man's voice, but pulled Achim and me even closer. The courtyard was dark; people could neither stumble nor fall because we were crowded like a herd of cattle rushing to their troughs. The only good news was that this very night we would be safe in Döbeln without spending another night in the crowded air shelter. Our comfortable feather beds in the upstairs apartment hadn't been slept in for weeks.

I don't know when we learned how badly Dresden, thirty miles away from us, was hurt. A few weeks later, the Russian war machines rolled into the eastern region of Saxony. Without phone connections or reliable radio reports, we didn't know what was happening from one day to another. As programmed, we trudged up and down the stairs to and from our underground existence.

Schools had been closed since 1944. I had recently turned six and attended first grade for only a few months. Now, I should have been a second grader, but hardly experienced public school while in Döbeln. I was too young to comprehend what war did to us, but lived in a constant state of confusion. The rapid changes robbed us of our previously felt sense of belonging. Besides, nobody counseled children in those days. Kids had to shut up and stay close. Fortunately, I owned some books with colorful pictures, especially a children's Bible which I studied with interest and carried it under my arm for comfort. On other occasions, I chose one of my dolls and held her close to me.

One day in May of 1945, I was excited because we were going to the movies that afternoon. We looked forward to this weekly event and dressed in our Sunday best. The children's movie usually presented some of Grimm's fairy tales in black and white on the big screen. We'd already seen *Hänsel und Gretel, Der Frosch König, Rapunzel, Schneewitchen, Die Goldene Gans.* Our entertainment was total fantasy and a substitute for candy or chocolate.

Before we could watch our feature, we had to see the obligatory *Wochenrundschau* (Week in Review). Children didn't care about politics of course. But we had no choice except to endure the awful, loud, screaming speeches of Hitler and Goebbel, the propaganda minister. If the grownups' world was in denial, our world, kids and adults alike, would soon disintegrate around us.

On a boring Sunday we loved to go to the movies. Other choices would have been a long afternoon walk, feeding of the ducks in the city's park, or flying kites. Therefore, we endured the propaganda.

Before we left the apartment, I heard the radio and actually paid attention this time, for something sounded quite different than usual. Our *Volksempfänger,* the name of our common radio, was our main information, though it came as censored communication.

Previously, I had managed to block out loud gobbledygook, but on that Sunday in May 1945, the atmosphere suddenly seemed filled with dangerous electric sparks. Did I also watch Mutti's face or watch our maid's sudden stalling? I don't know, but I picked up on *something* different.

"Germany has surrendered!" The radio announcer declared.

They canceled our movie.

"What happened to our fairy tales?" My little brother whined.

We could have celebrated! But I was mad. All this stupid dress up in vain. It was promised to us. The grownups were so busy with their stuff. Would they, *please* explain? Mutti seemed to have forgotten about our afternoon trip to the movies. How strange it was. But why would she ignore Achim and me?

I saw Onkel Dietz whispering to my mother and giving her some lengthy instructions about flags and alcoholic beverages stored in the basement. I couldn't figure out the adults' actions and clandestine conversation. Days later when the occupational forces marched in, I started to understand.

Our basement living had ended. Thousands upon thousands of refugees came our way. The streets filled with caravans of disheveled looking people. They came riding horses, buggies, bikes, or on foot. They walked, limped on homemade crutches with crying little children asking to be carried. The war cripples mixed in, barely hanging on to life. Old people struggled as though they wished to reach their restful graves. Young mothers resembled grandmothers, pushing strollers loaded with bedding, pots, pans, and other pitiful belongings.

Where did they all come from? And what was their destination? We children didn't know. I thought Grimm's fairy tales had all turned into horror stories. Little did I know, this ghastly fairy tale scene was a preview before the real horror show. I must have stared in space, overtaken by shock.

One of those homeless families lived with us for some

time. They crowded into one little room. They spoke a strange kind of German from the East. Grandfather, Grandmother, Mother and two little children lived with us and slept on the floor. Mutti let them use our kitchen and bathroom. She gave them all extra bedding and pillows for about two weeks and shared food and clothing. The neighborhood warden required people with enough living space to house refugees, my mother understood their needs and willingly obliged.

"They are human beings too," She reminded me. I seemed to ask too many questions.

I slowly appreciated my mother's charitable ways.

"Go in there and talk to the children." Mutti urged me, while I was standing around, confused about these foreign looking intruders.

"I cannot understand them," I protested.

"Go in there, now, and be friendly. This is all."

What to do, if they cannot understand me? But to my surprise, they understood my Saxonian dialect better than I understood their East Prussian tongue. Yes, we made friends, and I shared my toys with the children. Later, I mourned the disappearance of my special doll *Marianne*, the unique black skinned beauty from France. But she gave comfort to a little girl who needed it more than I did.

These poor refugees had moved through a harsh winter. The Russians evicted them, and rearranged the map to favor Russia. They also pushed the Poles westwards and gave them a new country further west, former German land.

The father of our hosted refugee family was absent. They didn't know his whereabouts, or if he was still alive. We never found out. By the time our temporarily adopted East Prussian family moved further west into Germany, the

Russians closed in from the East.

For weeks, the scene of more refugees streaming through the streets repeated itself. To behold the misery on a daily basis dulled our senses. We lived like real characters in scenes of a continuing drama. It was like a scratchy, old LP that jarred our nerve endings with constant irritation. The broken needle scratched and screeched.

Homeschooling

Attorney Walter Dietz housed his law office inside his spacious apartment. But during the war years, his business had declined. He was originally a criminal defender, but during the war his work load systematically dwindled down to nothing.

Thanks to Mr. Dietz Sr. and his patience and love for us, I learned to read easily and could recite Latin before memorizing German poem. Since Walter was at war, Onkel and Tante Dietz gave us all their loving attention. I was taught to read and write while having fun and playing around. Learning with Uncle Dietz was fun. No rules, but discipline was implied and never mentioned. Especially after our vacations at the Silesian estate, I was eager to resume my studies.

After lunch, he took his nap on a droopy old couch. A tapestry hung behind the canopy depicting a forest scene with a roaring stag and his deer family, and little rabbits jumping through the grass. I thought about this wall hanging, because in later years, I developed a disdain for such art work. But it fit the Dietz's decor. My brother and I climbed the attorney's resting body. We couldn't do too much damage to an old suit with soup and gravy-stained vest.

Tante Dietz, a pleasant and plump little gray haired

lady, shook her head. To her, this idyllic picture of her husband resting was quite normal, except now he had two children climbing on his belly rather than one. She had become used to mourning: bad times, a son in war, her mother had died, and her husband yearned for his pre-war prosperous law practice.

Onkel Dietz was short, only five feet four inches. He had a demanding presence, and I noticed not only Mutti, but other families in our apartment building, paid attention to him. He was respected. His bass voice sounded pleasant and melodious, but I knew he could change when he needed to shock criminals. But to Mutti, Achim and I, he was a gentle and smart man.

My mother was pleased about the public school's closing and welcomed Uncle Dietz's home instructions. It couldn't have been more convenient. Besides, Mutti not only watched our scholastic achievements but also listened to the older Dietzes for advice. Both of them represented our pseudo grandparents. I don't recall if I ever told my Omi how much I loved our neighbors. Who knows if I would have made her jealous or not?

In spite of perceived normality, I saw things changing in front of my very eyes after May 1945. Suddenly, the happy beat of the marching music from parading German soldiers stopped. We noticed how all the German soldiers vanished from town. The local barracks stood empty. Onkel Dietz interrupted teaching one day and said he needed a short vacation to sort through legal papers. I saw him packing boxes with heavy *Leitz* folders, and I noticed how he conferred with Mutti and Tante Dietz. I didn't know what was going on.

The Russians are Here

World War II ended badly for Germany. Hitler had committed suicide in his Berlin bunker and left his nation to fend for itself. No jubilation. No more marching bands. Instead, a lingering fear was in the air, of anticipated punishment, and the fear of unknown judges. What was coming next?

The waving red flags vanished. This significance of missing *Deutsche Fahnen* (German flags) escaped me totally. I learned this when the first Russian soldiers entered town.

In rapid succession things happened that made no sense. For instance, old, rotten German uniforms lay muddied and scattered along the riverbank and piled up under the Mulde's bridges. We lived close to the river, and crossed it almost daily on our various walks going shopping or strolling. We craned our necks over the bridge's balustrade to see if by chance we discovered dead bodies washed up.

When happenings appeared to be too strange, I didn't ponder the how and why. As any selfish little kid, wondering mostly about my very next meal and our next treat for this day, I turned into a passive observer. German civilians surrendered peacefully with white sheets, hung in place of the former red Nazi flags. The block warden instructed us to hang any size white sheets out of the window to express our peaceful surrender. However, German soldiers were still hunted and searched for in many private residences, including our apartment building.

How blessed an ignorant child's mind works in the middle of disaster. We became curious observers of a new kind of people sneaking into town and witnessed a stream of wild looking soldiers with slanted eyes and dirty worn uniforms, stomping their Army boots in rhythm on the echoing asphalt.

No more happy marching songs: *"Auf der Heide blüht ein kleines Blümelein, und das heißt Erika."* Adults were scared and pulled their children away from the windows. *"Weg vom Fenster"* (Away from the window).

All I heard was: "Good God, they are sending the Mongols." Supposedly, the Germans were afraid of the "Yellow Thread," and therefore seeing them in groups served as a psychological ploy, since they had never seen Asians. Many people didn't realize that Mongolia was also a Russian province.

It reminded me of the Old Testament's Bible story when the Red Sea drowned all Pharaoh's troops. We would be drowned, and erased from the earth. All of us killed without bombs falling from the sky!

The following days and weeks brought *Angst und Schrecken*, (shock and despair). We peeked from behind drawn curtains. Some obscure creatures with flickering flashlights broke windows and climbed into the movie house. Our apartment on the third floor wrapped itself around the corner from Moltkestraße to Hauptstraße, thus giving us a peripheral view which included the theatre and the movie house.

From the children's room we were able to see along the stretch of Hauptstraße where months earlier German soldiers marched. But now, the scary Mongols moved slowly into the inner part of the building, probably expecting some Barbarian monsters attacking them out of the dark. What were they trying to find there? Gold?

My mother whispered to Mr. Dietz who stood next to her, comforted her with his presence. He could interpret everything, not only recite Latin poems.

"Well, Mrs. Hunger," He tried to explain, "This is the beginning. The Russians want to intimidate us. They know we fear the yellow plague." He was referring to the Mongols.

As it turned out, this was the truth. The Mongols didn't kill people. They snooped around and climbed into buildings which appeared ominous to them. They searched for German soldiers. Most likely, they had not seen the muddy, discarded uniforms by the river. It was understood that nobody would communicate with Mongols.

In a day or two, the white-skinned Russians entered the town. The Mongol troops disappeared. But the Russians stamped their hammer and sickle, a triangular emblem, on everything cherished. The old capitalistic lifestyle collapsed in front of our eyes. A new regime cleaned out the old house with an iron broom. Our law books got spit on, stepped on, and swept aside.

By the end of May, Mr. Dietz closed his law firm. He went up and down the stairs, knocking on residents' doors and advising young mothers how to protect themselves against the occupier. I heard him outside when he stopped at our door saying, "Mrs. Hunger, you better go down in the cellar and break every bottle of wine or cognac you can find. The Russians are making house searches. Hordes of them. They look for booze. We don't want them drunk in our house. They'll come searching. Hurry! Break every bottle as fast as you can."

Attorney Dietz was clearly our civic leader among the apartment building's tenants. My mother trusted him with her life and hurried down to the basement. I was right behind her and watched Mutti shatter wine, Champagne or any other bottles containing alcoholic beverages on a pile of coal. The coal was our heating supply as important as food reserves, potatoes, apples and canned good, all sharing the same storage stall. Soon, the fruity, rich alcoholic scent permeated the unlit basement. Shards of glass scattered about, it was a stunning, surreal unnecessary mini war exhibition.

In her anxious destruction mode, my mother hadn't noticed that I had followed her into the basement. She turned to me and warned, "You better run upstairs and mind your brother. I'll be right back! Go now, and do shut the door behind you. I have the key. I'm worried that you sneaked out without closing the door. Go now, girl, run."

Shortly thereafter, I heard more smashing of glass. It came in different intervals and made slightly different sounds.

I thought, "Wow, Mutti wasn't done yet and had company from other residents who went crazy. Vati will be so mad finding his French Cognac all gone."

Less than an hour later, renewed commotion filled the stairwell. This time, it was a stomping noise and repeated banging on doors, accompanied by angry commands in an even angrier foreign language.

At last, the Russian had entered our building. Frightening, harsh voices shouted and demanded and some meek little voice responded. We listened, my index finger over my mouth as I faced my little brother. We stood there motionless like petrified wood, when a sudden loud noise echoed upwards to the third floor. Another bang and crash followed. It came from just one flight beneath us. I imagined broken windows. Then total silence.

Mutti reached for my brother. I grabbed my mother's hand, and her grip felt uncomfortable. We huddled, forming a human bundle with fiercely beating hearts. Six trembling feet remained frozen in place and seemed to belong to somebody else. Our combined bodily heat mixed in with fear for our lives created a sensation of rolling lava from a spewing volcano.

What is wrong?" whimpered my brother. "Quiet!" Mutti hushed. "Hold still, they may pass us by."

Time stood still. What were we waiting for? A sudden knock on the door interrupted the suspense. I imagined several broomsticks hitting the wooden door frame. We waited and listened for more to come. What did we expect though?

Among some unintelligent babbling and shouting, we clearly distinguished Mr. Dietz's assertive voice:

"Mrs. Hunger, you better open the door, or they will shoot it down."

Mutti opened the front door. Lord have mercy! Three stocky Russians stood there with their machine guns pointed at us. One of them had his uniform's sleeves rolled up and exposed several watches, one placed on top of another one.

"*Uri. Uri. Uri.* Soldati, Soldati!" *Uhren* in broken German meant watches. No questions asked. They wanted *Uhren und Soldaten,* watches and soldiers.

Apparently, the Russians hunted the very last un-surrendered German soldiers. It seemed odd to us; but to ask questions seemed even dumber while staring into a gun barrel.

The soldiers pushed us aside and entered our apartment. We got pinned between the old entrance table, now void of Hitler's photograph, and the wall. He was gone, and the Russians forced their way in.

The young fellows elbowed their way first into our living room, machine guns stuck to their bellies as they waved them side to side in repetitive rhythm. Mutti, Achim and I were herded like cattle.

"Move straight ahead," one Russian motioned with his

head to the others to move along like perplexed calves.

"*Deutsche Soldati, soldati.*"   The tallest of the Russians pointed to the bathroom door next, kicking against it with his knee-high boot, because he wasn't about to relinquish his machine gun when maneuvering his body sideways.   It seemed as if he were asking for assistance: "Hey, woman, help me along or else!"

"*No soldati* here," Mutti tried their lingo in vain.

They proceeded, totally ignoring Mutti, one behind the other.   Our bathroom was T-shaped, wide at the entrance where a lion-footed bathtub stood.   A narrow path led to the far end with the commode.   Too closely together, the soldiers almost stumbled over each other fitting side-by-side in the narrow part of the bathroom.

The younger one, probably not older than seventeen, tried to bend down to look under the clawed enameled bathtub. He poked behind the water heater and examined the toilets, every time using the gun like a blind person uses a cane. The scene turned comical and the young Russian moved back and forth, probing with his machine gun under a free standing bathtub and a water boiler.

One soldier flushed the WC, the water closet, or toilet, which surprised the soldiers. They stared down into the bowl. The second soldier copied the first one, and the third one followed their example.

They slowly relaxed their machine guns, and I dared look at their faces for the first time. I noticed two blue-eyed soldiers and one Russian with dark complexion and brown eyes. All wore funny looking boat-like caps with red emblems on them. Most likely, it was the hammer and sickle. I felt like they were in fact Russian, but definitely not monsters.

"What's so funny about our commode?" I wasn't sure.

As I made my observations, they laughed among themselves. The major danger was over, at least for now.

Mutti relaxed and pushed us gently forward out of the bathroom. The men followed right behind us. By now, their guns hung by their sides, and they entered the master bedroom. Miraculous transformations made them appear like nosey relatives who hadn't been around for decades and felt like studying all the pictures on the wall. Every photograph was removed from the dresser and studied. They chuckled and examined the people shown. Whatever they thought and said, it was impossible for us to even guess.

At this point, the young Russians had concluded that this mother with her children were harmless. One man motioned with his elbow in the direction of Mutti's huge wardrobe. He smiled with a gleam of golden teeth.

"Open it!"

My mother obliged and turned the key of the freestanding German wardrobe. The shortest soldier took his machine gun and sorted the clothes, slid Mutti's dresses and suits from one side to the other and checked out her blouses and skirts. They acted like they had never seen women's clothing.

"*Oh, schön,*" meaning very pretty. The Russian comrades whispered to each other like planning their next strategic move.

We had no idea what they said, but a few days later some Russian female soldiers showed up. They rang the door bell, and asked to be let in. The women knew exactly what they were after: Mutti turned on her charm with the female soldiers and gave them engaging smiles. Maybe officers by rank, they had better manners, didn't point machine gun at us, and pretended to negotiate while their pistols remained in their holsters. Mutti sighed with relief and demonstrated her most colorful outfits which happened to be the cheapest ones of her summer collection. They liked them all, piled them over outstretched arms and said in unison, *"danke."*

Our privacy was invaded numerous times. But nothing extraordinary happened to us even though many other people had their lives threatened. For instance, in our apartment house a bang coming from one flight beneath us some days earlier was a shot in the dentist's ceiling. The doctor hadn't been cooperating in opening his safe. The Russians knew that he stored gold for his crown work and weren't about to give it up. However, one shot in the ceiling made him quite obedient.

We found out later that this single bullet got lodged exactly under my brother's bed.

War stories of marauding Russians were plentiful. According to rumors, other soldiers had also fooled around with water closets in different people's houses. The modern invention of WCs was mostly unknown to the common soldier. Apparently, one fool studied the water bowl and determined it was good enough for washing potatoes. One flush and the potatoes were gone.

One of the big potatoes got stuck and caused a plumbing problem. As a result, one fellow was sent downstairs to check on his vanished potatoes. Similar stories circulated from other Germans who experienced Russian occupation.

Our personal stories with Russian intrusions didn't compare with other Germans who suffered cruel treatments and rape. A small town like Döbeln probably didn't scare the occupying forces as much compared to Berlin and major German cities that had their own resistance in place. One story of cruel Russian acts was told by a friend who lived about one hundred miles north from us. The family raised expensive race horses. They grazed on their land for lack of races held during the war. When occupying Russians arrived, they took interest in the horses, thinking they could use them for pulling heavy equipment. However, the horses resisted and acted "stubborn" since their race training was of different nature. The Russians shot them and threw them into a pond. By the time the family came back to check on their animals, they found half a dozen of their beloved animals floating belly-up in the water. How could anybody forget such cruelty?

Mutti had her own gruesome encounter with some filthy soldiers. Upon entering Döbeln, they broke into the police station to take up residence there for a couple of days. During their camp-out, drinking, and searching expeditions and stealing anything they pleased, they created a disaster within the building, including feces in the corners, urine on the walls, throw-up and discarded rotten food items strewn about. The stench of accumulated garbage stank to high heaven and the place needed a good clean up.

The Russian commander must have had some informant who gave him names of prominent ladies of the town. He intended to humiliate them with cleaning his soldiers' mess.

My mother was one of the ladies made to join the prominent cleaning team of the most atrocious filth any humans could leave behind. It was a lesson to the uppity town ladies! Mutti survived. She told us later that she took some old leather gloves along, because she wouldn't touch those animals' crap.

Scheisse was the word in German for shit; vulgarities were not spoken in our family. But she delighted in repeating

83

this word over and over when telling this story. It gave her relief. It gave her control. In the end, she threw her soiled kid leather gloves in the garbage. I imagined Mutti's attitude. "I have plenty more gloves, enough to touch other pigs, if necessary."

The Russians Settle in

A few weeks later, a relative peace set in. The soldiers had calmed down and were housed in the courthouse. Higher ranking officers took over elegant one-family houses, and when lucky, the former owners could remain there and serve them with cooking and housekeeping.

The courthouse, however, was changed. I had never seen feet dangling from the third floor window sills with their booted feet in full view. The soldiers dared their fate. Horses tied up in front of buildings were also a sight we couldn't get accustomed to. They simply pounded a stake in the space of a removed cobblestone. Pferdeäpfel (droppings) lay in heaps, and didn't get cleared away for weeks. What a sight to behold including buzzing flies emerging out of nowhere. How insulting to proud townspeople who loved order and neatness. We felt insulted. I remembered this as a first-grader. It made an ever lasting impression.

Another day during this occupation, I looked out of our bedroom window down to Hauptstraße. I spotted a uniformed Russian soldier on a motorcycle, swaying dangerously from side to side, until losing his balance. The motorcycle's wheels turned wildly, and it flipped over on its side. The soldier lay with blood oozing from his temples. It looked like war all over again, but a self-inflicted one.

I stretched a bit further to witness the next amazing event unfolding straight below my spectator's spot. A short uniformed Russian came out of the downstairs' barber shop. He must have witnessed the accident right from his barber's chair. He strutted into the middle of the road swinging an extremely long bull whip. I had never seen a horse whip before. It had several knots in the strap.

As I learned, it was the Russian commander who carried a whip to keep his soldiers in line. He had visited the barbershop downstairs when the accident happened. Short and fat as he was, he looked from my vantage point in the third floor like a bouncing beach ball with a huge whip.

The commander used a bull whip and hit the bleeding soldiers at least three times. The crack of the whip echoed up the apartment building and made me shiver with fright and disgust. There were too many strange habits among the Russians that didn't make sense to me. They prevented me going back to public school. How much had I loved school, and now I observed the world from an upstairs perch.

"Ouch!" I called out. "Why hit him, and so hard? He is already hurt." More blood oozed from the fallen man's face. I felt sick to my stomach when to my surprise, the fat commander bent down and checked the hurt soldier who obviously hadn't been killed by the fall and had survived the additional lashes.

It was too much to see and comprehend. "Mutti. Mutti." I hollered. "Come see. One Russian is killing another Russian."

I made room for my mother at the window. One look and my mother summed it up with her statement: "Serves them right. You see, the Russian Commander is corralling all drunken, no-good soldiers. This guy must have stolen this motorcycle, drunk and all. He just received his well deserved punishment." This was swift justice according to Mutti.

85

"Hmmm," I said. But I didn't grasp the severity of the actions.

As a child, I didn't understand my family's internal struggles, but I would soon see emerging changes that would scar our family forever. All of us, old and young, would never be a complete family, nor would we ever vacation at our estate in Silesia again. In the coming years, we would have to join thousands of refugees and have-nots to save ourselves from communism.

Red Apron

Summer 1945. The long, red flags with the infamous *Swastika* emblem in the middle were gone for good. Mutti had ripped up the material, destroyed the black center, and stuffed it all into her sewing basket. She made sure we didn't have any Nazi trophies for the Russian soldiers to take back home.

One summer day Mutti decided to sew a *Dirndl* for me. It was light blue with an array of little scattered flowers. Bavarian tradition required an apron worn on top of the *Dirndl*, and a contrasting color was a must. The trick remained where to find appropriate materials after the war. A stack of my grandfather's pre-war fabrics we had at home contained a variety of delicately printed cotton. Mutti sewed the dress overnight and rummaged in the cabinet for the contrasting apron material the next day.

Mutti's eyes must have flickered when she concocted the idea of a red sateen apron. What a better use for an old Nazi flag than turning it into a lovely girl's apron.

I paraded my new treasure around my girlfriends. Everybody admired it and wanted one just like mine. My mother blushed and whispered the secret to a lady who lived in the apartment above us.

"Not kidding!" she exclaimed. "Who would have thought of this? Adolf Hitler would turn in his grave if he knew what happened to his sacred flags!"

The woman thought for a moment, and asked, "May I beg you for a piece of special flag material, Mrs. Hunger? Katharina would love to have one exactly like Mani's."

My memory was refreshed when many years later I browsed through the old photo albums. Katharina wore a *Dirndl* identical to mine. Wrapped around her waist was an apron, hanging way down from her tiny frame. It almost touched the ground. Hilarious. Of course, it was made from the very same recycled flag. We didn't have colored photography then, but the authentic Nazi flag was given an unexpected afterlife in black and white.

Wartime items such as parachutes were also successfully recycled. Unused parachute material came in handy, and Opa had manufactured thousands of them. Its fabric was simply artificial silk. Off white. It felt exactly like natural silk.

The excess parachute cords turned into another special find! The most fascinating activity was the unraveling of the parachute's cord. We tied several meters of cord on a doorknob, strung it diagonally across our large kitchen, and then piece by piece, one thread at a time was isolated, cut and pulled. A second helper assisted in assuring that each string stayed taught while isolating and pulling individual strings. This tedious labor was rewarded with the final product: a neat and manageable ball of yarn.

I was allowed to help, and rolled endlessly until the right size ball emerged in the shape of a grapefruit. Similarly, I assisted in unraveling old knitted sweaters, which we used for new caps or gloves. Often, we combined two colors of previously knitted or crocheted garments to transform them into brand new accessories. Early on, I learned the art of knitting, crocheting, hand sewing, and needlework. Nothing was perfected over night, and I spent years under adults' scrutinizing eyes learning to do it all correctly.

We also came up with other inventions after the war ended. The strangest of all was artificial whipped cream. One of the children in the building had a birthday coming up. My brother was also invited. Katharina's mother shared her great recipe for whipped cream and of course Mutti tried it out. Does potato meal sound like a basis for cream? Mashed potatoes come to mind, but whipped cream? The "potato" whipped cream was a hit, and the little guests gobbled it like it was the real thing.

In spite of war and Vati's absence, we always enjoyed birthdays with lots of goodies. Nobody complained. We didn't remember how cream was supposed to taste, so we couldn't know the difference. We had great fun. Sad to say, however, Mrs. Wüstefeld's war invention never made it into post-war Germany's cookbooks.

From East to West

Late in 1945, schools reopened. I was pleased to see the same children I knew from the few weeks I attended first grade. Nobody laughed at me anymore for not knowing how to salute and no one wanted to be reminded of the old *Führer*. Selective amnesia worked splendidly under a new regime.

When I saw our teacher, I felt sorry for her. She looked much older than my Omi. After she introduced herself, she begged the class to ask our mothers for sewing items such as needles, threads, and scissors. Extra paper and pencils. The list went on. At home I told Mutti, "My new teacher has holes in her stockings and needs to mend them with yarn. She is poor, and we need to help her so she can teach me."

"Very amusing," Mutti told me. "Don't worry, you are so advanced with Uncle Dietz's instructions, I could actually keep you at home. You'd learn more at home than in that pitiful school. Come to think about it, we've had nothing but problems there. First, we had to put up with that Nazi principal and now the new folks, who try to convert every child to communism." Mutti stopped.

I had no idea what Mutti really meant.

"Nobody will take notice if you are there or not. They are so disorganized. Besides, your new teacher has no idea what communism is." Mutti turned away from me with a dismissive hand motion.

"Goody, goody, you take me out of this school. Do you really mean it?" I was so flabbergasted and happy that I danced around. "Imagine, reading with Onkel Dietz and learning Latin verses, and singing silly African songs."

Mutti snickered, "Mani, tell me your latest Latin quote Onkel Dietz taught you."

"It goes like this."

I posed, stood there with my pleated navy skirt, white knee socks, and a white blouse with round collar, looking like a student from a parochial school.

"Difficile est tenere quae acceperis nisi exerceas," I quoted.

Mutti shook her head in amazement. "And it means?"

It is difficult to retain what you may have learned unless you practice." Onkel Dietz's words rung in my head. I recalled how sad he was when he talked about his son. "Bella detesta matribus." I told Mutti.

"What does this mean? she said. I figured that Mutti knew this quote.

But I informed her anyway: "Wars, the horror of a mother."

To my surprise, Mutti pulled me close. I couldn't remember another time that she hugged me. It felt odd. She told me that I would soon see my father, and she had to leave for a couple of weeks to visit him. Staying with Onkel and Tante Dietz during her absence would be fun and a great help to her.

Mutti prepared me for her escape from East Germany. But she had to be careful what she told a seven-year-old child about crossing the eastern border. A slip of the tongue could have spoiled her flight. Therefore, Mutti designed a trial run which didn't involve us children. Traveling by train and walking long kilometers through fields and forest was neither suspect nor difficult for kids who were physically fit and used to doing so.

The time between the Russian occupation and the following twelve months remain foggy in my memory. Different important events competed with each other. Therefore, the sequence of events got lost like keys dropped in murky water.

However, I recall one more visit to Olbersdorf, which was close to Zittau. Opa was now a part-time employee in his own factory which earlier had been taken from him. Omi looked sad when she explained that we would never go back to Schosdorf.

"Child," she started. "Strangers took our land. Tante Annemarie had to leave. Within a few days, she and cook Suse packed important belongings and made their exits.

Remember *Ahnfrau*, the friendly ghost, warned them all along, actually weeks before the Russians came."

Too painful to grasp this new reality. I understood changes by looking how my grandparents lived. The downstairs villa was occupied by Russian officers who allowed the Wagners and Tante Annemarie to live upstairs and make a nook in the bathroom for cooking. We were asked to speak in hushed voices and warned not to open any downstairs doors.

Omi added, "We are *enteignet* (disowned), no more capitalism, only communism. And all people will be the same and have the same."

"No!" I cried. "That is our house, and our stuff. How can they take whatever they want?" Communism didn't make sense to me.

"Shhh. Mani, please speak quietly. We lost everything but our life, thanks to God." Omi consoled me by laying her hand on my shoulder.

I felt relieved that Omi regained a faint smile. As she moved her hand down to my waist and pulled me closer, I knew things would be fine again someday.

Omi bent her head closer to mine and whispered, "But I have a surprise for you. Let's go together into the garden. I have new animals you'd like to see. Cages of rabbits and Guinea pigs Omi's new-found cheerfulness showed. Her face had make-up with rouge spots.

Hand in hand we walked down the gravel path to an out-of-the-way corner of the garden to see Omi's new little animals.

"How cute, Omi. I never saw a Guinea pig before," I exclaimed. "Can I hold one?"

Before long, I held Peter, the Guinea pig, who looked

91

like a Calico cat without a tail. "Omi, I love him. Can I keep him?"

On the train back to Döbeln, I held Peter in a wooden box with penny-size breathing holes and carrots and water in small porcelain bowls. We made it home with little trouble. But Mutti remained an unwilling participant.

"How are we keeping that animal? We only have a balcony in the back," she said.

"Good enough, right next to the kitchen. Perfect." I tried to allay her concerns.

Much later, I found out that those Guinea pigs were specifically raised to supplement meager meat portions during that time. The farm was gone, and no food to be had anywhere. Ration stamps for food remained. Food staples ran out across the country. Transportation was halted, and railroad tracks were ripped out and shipped to far off Russia. What were families supposed to do next? Steal food from the fields? Many people did.

Every day, we went out to search for food. We visited farmers outside town and talked them into letting us pick up apples, those that had prematurely fallen off because of worms and other insects. We picked dandelion leaves and made salad from it. Elderberries were guarded like treasures. On our afternoon excursions we wandered around and searched for berries which we used in soups and desserts, thickened with cornstarch and a pinch of sugar when available.

I realized, over half a century later, that my beloved Guinea pig must have become victim to such human survival instincts. I cried thinking that my sweet little pet supposedly was shipped back to Omi's house, because we were getting ready to see Vati. Mutti told me that Tante Dietz couldn't stand animals that reminded her of rats. Though I argued against such an assertion, I believed it.

During our daily scavenger's hunts, I learned about nature. In a few weeks, I was able to distinguish between poisonous or acceptable mushrooms. Some red berries on bushes were taboo to touch. "Bird food only," I was told. The potato plant could be poisonous. Any part of the potato plant growing above the ground was unsafe. I knew people who went to outlying fields and stole potatoes, digging them out of the ground and carrying them in large burlap sacks home. We never joined those tote-carrying folks, the potato *Klauer* (robbers). That would have been beyond Mutti's dignity.

Big laundry days were adventure days. They happened about once a month and were quite an educational opportunity. The washhouse was accessible from the courtyard with descending stairs, which looked to me like the dark opening of the apartment building's bowels. Tenants took turns in using this location. A coal-fired, low-sitting stove was heated up. Above the stove, safely connected, sat a huge vat with removable lid. The women held a water hose and filled up the tank with running water. All white cotton laundry, bedding, underwear, table clothes and towels, were boiled – detergent added, and one woman stood on a stool, long wooden paddle in hand, stirring the laundry like it was a witch's cauldron.

Usually two housewives worked together. By the time the laundry boiled, the whole washroom was filled with steam, and wandering little kids would find themselves lost in sweltering billows. I imagined riding vicious waves in the angry North Sea.

"Ship ahoy!" I heard. But no, it was Mutti shouting, "Children are off limits here. Play in the courtyard. You have a ball."

And so I played with my little friends. I had Katharina, her little brother, my younger brother and Renate Holzapfel, who played with me in the courtyard while the women carried out baskets with laundry to a designated grassy square. Surrounded and secured by a short chain-linked fence, it was solely an area for drying clothes. But I distinctly recall at least one incident when I played tag with Renate, running between snow-white sheets and underwear flapping in the breeze. We ran along the rows and turned at the end of the line. At this spot, I lost my balance when maneuvering around the pole into the next lane and touched one wet sheet which my grubby little hands. Unfortunately, I left an imprint behind, telling the world that Manuela was here.

"Let's quit. We can play ball outside this garden." I knew I was in trouble if Mutti or her helper found the print. But I was never found out. For the most part, I was a well-mannered child who desired to please.

At the end of one dramatic wash day, we children had the reward of eating *Dampfnudeln* with butter and cinnamon. It was made out of yeast dough and steamed in a large pot with milk on the bottom, some sugar and butter added that would caramelize in the cooking process. It was prepared over low heat, and once in a while Mutti would listen closely to a faint sizzling sound that indicated the dumplings were done. She and her contemporaries cooked those specialties with expertise which I remained incapable of doing up to this day. Sometimes, when the season was right, Mutti filled these dumplings with pitted prunes.

A few days after the washday, we had an appointment at the electric mangle. Sheets or clothes were inserted under a heavy, four feet wide solid wooden cylinder and rolled out on the other end, nicely pressed. Renate Holzapfel's mother operated such a business. I went along to help place pressed towels and table clothes in a willow basket.

"Careful, careful," I heard. "You must place the laundry gently and make two neat stacks side by side." There was another woman, in addition to Mrs. Holzapfel, who fed the clothes on the operator's side together with a young girl, probably another *Pflichtjahrmädchen.*

The night before carrying the laundry to the mangle, we sprinkled it and rolled every piece into a sausage. I called it marinating. Low and behold, the wooden rollers flattened all the sausages into pristine and spring-like meadows of white clover, stoking my fantasies, which included the outdoors and dreams of vacations on the farm.

WE TAKE NO RESPONSIBILITY FOR CHILDREN. The sign warned of the danger. I wasn't to touch anything but the already folded stacks in the wicker basket.

In between our folding, I sneaked around with Renate. Every time I came, she offered me a piece of fruit. An apple was a delight, especially since it never let me forget Renate's last name Holzapfel which actually meant wooden apple. When we sat in a quiet corner chewing on our seasonal fruit, I admired Renate's brown braids reaching way beyond her shoulders. Tiny curls had escaped her braids and coiled around her rosy-cheeked face. When we left, I missed her, and I kept one postcard she wrote for my birthday.

Stuttgart - The American Zone

My mother sneaked over the border from East to West Germany and back again for practice. The second time, she picked up some belongings in order to escape for good. It was summer 1946. Vati had devised a plan and apparently knew a wooded and isolated border area where the Russians didn't patrol. Mr. Salzer, Vati's unemployed war comrade, agreed to be both a guide and accomplice to take Mutti to the south side of the border. They crossed the state line somewhere in northern Bavaria and then took a train further south to Stuttgart, so Mutti could reunite with Vati and make future plans.

Americans and Russians had stopped being allies. Communication between the Russian and American Zones turned more hostile by the passing days. The American Zone in the south was a desired area to flee to after the war. It was preferred to the English or French zone. The American's reputation for humane treatment of prisoners and civilians was well known. They also had more available resources to restore some resemblance of normality in the destroyed country.

After a few weeks, Mutti came back to Döbeln. Whatever transpired between her and Vati while together in Stuttgart, or what future plans they discussed, Mutti didn't tell us. I had no idea how we coped with our goodbyes to family, friends and neighbors. White lies and wishful thinking helped us swallow the bitter medicine of leaving. We deserted the present, familiar life with aching hearts and embraced the scary plunge into the unknown abyss with bravado. How we crept and crawled through the dark forest along the border, I don't remember, but we made it to the other side, to freedom.

We fled to a refugee camp. Some images of going through it will never leave me. The refugee camp was an old castle with winding stairs leading up to large converted dormitory. Along the way, we saw this huge community bedroom, human waste in corners half-covered by bunched up pieces of newspaper.

Rows of rough hewn bunk beds held children and

adults, some dying. People were stacked side by side and in layers, on the top and the bottom with hardly any space between them. The scene looked like a heap of humans. They were in different shapes and sizes and different ages, but all piled up like rubbish waiting for the next garbage pickup.

I was horrified at having to sleep next to an old, smelly man—unshaved—who hadn't been touched by a washcloth in weeks. I grabbed a scratchy green army blanket, which consoled me a bit, but not enough to keep me from crying for my mother.

"Where's my Mutti?" I felt desperate.

A raspy voice answered. *"Deine Mutter liegt unten."* (Your mother sleeps below).

I wanted to see her. How could I trust anybody to tell me the truth? I wondered if Achim slept right next to Mutti? Fear of abandonment came over me and strangled me with squeezing hands. Did Mutti answer my call or not, I couldn't recall later. I cried myself to sleep. Nobody cared.

During the night, another fear paralyzed me. How would I find the bathroom if necessary? And how would I climb down that bunk bed? The castle was dark, only a single light bulb dangling from a high ceiling. I would step into human excrement even if I could get out of this bed. The night was filled with nightmares, but when I opened my eyes, I saw daylight braking through narrow windows. I saw Mutti standing beside her bed, reaching for me. She must have called my name to wake me. I was glad to escape my night horrors for good.

We proceeded without washing or cleaning our teeth in order to get in line with other strangers. My hair was uncombed as we stood with other bedraggled individuals and mean-looking nurses with red crosses on their sleeves. They jabbed long needles into each of us as we moved along the line. Everybody had their left upper arm exposed. Herds of human animals vaccinated.

There was another line - and another one - how many more, I didn't know, but I was pushed from behind to go on. I was petrified like a calf being loaded on to a truck it had never seen before.

We gave the authorities Vati's legitimate address in Stuttgart. He had given Mutti papers earlier, verifying his employment as a translator for the American court. Official papers with stamps and signatures allowed us to travel south with the next available train. Something with this bureaucratic procedure prevented my mother from obtaining refugee status. We actually lost all future existing State benefits which in the moment of total confusion seemed irrelevant. We had no way of imagining our future.

We waited many long hours for a train to reach Stuttgart. In the American zone, railroad tracks had not been removed, but many tracks had been bombed. The trains ran on one set of tracks in one direction on one day, and back in the opposite direction the next day.

When we heard a train approaching, we saw it was a cattle train. No windows, just a large sliding door with manure splattered everywhere. It didn't matter. People piled in, falling over each other, mothers holding on to their children. There we hovered again, in post-war emergency transport. Again, there were no bathroom facilities. People pushed their way through to the designated corner used as a toilet. A sliver of light peeked into the dark bowel of human misery directing us to the bathroom. Years later, when I saw pictures of the Holocaust, I knew exactly how those children must have felt when loaded into cattle trains. But our destination was much different from theirs.

We arrived at Stuttgart *Hauptbahnhof,* according to a sign. But nothing appeared recognizable as a viable city. The former majestic building with glass dome that used to welcome traveling passengers was gone. Nothing but ruins, rubble, and disheveled human figures rushing about like disoriented, angry bees whose hives had been removed. The major war clean-up was in full swing. *Die Trümmerfrauen,* woman who specifically salvaged bricks out of ruins, had already cleaned broken bricks which they sorted, stone by stone, for possible reuse. In a way they resembled a version of "Rosie the Riveter," but not as clean and pretty as the WWII advertisement led you to believe. Cleaning out the ruins was dirty work, and the women looked like our scrubbing woman in Döbeln. The women in Stuttgart had soot-smeared faces and were clad in rags from head to toes. A chimney sweep would have looked cleaner and more attractive.

At the age of seven, I had never seen the physical destruction of war until this precise moment. This was a nightmare during waking hours and it wouldn't end. I remember a streetcar ride, down Königstraße, and seeing windows blown out. I could touch the devastation, but I couldn't grasp it. It was a horror movie in black and white, X-rated at best.

A formerly majestic shopping district was unrecognizable. Stuttgart had two castles, one referred to as new and the other as old castle. Less than half a kilometer from the train station, they had been burned out and looked like a structural skeleton whose heart had been violently ripped out. A row of still-standing Greek pillars in front of what once was a palace pointed fingers heavenward and lamented the results of 53 air raids which dropping estimated

184,000 bombs during September of 1944.

The streetcar ride went on for 20 minutes until we reached our destination. The neighborhood, called Hesslach, was a predominantly blue-collar district, and probably the least desirable in Stuttgart. But soon, I was immersed and learned so much about its people and opportunities to grow in spite of my initial adjustment difficulties. For the first day though, the beautiful Swabian city, in the capital of Württemberg, was covered in a black mourning robe. I was overwhelmed by emotion. I was tired, sad, and missed what we had left behind: a predictable life without ruins.

Vati was nowhere to be seen. Mutti apparently knew where to get off the streetcar and pointed up a steep hill. "Up there, about three blocks away is where we will live." She sounded like a robot.

"That's a mountain, isn't it?" I was befuddled.

"Didn't you notice, Mani, that Stuttgart is surrounded by hills, woods and vineyards. We rode along the bottom of the valley, and now we climb the first hill."

Mutti tried to explain new sites, still unfamiliar to her. She dragged my brother and I along. We must have looked like a couple of rag dolls, limp and exhausted from the many new impressions we couldn't process all at once. Achim was totally mute. Climbing the hill, I lost my voice and memory as well. I tuned out the general destruction along our way. Too tired to focus, I trudged uphill with my last strength. I tried to block out all depressing sights and prepared for the new revelations ahead.

I was so shocked by all the devastation I had seen riding by streetcar. I looked through blown out windows and observed hundreds of bedraggled people everywhere.

"Why did we leave our beautiful place in Döbeln?" I

asked. No answer.

"Your Vati is expecting us," Mutti said.

"And why wouldn't he be at the station?" I wondered.

"There are no reliable train schedules these days; I'd say was his excuse."

Mutti apparently knew her way to our new apartment, so I stopped worrying. Within half an hour we had reached No. 10 Dornhaldenstraße, our new address.

Vati had insisted that we escape East Germany to join him in the American Zone. We found out that he had been a German POW under the Americans, but found employment with his captors. His language skill and lack of association with the Nazi party enabled him to make a decent living for us. It had felt right and plausible that Vati wanted his family to join him in Southern Germany.

The day we arrived in Stuttgart, Vati welcomed us to our apartment. Full of hope we had met up with Vati. He handed Mutti the keys and left within the hour. Did we have a heartfelt embrace with Vati after two years of separation? Truly, I cannot remember. Too many negative feeling were engulfing me, and I was unable to accept any of them, I wondered what other ruinous scene would open in front of my eyes.

Pondering hurtful events, passing through the refugee camp, leaving behind our relatives, our friends and belongings, I preferred not to notice, to feel or to see. I believe Vati kissed us with a vague kiss on the mouth, his usual routine; it did nothing to sooth my longing for his reassurance and his love.

After this first hello, we saw Vati merely coming and going, only bringing food and children's clothing, or stopping to give instructions. Nothing felt right or secure for us. We learned that life could be cruel and disappointing. Our happy welcome was cut short. Mutti spoke in short commanding sentences. Vati and Mutti hid their own feelings for one another from Achim and me. It was hard for me to learn about their grudges and unhappiness. Vati acted very angry, never shouted, but lectured Mutti endlessly with sophisticated words that I didn't grasp, like a school teacher talking to a stubborn child who refused to do his homework. Mutti would cry a lot and threw up her hands in desperation as to say "What now?"

Getting Acquainted With the City

A couple of days after our arrival, we walked down a steep hill, one of many in the town of Stuttgart. The streetcar Number One stopped at Schreiberstraße.

"Just in time," my mother whispered, as she hopped into the streetcar, turning to make sure I was right behind her. Then she stopped at the first handrail to let other passengers pass into the seating area. A stranger, who had entered right behind us, caught my attention. Big city living was a new experience to me coming from Döbeln. I wasn't experienced in people-watching. Since no seats remained open, we stood there holding on for support. Signs saying *"Bitte festhalten"* reminded passengers to be secure.

The man stood there as well. He studied my mother from top to bottom, then reversed his movement and stopped, resting his eyes on Mutt's slender, nylon-covered legs.

Why are you staring, this is *my* mother? I thought. I realized, sometime later, that my mother was a strikingly attractive woman. In her thirties, Mutti was dressed in a pre-war exquisite outfit which made her look better than most women during 1947. The whole center of town stood destroyed. Only the roads and the tracks for the streetcar were cleared of debris. Women climbed around house ruins, gathering usable bricks, chiseling off old mortar, stacking them neatly up in rows. Mutti looked so different, and people gawked because she seemed out of place.

Riding the streetcar line number One to downtown was new and impressive since in Döbeln, we had no public transportation and walked everywhere we had to go. It was obvious; our life in the American Sector of Germany was going to be different.

This was my second trip on the streetcar in the huge city. My mother had become my only adult reference and safety. Mutti took care of us while in Döbeln; but I always compared to my Omi who allowed me to live in a boundary free wonder world when we stayed on the farm in Silesia. Somehow, at the age of eight, while riding that streetcar, I knew things would never be the same. Mutti, in contrast to Omi, was a strict mother and had a no-nonsense approach. I knew when we fled East Germany, weeks earlier, our family structure and life had been disrupted forever. A hard puzzle piece was falling in place.

Mutti's presence grew more important to me. It was a healthy change. But I still felt all alone in this southern city of Württemberg. It is located along the Neckar River, surrounded by hills and thousands of vineyards. The inhabitants die *Schwaben,* spoke a strange dialect. There was nothing inviting here for a child. No peaceful streets with cobblestones or friendly folks greeting us. Here, we rode in the crowded streetcar with sweaty, unfriendly people. Today our plan was to shop for a pair of leather shoes for me to wear to school.

Refugees had been pouring in since the end of the war. The Swabians of this area treated "intruders" with mistrust.

Housing was scarce, and thousands of bombed-out apartment buildings were years from being rebuilt. The shortage of food was staggering, and the government couldn't keep providing basic needs for the citizens.

I tried to understand the language people talked around us, but couldn't make out a word! "We are in Germany, aren't we?" I asked my mother. *The kids at schools didn't seem to like me. My Saxonian dialect made me a laughing stock.* I was more confused than hurt. Mutti must have picked up on my thoughts, for suddenly she said, "Child, you best speak High German."

"Yes, Mutti, I shall try."

"In time, you'll pick up their Swabian dialect. But if you'd speak like I do, like the Prussians do, you'll never have trouble communicating anywhere in Germany."

Of course, Mutti was correct, because the standardized German language was High German mainly spoken around northern Germany where she was raised. The Saxonian dialect was ridiculed by other Germans though it was actually more related to High German than any southern dialect such as Swabian or Bavarian was. All Germans learned to read and write in the standardized form, but hundreds of variations existed.

More worries overcame me. The train's rattling faded in the background, while I thought about my language problem. Mutti wants me to speak like a Prussian. Not so good. Maybe tomorrow the girls in schools will notice my nice new shoes. Let's see if Mutti will allow me to wear them, or if she will make me save them for Sundays only. And where is Vati? Doesn't he want to live with us? Did he give Mutti money to go shopping today? Everything is strange.

"Mani," I heard my mother. "You need to be right

behind me. Next station we'll get off, *verstanden?*"

I understood, and answered in a low voice, but I was more absorbed with our new living experience in Stuttgart, in the state of Württemberg. I slowly followed Mutti. How I missed Omi and Opa.

"Wilhelmsbau!" The conductor called out.

"Hurry," my mother reached for my hand and pulled me in the direction of the exit.

I jumped out of the streetcar, and Mutti cut me a look as if to say "we are now in the big city, watch out!"

Even though new in the city, Mutti was moving through city crowds with the apparent command of a general.

Every day, like the lifting of the fog, things came into focus and made a little more sense. We arrived from East Germany carrying only a few belongings. Somehow we had arrived at the bombed train station of Stuttgart, and took this very same streetcar Number One in the opposite direction. I recognized the many different lines and read with increased interest the posted destinations.

My mind went back and forth between our new home. I worried about my parents' relationship. It seemed like days had gone since my father had advised my mother.

"Mani looks pitiful with those doubly repaired straps on her shoes," Vati had shouted over his shoulder. Once again, he had been in a hurry to leave our apartment. "Make sure you take her to Wilhelmsbau as soon as possible. The best shoe store in town." He looked angry and had some unfriendly sounding words with Mutti. It made me flinch. *Why do they have disagreements? We used to talk differently around Omi and Opa. Have I caused them to act like this? Why do they want to replace my old shoes?*

"*Paß auf* (Pay attention)!" Mutti said. I was absorbed

in thinking about my parents' discord, as I stumbled along. People were pushing, shoving and running to catch another streetcar.

"We are crossing the street right here," my mother said, grabbing my arm, and pulling me in the direction of a store opposite from where we left the streetcar.

The shoe store announced in big letters: ELEFANTEN SCHUHE, which is a trade mark for a good, quality shoe company. However, this fact wasn't explained to me, and I worried about having to wear oversize shoes which they called elephant shoes.

"Can I help you, Mum?" an approaching sales lady greeted us.

Mutti took a deep sigh and answered: "We have a major foot problem with this girl."

She suddenly sat with a sad expression. I remember her teary light brown eyes and drooping shoulders. I couldn't understand what was going on. Where was her earlier good mood? I sat next to her, and Mutti arranged her purse next to me and regained her previous cheerfulness.

"She has her father's exostoses (extra growth of bones) on her feet, legs and knees. Imagine!" The saleslady must have looked puzzled; because Mutti belabored her statement adding, "That's hereditary stuff." She made an apologetic hand motion.

Was I handicapped? Is that why I needed elephant shoes? What about Vati? I thought she must be upset with him.

My mother's complaints continued. "On top of this," she curled her lips, "my daughter has those large, wide feet and children's shoes rarely fit her.

While in my chair forlorn, I yearned for my old worn

out wooden sandals. I glanced at Mutti's pretty cork shoes, white leather wedge, toes exposed.

Mulling over disturbing feelings once more, I sat there perplexed. Wow, more bad news, I thought. Not only do I not speak proper High German, but I also have those bone problems. I used to run and play, climb trees, and keep up with rowdy boys, and suddenly I am a crippled child with elephant's shoes. I wished my Omi were here.

Close to tears, the clerk motioned me to an x-ray box. The machine had the appearance of a lectern. On its wooden structure there were footprints. Distracted by the saleslady's attention, I felt better. Some small amount of confidence returned, as I stepped on the footprints and my feet were measured. Width and length.

The clerk returned to Mother's seating area. "Everything's in order, my Lady, we have nice and sturdy *Elefanten Schuhe* for your little girl. I promise we are on the right track."

She touched my shoulder slightly as if to cheer me. It worked. I felt better as she hurried off in search of those promised shoes.

Mutti sat next to me, but she could have been far away. Her head had turned, and she was focused on the store's entrance. I wondered, *what is Mutti thinking now? Why isn't she happy? Is it our 'extra-toes' problem?*

The clerk returned and, touched by a familiar fuzzy Christmas feeling, I slipped into several different pair, and considered which color to choose. Some oxblood-colored footwear looked and felt especially comfortable. When the shoelaces were nicely tied, the clerk patted my instep and said, "Let's try them out, little lady. Walk up and down on this red carpet." I did what I was instructed to do. I walked around

107

and repeated the trial a couple of times, quite pleased with the new shoes. I remembered thinking, *is this how real leather shoes feel? How did my old pair feel - did I ever wear wooden shoes?*

Mutti perked up again as I smiled. The choice seemed perfect. But she still looked doubtful and asked me, "Mani, are you sure they fit?" Mutti's eyes widened and a slow grin crept into her face as I nodded. "Thank you. What a relief to have this purchase done." Mutti paid and shook hands with the sales lady, then walked to the store's exit, I right behind her, watching Mutti's skirt whip to and fro with every step she took.

I stretched out my hand to say goodbye. By now, the clerk clearly ignored me, obviously more interested in admiring Mutti's outfit. She wore a black silky body-wrapping jacket with peplums and long sleeves. Mutti knew she was beautiful, but at least I was no elephant. That day was memorable in many ways. However, my self-consciousness about my shoe size lingered on for many years. My mother had managed to convey the message that I was ugly and difficult to fit. She had said, "You're a lot like your father."

Was that a good or bad thing? I wondered.

Shocking News

July 1946. It had been only a day or two after our shopping trip for my shoes when the bad news was finally revealed to me. Vati asked Mutti for a divorce. She was in total shock and disbelief when he finally told her. Surely, Mutti knew that something was amiss when Vati didn't spend the night with us, but she didn't say a word to me. Soon, I learned that Vati would never live with us again. He had a plush apartment on the Westside of Stuttgart on

Rotebühlstraße.   The house he lived in had escaped the bombing raids, and the main entrance and vestibule were covered with marble.   A castle compared to our apartment building.

Mutti's anger showed. She ran around the apartment, slammed doors, wailed and shouted. I couldn't console her as she pushed me away to be alone.

"I have followed him and brought his two elementary-schooled children with me."

I started to cry, too.

"I escaped and endured a dreadful refugee camp." Vati left the apartment. The realization of being all alone with a sobbing mother, Opa and Omi so far away were too much for me. *Where was Achim all along? Apparently oblivious and playing in the bedroom while I had to be the older one, the one to witness and endure such a disaster?*

"All along, he wanted a divorce," she went on. "He had planned to leave his family. Was I stupid? Was I blind?"

"No, Mutti, you are neither." I came closer to her and grabbed her around her waist.

Long minutes elapsed – and they turned into hours. I didn't know how Achim found out, was he eavesdropping? But I knew one fact; Mutti had no chance of negotiations. Vati was in a hurry to be free of us. He vanished from our lives like the sun sliding behind the clouds.

Now, only the hope to live and prosper in the free American Zone uplifted us. Mutti's pain remained, but the shock of Vati's leaving lingered on. It was devastating. After all, life had promised to be good again.   We escaped communism, but didn't want to lose our father. Achim and I had only known him shortly during the war, one week at a time when on leave. I'm sure he said goodbye. It felt like a casual visitor who passed through without any emotional ties.

Mutti mentioned how betrayed she felt over and over. "He tricked me out of East Germany to get the divorce papers signed, nothing else. How else could he have obtained a divorce?"

I had no idea either. How could I understand the complications fleeing within one's own country and being required to have legal papers to take a train somewhere else in Germany? We had a beautiful apartment in Döbeln that was close to our relatives; why leave everything behind?

Many German families were torn apart after WWII, and many women had lost their husbands. One of them had lost her fiancé and swiftly grabbed my lonely father. Four years of separation irrevocably hurt my parents' marriage.

The New School

Before our arrival in Stuttgart, Vati had Achim and I enrolled in the new school. I was arbitrarily placed in third grade without transfer papers from Döbeln since officially Mutti never withdrew us from that school. With so many refugees pouring into the West, bureaucracy lagged behind, and nobody worried about a few more students. It was but a few weeks before the summer vacations started. Traditionally, our school years ended around Easter time.

Shortly after the purchase of my new pair of *Elefanten* shoes my mother collapsed.

During our stay at the refugee center, Mutti had contracted hepatitis due to poor sanitary conditions, a weak immune system, she was obviously compromised. But the final outbreak occurred a few days before Achim and I were to enter *Lerchenrainschule*.

Vati had to make fast arrangements for both of his

estranged spouse and children. Being new in town, we didn't have any friends yet, nor relatives to help out when in need. Suddenly, my brother and I were hauled away to live with my father's cleaning lady, a total strangers to us. Vati's cleaning lady lived close to our new school, and he convinced her to take us in until soon approaching summer vacations. Achim and I could walk safely from the cleaning lady's house to school.

Lerchenrainschule was nestled into a green mountainside. It looked picturesque from a distance. However, being dropped off on my first day with thousands of dirty, smelly children was traumatic to me.

Since Mutti was hospitalized, Vati picked up Achim and me and drove us to school. His white sports car drew attention and was a painful contrast to how most people in this neighborhood lived. People were starving, and nobody else drove a fancy car. Here we were new students and didn't need gossip to welcome us. I wanted somebody to hold my hand to help me blend in. He could have walked Achim and me to the school's entrance, but instead he dashed off in his sporty little car. Vati was always in a hurry to be somewhere else. After this day, we learned which streets to take. In fact, this was the first and last time Vati drove us to school.

The public school was a place to hold war-damaged, hungry children. Eventually we were sorted out by some helter-skelter procedure. I felt like an injured antelope in the middle of some carnivorous wild African animals. The roar was missing, but I was all alone, misunderstood, disoriented and scared as a lost antelope. I felt I was a new arrival at the zoo. I remember incredible times of growling stomachs, lack of soap, toothpaste or books, notebooks or loose paper. Crowds of children huddled and shared ancient, yellowed-by-

111

time textbooks which were printed in the old-fashioned German script. To me, it was like a book of *Seven Seals* (Revelation), and very difficult to decipher.

I could easily hide with that many undocumented kids. The teacher didn't realize I was lacking math skills. With Uncle Dietz's teaching methods, math was more or less ignored. When it was discovered in Stuttgart, an old retired teacher instructed me during summer vacation, and I made up two grade years of math.

Discipline was strict and learning sporadic. We suffered shortages of books and supplies of any kind. For hours on end, they kept us busy by having us copy sentences and rules off the black board. Anxiously, we awaited the bell to ring and the end of monotonous rote learning.

First, I sat next to Hannelore. She was gorgeous, with a sweet smile which complimented her quiet disposition, and her pink cheeks gave her a wholesome look. Her long thick, blond braids hung down her back, and she managed to keep them away from the inkwells, found in every desk. I wished I had thick hair like hers or something that resembled braids. I had asked Mutti many times. "Can't be done, it is too thin."

In contrast, my hair was short and dark brown. Simplicity and practicality was Mutti's attitude when rearing a nine-year-old girl. No fanfare, no ribbons, laces or bows. 1946 meant digging out from ruins. We wore recycled clothes, some outfits dating back to my grandmother's day, twenty-or-so-years ago.

This post-war upheaval in Stuttgart thrust us into an unaccustomed environment. School was totally bewildering. Adults were busy finding jobs, food, and especially housing. They didn't explain how to survive. We lived in poverty, surrounded by dirt and unfriendly strangers. I felt like an orphan, waiting to be adopted by a caring family.

Helga

On my second day of school I dawdled, and the cleaning lady pushed me out the door. Achim had left already. I thought he was rather brave to go alone.

"You'll be late and make a bad impression, if you don't leave right now. Your father will be mad with me." *That would be grand*, I thought – *it would show me that he cares.*

Ever so faintly I said, "Yes, yes," and swung my boy's black satchel over my back and headed out. I disliked that bag which had a long flap. Girls' school bags came with short flaps. Cutting off half of the overhang would have easily solved the problem for me, but Mutti had told me earlier it was tough leather and couldn't be done. I was upset. It didn't seem fair, besides she was in the hospital and wouldn't see the other children teasing, pushing and shoving me around in the school's dark stairwell and laugh at my funny speech. I felt bruised before I reached my classroom on the third floor. Achim entered another door and entrance since boys and girls were separated by different wings of the building.

My first day there had been a nightmare. But in the hope of leaving our apartment a bit later this today, I assumed I'd miss the crowds when the doors opened to the school house and hundreds of children stampeded at once.

I watched landmarks to guide me on my second day. It was a fifteen-minute walk, one cross-over at a busy intersection, before I climbed a steep road with a bakery shop on the right side, followed by another five minutes on a side street, before I faced my frightening experience of entering the school building.

113

I mustered all my courage and kept going. I was alone, and with clammy hands I held on to the side straps of my satchel for moral support. I heard somebody coming from behind, apparently in a hurry, with heavy staccato breathing.

In fact, it was an angel catching up with me.

Little girl, stop." I heard a Swabian dialect.

I followed the voice and looked at a girl, almost a head taller than I with blond braided hair and twinkling blue eye, and I figured she was about two years my senior.

It was immediately apparent that she was not one of the rude children I met the previous day, because she said, "You look so scared. Are you from over there?" Pointing in an imaginary eastern direction and indicating that she meant the Russian sector of Germany. She used the German word *drüben*, over there, rather than saying East Germany.

"Did I really show my apprehension?" I wondered, but said, "Yes, we are new here. We came from Saxony."

The girl walked next to me and told me that her name was Helga and she lived close to the vineyards. She stopped a moment, held me by the hand and continued, "Oh, you poor little Spatz? You're so little and *von drüben*. And where do you live now?"

She called me a little sparrow? I wasn't quite sure of our short conversation. Her dialect confused me. However, I noticed she didn't react to my Saxonian twang which was closer to High German than her speech. The people from Saxony spoke with an upwards intonation ending of every phrase and sentence and added unfamiliar vocabulary to the standardized German dictionary.

I did the polite thing, loosened my shaky hands from my satchel and offered a handshake.

"I'm called Mani."

"Pretty. And in what grade are you?" Helga wanted to know. Helga was shocked to hear that I was in third grade. She marveled that I was so small and too young, and couldn't comprehend that she was more than two years older and went to third grade as well. She explained that the war kept her from either going to kindergarten or first grade. Her mother had left Stuttgart, to evacuate to rural Bavaria and escape the bombing. By the time they returned, several schoolhouses in the Hesslach area had been destroyed, and therefore so many children were piled into this Lerchenrainschule. "This school is a horrible mess."

We reached the school hand in hand. I insisted on walking the longer driveway rather than taking the shortcut of hundreds of stairs on the other side. She couldn't quite understand why, but I admitted now that I was indeed afraid of being pushed down and overrun by rude children. I felt better already and convinced that a protective angel would get me unharmed to my classroom.

The bell rang as we turned into the hallway on the third floor.

"How strange that we are both in Fräulein Moos's class. And I didn't see you yesterday," Helga said. "Why wouldn't she introduce you, she's such a nice lady? And my Mama knows her family. They have a flower shop down on Schreiberstraße."

Before we entered the loud classroom, Helga assured me she'd talk to Fräulein Moos right away and promised to wait for me at break time and dismissal for the day.

"I bet you, she overlooked you with over forty students in here, and some more coming and leaving all the time."

Carefully, I forged my way to the back of the classroom. I shared a desk with a Hannelore, who was very

115

nice and quiet.

"Guten Morgen," I greeted her, and she replied, *Grüß Gott."* This was the customary way in the southern states of Swabia and Bavaria. A bit more inspired by my new friend, Helga, I decided I'd switch my greeting to *"Grüß Gott."*

Looking around, I became more aware of my surroundings than on my first day. The windows were bare, no plants on the window sill, no pictures on the wall, except a board with hanging papers that dangled in a helter-skelter fashion. The teacher's desk was slightly to one side of the black board and an invitation was written there for our parents to attend an evening meeting.

"This means?" I looked at Hannelore.

"We have to copy this, Mani," Hannelore answered and kept on writing.

I realized that we had to practice our handwriting. It made sense to copy this invitation off the board especially since paper was preciously scarce.

"You take this home today and hand it to your mother," Hannelore added.

So my second day started with copying a note in my best cursive handwriting. I saw Helga sitting way up in the front at the second desk next to the window and was able to observe the whole scene of restless little girls. Boys were grouped in another classroom which seemed more practical in 1946.

This day was much improved from the first one. Nothing unpleasant happened that I remembered. By the end of our school day, Fräulein Moos called me to the front where Helga joined in our conversation.

"Hallo, Manuela. The office just gave me your enrollment papers. What happened yesterday is beyond me.

How did you slip in undetected?" The teacher asked me.

She's pretty and very sweet, I thought, looking up at her.

Fräulein Moos continued, "Your new friend, Helga, is an unusually compassionate and kind girl. I know her mother quite well. She volunteers carrying the church paper for the neighborhood. Has a heart of gold."

"Yes," I agreed, not knowing exactly about the compassionate part. Besides, I hadn't met Helga's mother yet.

"Manuela, that's pretty," I heard Fräulein Moos say.

Promptly I interrupted her with, "Call me Mani, instead. That's easier and I don't have to explain all the time. My dialect is enough."

"So it is, Mani. The class's dialect would be funny *"drüben"* as well." Fräulein Moos consoled me.

"Drüben" (over there) was the generic place where Mutti, Achim, and I had fled from. To the southern Germans' perception Russian-occupied Germany was merely a conglomerate of German states referred to as *drüben.*

Missing Mutti

Benevolent neighbors took us to see her at the hospital. Nuns in impressive black habits rushed through hospital corridors, spreading love and kindness. Their long, heavy starched bonnets touched their shoulders, as they whipped along corridors like barn swallows flying low. They were the Compassionate Sisters of the Holy Vincent de Paul. Those *Barmherzige Schwestern* originated in a tiny municipality of Untermarchtal south of Stuttgart along the Danube River. I still feel their happiness expressed as they engulfed us with their arms. Their embraces could not have come at a better time. The sisters must have been godsend to look after us.

117

The nuns took care of Mutti, while Achim and I lived in the attic with the cleaning lady's family. The tiny two-story house was built for low income people and its size seemed fit for Lilliputians. We stayed with them for about two weeks. Summer vacations had commenced, and Vati needed somebody else to look after us kids full-time.

After these temporary accommodations, we moved to live with the old parents of one of my father's war comrades, Mr. and Mrs. Salzer. They lived clear on the other side of town, far from the hospital. The times we went to visit Mutti in the hospital, the nuns hugged Achim and me and reassured us that our mother would be with us again very soon. My mother remained hospitalized for several more weeks which seemed like an eternity.

The Salzers were Swabians, typical folk from the state of Württemberg, referred to as *die Schwaben*. Although understanding their dialect was a hardship at first, both Achim and I had made considerable progress in imitating their language. We loved the Salzers, generous people with kind hearts. But again, their apartment was tiny. Their living room appeared to be the size of Omi's pantry. I thought they were poor, not grasping that I had been spoiled by a richer upbringing.

My brother was with me. We were physically close, as we slept in the same room, yet I have no memory of playing together. Did he hide his feelings from me? I'm certain, he wasn't happy either. But as a nine-year-old, I was focused on my own survival in an increasingly strange and complex world. He would need to write his own version, and tell how he coped with all the new uncertainties.

Mr. and Mrs. Salzer treated us like grandchildren. They fed us well with vegetables and fruits out their garden. I loved Mrs.Salzer's dried apple rings that she had strung up in the attic to dry. But Achim and I were allowed to pull a few from the string, a novel thing for us.

At night, Mr. Salzer came home from the brewery and allowed us to try a small glass of beer. He was the brew master at the *Schwabenbräu* and proud of his profession and specialized knowledge. My very first glass of beer was tasted in the Salzer household.

"Malt is healthy and good for children. You will get used to the taste, I'll promise." Mr. Salzer's eyes twinkled, and his wife nodded her head in agreement.

While at the couple's apartment, they saw to it that Achim and I would visit Mutti at the hospital, riding with us in the streetcar for 45 minutes.

Our lives turned in a new direction after Mutti came home from the hospital. We were so happy to have her back and being able to stay with her in our own apartment.

From what we have been used to it, it was crammed with only one bedroom, no central heat, and one toilet off the corridor. We washed ourselves in the kitchen with cold water and shared one commode. Our furniture was made up of odd pieces. Throughout 1946, living conditions remained dismal, and we coped as well as most other refugees. Adjusting to poverty felt like a jail sentence. It was a rough awakening from the have-it-all, sliding into the status of the have-nothings! Even though we had to search for food in Döbeln after the war, we lived in an elegant place, had our belongings, comforting toys, and consoling neighbors. Somehow, without expressing it, Mutti, Achim and I felt that this prison sentence would end one day. But it was much better than the refugee camp we had recently passed through, but in no way comparable to our place in Döbeln.

In contrast, my father had prestige and power. In 1946, this happened seldom. He could afford to employ a cleaning lady. Everybody in the neighborhood knew when Vati showed up with his grocery deliveries. His racy little white *Adler* car, parked in front of the apartment house, raised eyebrows. Private cars were mainly driven by the American occupational forces and a few dignitaries. People whispered, thinking perhaps, that he was a black-marketer. Funny enough, the children in our apartment building called it *Seifenhandel*. It is a strange sounding concept for a non-speaking German.

Vati had a comfortable place with his new lady and continued in his well-to-do status while we felt abandoned. It was as if the war never happened to him. He went through the proper motions, checked my mother in and out of the hospital, and made all necessary arrangements as long as the divorce was pending.

I had to accept the truth that Vati would never live with us again. I was also divorced from my father without my consent. Omi's voice in East Germany didn't count any more. Mutti and Achim had lost their vote as well. I was distressed, totally confused and overwhelmed by all our previous changes getting to Stuttgart. It seemed like I lived in an unlit basement without human contact.

Fall of 1946

Before school had let out, I had connected with Helga. We continued our friendship after summer. While in class, however, I sat next to Hannelore who was also a blessing to me. She seemed different from the others, pleasantly quiet and naturally accepting of me. I was a stranger, a refugee, and new to the neighborhood. Some children ridiculed me, or

120

better, they laughed at my sing-song Saxonian speech. I clung on to Hannelore to survive.

One day, a little package changed that miserable feeling. I recall the very day, as if it happened yesterday. To the children's surprise, packages appeared in the classroom, piled up in a stack to be divided among the third graders.

Hannelore and I received one box to share. In a flash, that meager-looking classroom was transformed into something rivaling Christmas. Wrapping paper flew, strings were loosened, and we girls unpacked curious little things wrapped in colorful paper. We spread them all over the desk. We did not hurry and admired everything from all sides. *Überraschung, wie Weihnachten* (Christmas surprise).

A moment of peace and contentment followed. Excited children chattered, no arguing was heard. We were awestruck!

Our fierce teacher faded from my consciousness. All of the many unwashed children around changed into perfect little cherubs. Hannelore politely and graciously divided the contents of the package. She smiled at me, and we nodded in agreement to our presents' division. We loved our Care Package.

It was absolutely unthinkable that wonderful and generous people had sent treasures to cheer us up. They lived so far away, in America, and they knew what we needed. My share of the package consisted of items I used for many years.

I was elated when I unwrapped the packet. There were colorful Lifesavers, which I devoured on the spot, one after another. Of course, eating was not allowed in class. I dared to break another rule! The day the Care Packages arrived from The United States was special and unforgettable to me and meant that anything and everything was possible. Such expressed love and care lifted me up and sparked my interest to learn more about America.

After eating the Lifesavers, I opened another present. A light blue comb emerged, its transparent, glossy plastic resembling nothing I had seen before. That sky-blue comb I'd received lived on forever. It magically brushed the clouds of my mind. I imagined it whistling and humming with air moving through its teeth. When I left for America, I retired the worn out comb with many missing teeth. In my imagination, the plastic comb continued glistening as if it was a symbol for a new homeland across the Atlantic. The magic comb still smiles in my memory with all its teeth in place.

I don't remember what Hannelore claimed for herself. I was totally self-absorbed and mesmerized with our gifts. She and I knew about sharing, and as we indulged in our private happiness, we did not compare. In later years, I lost Hannelore somewhere when changing schools took us in different directions. In fact, I hadn't thought about her until I recalled this event.

Another very special item had emerged from that Care Package. I found a small tube that I carried home and showed it to the cleaning lady.

"I was given presents at school. Look here," I told her and handed over the empty tube. I couldn't read the label, and when I was examining it earlier I had simply unscrewed the tube's cap and smelled its content.

"Peppermint. *Wunderbar.*" Interesting indeed, what could that be? I took a lick to find out.

"Hum. Pretty good! Hum. *Sehr gut.*" Not like those colored rings with the holes in the middle, but probably the next best thing to it. For awhile, I tasted and I pressed out more gooey peppermint. I licked it and tested even further.

When the cleaning lady finally saw the empty tube, flat as a run-over tin can, she wondered about the lettering. In fact, she had to ask a neighbor who knew a few words of English. When she came back with a questioning look on her face, she asked me, "And where are the contents, little girl?" She looked, puzzled and concerned, but apparently had forgotten my name.

"I ate it. It was peppermint…paste." I explained.

"Girl, do you know what you ate?" The woman's rhetorical questioning didn't fit my excitement.

Toothpaste! And no belly aches either. The revelation didn't dampen the exhilarating day it had been!

We clearly had no idea what toothpaste looked like in 1946, at least not the "modern" type out of a tube. We did have a way to clean our teeth, with a slightly different procedure.

Hard times had eliminated toothpaste, and modern Western ways were coming ever so slowly to the defeated Germans. Yes, we had a kind of toothpaste. With a damp toothbrush, we brushed over a caulk-like bar of pinkish substance until foam appeared. Primitive maybe, no fluoride, no peppermint flavors, no gel, only a hardy scrubbing motion, that was our toothpaste then.

Sometime later, my class wrote thank you-letters to anonymous American people. This small effort inspired us to start corresponding in our beginning English. Eventually, I had several American pen pals whom I wrote on a regular basis. This became an opportunity to study foreign languages and countries, and it also helped me gain a new view of the other side of the Atlantic Ocean. A future door was opening, unbeknownst to me at the time.

Vati had a plush apartment on the Westside of Stuttgart

on Rotebühlstraße. The house he lived in had still had its pre-war look of elegance. No damage anywhere. It was a virtual castle compared to our apartment building.

Vati lived with a strange woman, Else, on the first floor and a shiny brass plate on the door read "Dir. Joachim Hunger." He was director of the well-known Bleyle Company in Stuttgart, and Else worked for the same firm, running the company's *Konsum* (commissary) and selling affordable food the employees, unavailable on the open market. As manager of such precious commodities, she was a powerful woman. She even started sending bags with spaghetti, rice, and potatoes, and some candy for Achim and me to eat. I wasn't sure if eating her donations meant betraying Mutti.

The Bleyle Company's store was the place where Vati met Else. She pampered *Herr Direktor* with anything his stomach and heart desired, and more. He liked this female's caring attention, and was separated from Mutti for close to five years with only a few weeks on military leave. Before he knew it, he was caught in the spider's web and must have decided that Mutti was no longer a good wife.

In early 1947, we adjusted to the meager allowance from Vati. While Achim and I familiarized ourselves with a new school routine, Mutti could not escape her personal misery. The divorce left her facing an uncertain financial future. She couldn't be consoled, and her faith was gone, if indeed it ever existed. Mutti turned into an empty shell without spirit. The little spousal support from Vati dwindled fast. Our security was gone and she had to get over her depression and try to provide for herself and her children.

During our early years in Stuttgart, I remembered taking on the role of mother. I did our daily shopping, cleaning, and supervised my indolent little brother. It was a major task for me to become unspoiled from Omi's earlier doting.

Since our arrival, my regular meals had been what we referred to as the Hoover feeding at school, which improved our lives since leaving East Germany. During the years of 1946 through 1948, I was always hungry. At home, we started our day with stale bread broken up, sugar and hot milk poured over which made our specialty cereal, and it held me over until the best meal of the day which was served at school. A free lunch for students and teachers as well was sponsored through the "Quaker Relief Fund."

We referred to it as the "Hoover Feeding." An American study of the American Zone in southern Germany found that during the early post-war years, adults on the average had only 1,397 calories per day. One pound of cooking fat cost 200 – 400 RM (Reich Mark) ($50 - $100), and one pound coffee beans were 450 – 600 RM.

The food stamps for distribution of daily staples couldn't buy enough food. Neither produce, nor meats were available, unless people bartered, begged or stole. Consumers traded Persian rugs for eggs and butter. When the blue large canisters of "Hoover Feeding" were unloaded at our school, we spotted the canisters from the classroom's window and announced its arrival to the class. Even our teacher showed interest in her share and never chastised us for calling out.

The U.S. President Hoover encouraged the Quakers' good deeds after war. I experienced the movement of WW II, and was forever grateful to have received our best meals for the day. The program lasted for several years. President Hoover saw that large amounts of money were raised through the American Relief Administration to feed one million children in the American Zone of Germany. Our nutritious meals had a repeating menu:

Oatmeal with hot chocolate	344 calories
Peanut butter	450 calories
Bean Soup with meat	360 calories
Porridge with preserves	357 calories
Potato Soup with meat	313 calories
Hot chocolate with white bread	423 calories

Those favorite foods still tickle my taste buds. I loved everything. The peanut butter, unknown to us 'till then, was among our favorites. It seemed that good things happened to us children all the time.

One day, I was lucky to receive a banana from an American military chauffeur parked in front of the Zeiss Ikon Factory. His officer was shopping for quality lenses and related equipment. The young soldier sat in the car and peeled a yellow fruit, and I must have looked interested and puzzled. In fact, I had never seen a banana before.

"Here, little girl, take it." He handed me the peeled fruit. I took and ran like a dog which had snatched some forbidden food from the table.

"And you didn't say thank you?" Mutti questioned me in an accusatory way as I told her my story about this generous American soldier.

I don't remember exactly when the "Hoover Feeding" was suspended. But I do know that in 1949 I changed over to a parochial school. While there, we still enjoyed those daily scheduled meals. They had been our manna from heaven.

Food was always plentiful when we visited Vati. By now the end of 1947, another Saturday parental visit had arrived. Vati picked us up by car. It was rumored that Vati's neighborhood was in the infamous Black Market area of Stuttgart where people traded precious heirlooms and Persian rugs for cigarettes and coffee. Russian and Balkan Jews had quickly moved into this post-war market. While most of the German Jews had left, disappeared, or died, some did come back to reclaim their properties.

Mutti wasn't about to let us walk to the west part of Stuttgart, too far and too dangerous. But as I found out, the apartment buildings in Stuttgart's Westside neighborhood were beautiful, upscale, and safe. On the other hand, people with means and able to trade goods didn't believe that the Westside was to be avoided. I was confused by those supposedly devious Black Market dealings and Mutti's opinion of our convoluted living standards in Hesslach. Achim and I were another type of pervasive war victim - that of divorce. We walked timidly behind Vati and followed him wherever he decided to take us.

As soon as Vati closed the front door of his pretty apartment, Else appeared in the background. I cringed when she came closer threatening to embrace us.

"Not me, please."

I pushed Achim in front of me and tried to hide in an imaginary cloud to be lifted out of this place. I had seen Else before, behind her store's counter, officiating and ordering clerks around. She didn't look so short behind her counter. But standing in front of her, she stood not much over five feet. Two shiny cat eyes pierced me. Her face was outlined by a long scar, starting below the ear lobe and running to the corner of her mouth. She smiled at me, slightly contorted, and suddenly two curious dimples popped up to soften the otherwise menacing demeanor.

"Willkommen," (welcome) I heard Else say as she reached for my arm. I felt my heart beating alarmingly fast.

"Watch out for the devil," my inner voice pounded in rhythm with my heart.

I couldn't contain myself and started to sob uncontrollably. Nine years old, and I cried like a baby. Since I couldn't stop wailing and carrying on, Vati took both of us home. I don't recall giving an explanation for my tears, but I wasn't about to explain myself or apologize for anything. That ended our first official meeting at Mr. and Mrs. Joachim Hunger's apartment in Stuttgart.

Surviving Dangers

Kids climbed into ruins where by now wild flowers had started to sprout. Who would have thought that within a few seasons sturdy plants made their debut in this unlikely place? The burning nettles grew in patches and a candle-like, magenta flowering creation emerged as if to give us renewed hope for a better future.

Mother's Day was important to me. Of course, I didn't have money, and the pennies I earned cleaning Dr. Howorka's room, who lived with us for a while as a sub-renter, were spent on candy the very same day. I remembered that stunning magenta flower in the midst of rubbish and instantly dashed for the nettles. I climbed through broken and burned-out windows and doorways, sometimes giving way to underlying burnt metal and charcoaled wood. Why worry about getting too dirty when most of the soot from the bombing and flames had been washed away by many subsequent rain showers. With confidence, I climbed around, ignoring the possible danger of unexploded bombs.

Our afternoons were longer than those of American

students. Thus, we had enough time to do our chores and homework and still play outside. As a nine-year-old, I ran with groups of kids, boys and girls from the neighborhood. Thinking back to this time, I am amazed how fast the playing children found one another. We played "Cops and Robbers," and extended our roaming to the nearby woods. It was in the vicinity of our elementary school, nestled on the hill side. Surprisingly, the school showed only minor war damage, but the woods looked ravished and unkempt. Trees had been knocked down and burned by uncountable bombing raids, and a huge swatch of a formerly wooded area, stood naked, a no-man's land. We children claimed to be the new explorers, hiding and searching for "bad guys" and totally ignoring the real dangers of the ever present unexploded munitions.

Some bombs had left craters, now filled with water covered over by fallen trees. I balanced on a tree trunk and lo and behold, some of the other youngsters followed my example. I enjoyed acting like a boy, and I fought with the skirt of my cotton dress. We had not a care in the world. We lived in oblivion of the lurking risks.

For several years reoccurring alerts closed the schools temporarily. When construction workers came across left-over bombs and mines, all inhabitants of a designated radius had to leave their homes for up to two hours while the devices were diffused. We children responded to the warning sirens with jubilation of a school "break" and rushed home to engage in other dangerous games. Many single mothers, usually war widows, had to work, and childcare was unavailable. As long as the chores were done, and I was home before dark, Mutti wouldn't worry about me.

The following year, I learned more about the forest area. My roaming territory had widened. As Mother's Day came around, I convinced Helga to come along to pick the prettiest violets for our mothers. We told Mama Knosp that we would go for a walk on the path between the vineyards behind her house. Instead, I took Helga on a much larger detour to the shooting range.

"We cannot go in there," Helga tried to stop me.

"Yes, I know, but we are not going in there while the Americans are shooting," I told her.

The shooting range had been turned over to the Americans. After the war Germans were forbidden to carry fire arms, not even hunting rifles were allowed. The chain-link fence meant "keep out," and was not to be violated. I reasoned that I didn't care to climb over the fence either and rip my skirt, but there might be another way. We examined the fence line. I spied a possible hole close to the ground where we could crawl underneath. The day I took Helga on this forbidden tour, no shooting was heard, and nobody moved inside the fence. We came back with bunches of fragrant purple violets and presented them to our mothers on their special day of honor. I had instructed Helga, never ever to tell Mama about our explorations, out of fear she wouldn't let me come to play.

During summer, I expanded my activities. We had a very rainy summer that year; new creeks formed and ran down from Degerloch's neighborhood directly above the hills. On the bottom of the hill, the water collected in a crater, and we turned it into a make-shift swimming hole. About five children's busy hands formed a dam with smelly mud, sticks and rocks. We built a perfect dam. We pulled off our outerwear and jumped into the refreshing cool water.

That water was murky, dirty and stinky, smelling a bit like sewer. As children we were careless and dismissed the idea that the water was filled with unpronounceable germs. Mutti never knew. "But should she have known? Did she ever ask me where we played?"

Achim and I never knew if Vati even loved us. We demonstrated loyalty to our father and respected him. His attention was oftentimes negative, such as belaboring a poor grade in school, which was usually a "B" or comments about my appearance being too dumpy. Naturally, I thought I was ugly, unwanted, and not too smart. In later years when Mutti remarried and we had a stepfather, Achim and I knew that Papa Theo was consistent in giving his love and care without even having to say the L-word. Mutti never said, "I love you", as was the case with many German adults of her generation.

Adjustment Period

In fact, the housing authority deemed that our three little rooms were too much for a single mother and her two children and declared that we had to sublet the smallest room. A housing shortage, due to the millions of new refugees, made it necessary for our government to control living space. We knew this very well. Refugees from East Germany and eastern former lands such as Pomerania, East Prussia and Silesia, not to mention the Germans who lived in the Sudetenland and the Balkans, had been pushed west into Germany. All these people were looking for new homes.

Such was the case with *Doktor* Howorka who was doing his internship at Marien Hospital down the street. He was a young man, close to thirty and he came from the Sudetenland, an area squeezed between Czechoslovakia and Yugoslavia where many German-speaking folks lived. All of them were expelled from their homeland. We welcomed him, and Mutti told us we could have saddled with someone worse.

Achim and I slept in one bedroom. During wintertime the door to the living room - from where a bit of warmth escaped into our quarters - was left closed, we could actually watch the *Eissblumen* (Frost) decorate the inside of our windows. It was below zero degrees centigrade when these icy flowers blocked the view out of the window. Therefore, the door to the living room, where Mutti slept on a make-shift bed/couch, stood mostly open. A huge *Kachelofen* (hearth) with moss green tiles heated our home. We even boiled water in an inset and sometimes cooked apples with butter and cinnamon.

When Dr. Howorka joined us, the extra third room was lost. The adjoining door to our living room was closed off. The good doctor pasted the cracks of the door frame with plaster of Paris, using bandages dipped into the sticky solution to cover all the cracks. The keyhole was stuffed with cotton and plastered over as well. One way or another, he had his way of creating his own privacy. Besides, he wasn't dependent on our "central heat" since a new pot-belly-stove had been installed in his room.

His room was furnished with a child's bed and nightstand, a mini couch, little table, dresser, and a freestanding wardrobe. An ancient chest of drawers draped with oil-cloth, held a water pitcher and bowl. This creation became his special corner for shaving and morning toilette.

Achim and I found the doctor a little weird. He was tall, dark haired, and looked foreign to us. His German was also strange, and he used words we had never heard before. But with time, we got used to him. What I didn't get used to was the additional chores I was given: cleaning his room and making his bed. I carried the heavy pitcher, filled to the brim with soapy water down the hallway, occasionally spilling water along the way. Fifteen steps with a heavy load, swishing back and forth, was a lot for me. My mother never saw my struggles, and I didn't complain about the job. I was horrified how sloppy and dirty the man was. He left clothes strewn about, dirty and clean all in a single pile. The sorting was disgusting. Rubber gloves were probably used at the hospital for such work, but I had none. I used my bare hands, disgusted and nauseous.

One day, Dr. Howorka was in a good mood. Usually, I tried to hide when I heard him turning the key in the apartment door. But, soon after entering his room, he came out looking for me.

"Thank you, Manuela for cleaning after me." I was shocked to hear him talk like a polite human being.

"Yes." I hesitated. What else should I have said?

"Well, you seem to find pennies here and there that I drop. Why don't you keep them, no need to lay them on the table. I will drop them again."

I accepted my pay and celebrated by rushing downstairs to the Mom and Pop store to buy sour lemon and orange candy with his dropped change.

One day, an old lady, Miss Lächele, who lived in an attic one-room apartment, became my helper. For some unknown reason I had left the front door ajar, when I heard a female's voice call "anybody here?" I knew her, invited her in and explained that I was busy with cleaning Dr. Howorka's nasty room. I'm sure I made a disgusting face when I told Miss Lächele.

"You are cleaning that man's room?" She sounded shocked and concerned, but didn't elaborate further. But after this encounter, she volunteered to look after my brother and I during Mutti's absence and even helped me clean. Bless her;

she tried to instruct my uncooperative younger brother how to help just a little bit. I guess Miss Lächele felt sorry for me.

During that time I was actually anemic. My mother noticed my paleness and gave me a concoction of red wine mixed with raw egg and a spoon of sugar. Mutti indicated she couldn't take off from classes for a doctor visit. She relied on home diagnosis and home remedies. Besides, according to my mother, kids didn't suffer from headaches and belly aches. They were most likely caused by drinking polluted faucet water.

"That should cure it." She assured me. Every morning she handed me the doctored-up red wine, one of her home remedies.

To tell the truth, I felt more tipsy than cured. Even with a doctor in the house, it took some time before he initiated more influence. I guess he waited to be asked rather than assert his medical knowledge.

It actually happened when, during winter when I got very sick with the flu. Piles of featherbeds were loaded on top of me and I couldn't keep warm. I was shivering from very high fever. Mutti called on Dr. Howorka to come and have a look at me.

As he examined me, he was very stern. "Mrs. Hunger, your daughter is extremely ill and needs to go to the hospital immediately."

"Oh no, let's keep her here. I can't pay for the hospital. You should be able to look after her." Mutti had a way of convincing people and she used her charm on Dr. Howorka.

For the first time in my life I was given the wonderful medicine, Aspirin. As a result, the fever broke. Fortunately, I remained in bed over one week and during this time was convinced I would die. But I survived the ugly complications of the vicious flu. I was well again to do my duties.

Every day the same routine: first school, then shopping, cleaning, and then homework. Miss Lächele waited for us after school, and between noon and one o'clock she prepared a simple snack since we had our main meal at school. She helped me cut my chores in half. I loved that old lady and felt like living again.

"You keep everything *sauberle* like you'd expect Jesus to come any moment," Miss Lächele instructed me about cleaning and Jesus, and asked my mother to let me go to church with her.

Mother considered Miss Lächele odd. But, it seemed prudent to indulge the old lady and have a responsible adult supervise us during Mutti's work hours. Miss Lächele was never paid and was never there on a regular work schedule. She was there when needed and was a great help to me. In addition, Miss Lächele was like my Omi, a peacemaker. I was often upset over my lazy brother. Mutti gave me a daily list of things to do, and I followed it to the letter. Miss Lächele's encouraging words and help was gratefully accepted and appreciated. I felt overwhelmed as a ten-year old child and felt I couldn't please my mother. My brother, mostly in his own world, was a passive boy. I wasn't familiar with his strange behavior and lacked the necessary coping skills to deal with him. How could I ever turn into a responsible and caring sister?

"The old lady is crazy, but has good intentions." Mutti referred to Miss Lächele, and her point of view was harsh and never gave credit for good deeds.

Miss Lächele's brother and sister-in-law also lived in our apartment building on the third floor. The sign read

Seelsorger, pastoral work. Her brother wore a black suit and was employed by the State. Church and State had joined administrations, unfamiliar to American thinking. Mr. Lächele was a rather detached and serious man who rarely stopped to greet anybody, unless folks would stop him. It struck me how different he and his sister were. She was an angel, and he appeared to be an untouchable, cold official, far removed from any hands-on Christianity.

Thanks to Miss. Lächele, I got through a couple of difficult years. She also took me to Stuttgart's largest *Fußball* stadium the time Billy Graham toured post-war Germany. He visited in Stuttgart for one day. I was impressed to see thousands of people crowded into the stadium to listen to his engaging voice while his words were translated. Right then, I started to understand that religion should play a role in my life. After the mass assembly, I thought about the message of Billy Graham's inspiring sermon.

The crowd from the crusade took public transportation all at the same time. Miss Lächele and I walked home, probably five to six miles, faster than we could have by taking the streetcar. During that walk Miss Lächele talked about her faith and why her life was happy and fulfilled. She was very convincing, and to her credit gave me real moral support. At home, I was loaded down by burdens beyond my age and maturity. She reassured me of my role as a responsible older sister. I had openly complained about Achim who was a cute little cherub, but spoiled by Mutti, and he knew how to avoid work and get his way, no matter what.

All along, we were exposed to religion. The public school taught the subject at least one hour a week, parochial schools of course, even more. My mother admitted that religion was beneficial for youngsters, and she knew we would be safe attending Sunday school or going on weekly day-camps during summer vacations.

I cherished those organized church activities. In our specific case, it was the Evangelical Church, reformed Lutheran, in which my parents and grandparents were raised in. But it didn't matter, and all the teachers and counselors I met in these times, gave me gifts for life. We knew our Bible stories, participated in pageant plays, and grouped as if shepherds in the field. I wondered why no one recognized me as a potential "Wise Man" or a "Maria." But my mother remained aloof and uninvolved. The organizers needed blue or red robes and fancy outfits that only parents could provide. Accordingly, I knew I would be stuck among the group of brown-robed shepherds.

"To make a joyful noise" held yet further inspiration that I remembered forever. One summer, when going to day-camp, Achim and I rode the streetcar to Degerloch and walked for a couple of miles to the church camp. Then, school buses didn't haul children around. We acted responsibly, and had the exact change for the streetcar ride back and forth, allowing us to make it home every evening without a hitch. Nobody worried about us, and I came to believe that God was our protector. Most German children grew up this way out of the brokenness and the despair of war.

In church camp I found another pretty "angel." She probably was a senior in high school. She had shiny black braids down her back and beautiful white translucent skin, delicate features and a cherry mouth that made her look like the Snow White of Grimm's fairy tales. She sang like a delicate Christmas bell rings and even looked saintly when she prayed and praised God with the hymn "Beautiful Savior." She touched my very soul and made me cry.

She was also an artist. "Snow White" drew gorgeous flowers on strips of construction paper to make me a book mark. I used it until it crumbled in my hands. At a later time, I tried to copy the girl's talent and decorated homemade cards, and remembered "Snow White's" drawings.

Accepting My Parent's Divorce

By summer 1948, my perception of Else started to change for the better. In fact, she called Mutti several times at work to make arrangements for Achim and me to go places with her. Mutti said what audacity of this vulgar woman to call her up. But eventually, Mutti relented feeling powerless with our obligatory visitations. There was no phone at home, and letters couldn't be answered immediately. Else seemed to have reasons to call and "pester" Mutti at work. Truthfully, Mutti enjoyed her time alone, and during school vacations we were sent off without shedding any tears.

Vati and Else moved to Hamburg in 1949, where he started working for the Unilever Concern which produced famous Sunella margarine. With this change, our visits had to be continued via a five hour train ride.

Achim and I had our suitcases packed for our summer vacations in Hamburg. Else picked us up in Stuttgart, taking a short detour over Pforzheim in the same state where Else's family lived. As it turned out, her younger, unmarried sister and Else's son, Heinz joined us. I had never met her parents and brothers, and I took an immediate liking to them. We were warmly welcomed and spent a pleasant day in Pforzheim. I felt their closeness and couldn't help but wonder how a witch like Else descended from their midst.

Else's dad was also short with his right arm missing. Only a stump was showing above the elbow. During one air raid, low flying planes had shot at fleeing people rushing to the nearest bomb shelter. Mr. Wolf pulled his daughter, Else along. During this attack, Mr. Wolf lost his one arm, and Else's had her face sliced by shrapnel, explaining the scar I had originally wondered about.

Discovering these things, tears started to swell when I felt sudden pangs of guilt. How could I have seen her as a devil? "Else couldn't be that bad," I argued with myself. "Why misjudge her for the rest of my life? I need to work on my attitude and start acting friendly toward her." The woman Vati had married wasn't about to go away anytime soon. So I might as well call her "Tante Else," and everybody will be happy.

Achim and I were friendly with Tante Else's son, Heinz, and sister, Hilde. Although Heinz was Else's son, she required him to call her "Tante" in public. His last name was Wolf. According to Else, Heinz's father was a Wehrmacht officer who died during WWII. Heinz lived with his grandparents and in later years with his uncle's family. Having an out-of-wedlock child was still considered a disgrace, and didn't happen in so-called better families. To lie and cover up indiscretions seemed justified. As far as Achim and I were concerned, we liked Heinz and never probed with embarrassing questions. He proved to be a good companion.

Heinz was a few months older than I, full of energy and more experienced in the real world than we were. Most of all, we had sympathized with him, for he had his own struggles and rejections. When we first met, he was our leader and more familiar with that new family dynamic. Tante Hilde was a caring woman and a nurse by profession. She was now helping her older sister, Else, who needed extra help with three lively youngsters in the house and one on the way. Of

139

course, we kids didn't know about this and found out later when Joe Richard's birth announcement arrived by mail in February, 1950.

My favorite movie in those summer days in Hamburg was the Tiger of Eschnapur from a novel by Thea von Harbor. In 1938, this Indian epic was filmed and released in black and white. Its later version came out in 1959. The movie stuck in my mind forever. The difficulty of telling Vati the movie's plot with things never seen before, including wild tigers in the jungle, English colonial architecture and an exotic dancer named Seetha, was a task that almost spoiled my movie pleasures.

In the evenings when Vati returned from work, he quizzed especially Achim and me about the content of the movie we had seen earlier in the afternoon. Then he proceeded to correct our "horrible" Swabian dialect in which we children conversed. The message was equal to Mutti's: only High German, please.

Nevertheless, we kids had fun and played harmoniously and also enjoyed the freedom of playing in a large yard with the German Shepherd. The boys found discarded wood with rusty nails sticking out and old boxes to build a camp. The roof of our primitive house was a blanket that Heinz took from the living room. He felt more entitled than Achim and I. His mother, or sometimes called Tante Else, never scolded her son and handed him extra money each time I saw them close and whispering. One afternoon, he also confiscated a pack of cigarettes. Repeated puffs, inhaled in rapid succession, my stomach rebelled, and I stubbed out the cigarettes as fast as running from a wasp.

While vacationing in Hamburg, we learned to ride bicycles. When we left, we took our new bikes with us on the

train, which was common practice in Germany. I was in my
element and adored that new toy like a modern teenager would
treasure a car. Silver-colored and beautiful, I cared for it with
weekly cleanups and waxing. I demonstrated my new learned
bike tricks to the boys and could hardly wait to share it with
Helga. Mama Knosp didn't approve of dangerous stunts, and
she never allowed her daughter to even try out my bike once.

Helga's Home Life

My major support system became Helga's house and
Mama Knosp. Not long after meeting Helga; I was invited to
their home. She had told Mama Knosp, as I'd call Helga's
mother sometime later, that she met a new girl who needed
protection. After Mama inquired about my address and family
circumstances and coming from *"drüben,"* she learned that I
had a father who deserted his family and a sickly mother, her
heart melted. In no time at all Mama Knosp became my
second mother and treated me like her second daughter. In
fact, she showered me with the love and consideration I felt
was lacking with my self-absorbed newly single mother.

Helga warned me that her household was different.
That didn't prepare me for what I found. The Knosp house lay
nestled in former vineyards. It was a three-story family
dwelling with a garden behind and below them, filled with
goodies such as trees producing cherries, apples and pears,
also vegetable gardens including a variety of flowers with
many unfamiliar names. Compared to our apartment living
across from the factory's entrance, this unbelievable dwelling
seemed heavenly.

Helga's home at 89 Eierstraße became my new home
away. I overlooked the long cracks on the house and the
crooked, sagging stairs leading up to it. The paint was peeling

141

upon closer observation; and the doors creaked needing a hard push before they opened. However, the house had survived the bombings while two houses down the street were in ruins. It seemed to me that every third house had visible war damage. The Zeiss Ikon Factory, located between our apartment building and Helga's house, had only half of its original buildings standing.

Other than having to climb a steep hill, I lived but an easy ten minutes from Helga. After my chores at home were done, I was free to visit her.

I met several unexpected people there. Frau Knosp answered the door bell with a checkered blue and white apron around her full waist. She had black, dyed hair clearly showing grey growth and a pinkish skin. She looked older than my Mutti.

"Come in, Mädchen." She also called me girl, not sparrow, like Helga did.

I thought they have their way of being nice and polite.

I smelled hot cocoa. Although I had eaten a snack at home, I was still hungry. A slice of bread with only mustard spread across it surface had not been very filling. I entered the living room where Helga fed an approximately ten-year-old boy who sat in a rough-hewn highchair with a bar across.

"This is Rolf, my little brother. He's sick and never will be well again." Helga explained his condition in a matter-of-factly way. I was stunned.

I realized that the little brother was suffering from a multitude of handicaps. Rolf was apparently upset with my new face and immediately started to have a fit, knocking the spoon out of Helga's hand and then pushing the cocoa away, spilling the hot liquid all over her dress.

"Ouch, that hurts," Helga gasped.

Mama Knosp entered the room with a freshly baked *"Kugelhopf,"* a yeast-based cake that smelled heavenly.

"So eine Sauerei," she cried and pulled a handy rag out of her apron to dry the worst of the spill. What a mess, she had said. It happened every time I came to visit, but Helga and her Mama remained calm even though Mama said *"Sauerei"* many times.

I had never seen a mentally handicapped person up close. With time, I got used to Rolf, but I made sure that I wouldn't sit too close to the highchair. Helga and her mother talked to the boy with loving words. He only grunted. His language skills were those of a toddler at best. I didn't understand him, but his caretakers apparently knew what he wanted. Sometimes Mama Knosp sounded rough, but her eyes still twinkled. When she spoke to me I detected two slightly crossed front teeth. I knew she could be charming, but for the most part she appeared like her war-damaged house, but yet with an indestructible exterior.

Soon, I became part of her family and she gave me short commands to run to the kitchen to fetch something. Other times we were asked to clean the kitchen or pick seasonal fruits or vegetable in the garden.

"Mädchen, you better get used to it. When you're here, you're family. Hurry, and get me the sugar and the basket of bread." It didn't matter to me at all, for I wasn't alone here, had Helga next to me, and was instructed how to cook Swabian specialties. Besides, my body filled out, and my hunger pangs went away.

Of course, I jumped to every one of Mama Knosp's requests. After a while, I felt loved and secure in their house and didn't care to go home when their grandfather clock struck 6:00 p.m. In fact, I wanted Mutti to be warm and embracing like Mama and listen to me when I told her something important. I hated her notes, saying "do this, do that, and do not forget to do and make sure your brother…"

After getting used to the handicapped brother, another surprise awaited me at their house. Two strange men lived in the Knosp house. They were typical sub-renters during this time. I was used to ours. Even at our apartment, small as it was, the housing authorities mandated to sub-rent to a single man.

The men at the Knosp's were war invalids without families. One lived upstairs in an attic room, and the other one in the basement. Herr Zoller was the shorter man who limped with an artificial leg and sang in a men's choir. I had heard him earlier singing loudly by the open window. Herr Lemke was the taller and skinny one, with a nervous tic who made jerky movements and spoke an eastern-sounding German from the former East Prussian area. I learned that both were captured by the Russians and had suffered severe injuries.

"Don't get scared when you see them and when they talk to you. Mama says that they have body pieces missing, some you see, and some others are hidden."

"Really," I was dumbfounded.

One day, a legal holiday, both men sat in the Knosp's dining room when I dropped by. Herr Zoller was home from work, and Herr Lemke was home as well, sorting through a box of small figurines.

"What you got there?" Zoller asked Lemke in a rather rough tone.

"Geht dich einen Dreck an (Shouldn't mean dirt to you)." I was shocked to hear such impolite language. Lemke said that it was none of his damned business.

Mama Knosp jumped out of her chair and intervened

like a school master.

"Both of you shut up and act right at my table. I cook and wash for you. She shook her head, wagged her index finger, and gave Herr Zoller a stern look when she scolded him. "Your tone is also unacceptable, Mister. I admit that you sing beautiful songs, but when you speak you are offensive and sound like a big klutz. Remember this: The tone makes the music."

Wow, that was new to me. Adults reprimanding adults. With the embarrassment of this episode, I motioned to Helga to step into the hallway.

In the hallway, we stuck our heads together and whispered. I needed more information to understand these strange men.

"Mani, old Lemke is a Prussian, and Zoller a Swabian. They never liked each other. Besides, Lemke is a refugee and Zoller a local man, so Zoller thinks he has special rights. But I tell you; even his family rejects him, because he talks ugly and disrespectful to them. The man is filled with anger."

It made sense to me. "But where was Lemke's family?" I asked.

"Good questions, but we do not dare ask him, because he goes into a rage each time we ask. So Mama remains quiet. I tell you, Mani, it's bad enough when he screams at night so loud that we can hear it echoing through the house. He must have the world's worst nightmares," Helga explained.

"What did Herr Lemke have in his box?" I was curious.

"Mani, he is a good painter and buys lower grade Hummel figures which he restores. Actually, he does beautiful work. Nobody can tell that these are rejects. And then he walks up to Degerloch where the American officers

145

and their families live, and he sells them the Hummels cheap and faster than they demand. Nobody can undercut his prices. Therefore, many young soldiers take souvenirs back home. He also tells us that the American women collect them like crazy."

"Wow," I said and couldn't quite understand such dealings.

"So Lemke is an artist, but he cheats, doesn't he?"

Helga had a puzzled look on her face. I explained that it seemed to me his dealings were fraudulent, because he pretended to sell a prime product whereas his Hummels were glued and painted over to hide the defects.

Another day, Helga and I studied our English that was offered as enrichment. We were repeating the word, "Ice cream," when Herr Lemke, painting at the end of the table, suddenly jumped out of his seat and flailed his arms, shouting, "No, no, Dummköpfe, it's supposed to be 'Itze crame.' We knew right away that Lemke was wrong and we had pronounced the word correctly.

I looked questioning at Helga who motioned with her index finger, tapping around her temples. In German sign language, this was to say, "He's got a bird living in his head," or he's a bit crazy. Herr Lemke returned to his quiet painting activities and ignored us, and we ignored him, never to mention ice cream in front of him again.

Some weeks later Rolf was sent to a state-run home. Mama Knosp visited him every weekend. I noticed that she was relieved and started to laugh out loud when Helga and I did silly things.

One day, I tried to jump over their spiky wooden fence bordering the street. I looked for a shortcut on my way home and jumped, slicing my gathered skirt. Very upset, I returned to the Knosp's house and begged Mama for needle and thread. She obliged and watched how I, an eleven-year old, was mending the ripped triangle.

"Does your Mutti know what a nutty kid you are?" Mama snickered.

"No, she doesn't know what I do half of the time. If she knew, I couldn't leave the apartment and would have to watch my brother doing nothing."

"Mani, before you leave, go and pack up fruits from the kitchen and take them to your brother. That will distract your Mutti from the ripped skirt, at least for a while."

Soon enough, I learned my way around. In my close neighborhood I also found girls in the surrounding apartment buildings to play. Boys played in the street, and I stood watching until I was invited into their games. I became so busy with my explorations and my chores at home, that I spent less time at Helga's. At least twice a week, I walked or pushed my bike up the street to Eierstraße. Coming back, I let gravity speed me home and raced down the hill within minutes.

Playing with dolls became trickier. Helga and I had done this for a few years. I didn't care to show other friends around the apartment building that I still played with dolls. Carrying all my toys to Helga, I didn't dare push a doll carriage around for fear of the boys seeing me. So I loaded up everything, placed it all in a blanket, and slung it over my shoulder. For months, I left my dolls and play "house" items at Helga's house.

"Hey, Mani, how many more toys do to you intend to bring here? Once in a while you should take your stuff home." Mama was right, but in reality I was finished with dolls and kept them around for looks only. They were safer in

147

Helga's care than in our apartment, especially when my cousins Barbara, Renate, Doris and Jürgen came to stay.

Helga became a life-long friend. We shared the pain of divorced parents, overcame that dreadful shame, and walked arm-in-arm to school. Even when I moved to Mannheim in 1951 and later to America, we never lost contact. The same is true for my cousins who stayed with us for a while after fleeing East Germany.

Mutti Learns a Trade

I had blocked out the time between Mutti's hospitalization and her entering the work force. Ever so slowly, we had to get used to a new life style. Mutti learned skills for the work force and struggled with childcare and household chores.

Originally, Mutti had no marketable skills and needed to learn typing. The new Deutsche Mark commenced in 1948. One hundred German Reich Marks turned into only ten of the new *Marks* overnight. My mother's divorce settlement, paid a few months before this change over, was suddenly devalued to nothing. The child support was specified in DM (Deutsche Mark), one-hundred per child. Even in 1948, twenty-five dollars per child wasn't very much.

Das Arbeitsamt, offered classes in shorthand and typing. With a borrowed *Olivetti* typewriter, Mutti practiced every evening, hammering away into the night. She attended day and evening classes. Achim and I stayed at home alone at night, and both of us wore a house key around our necks during the day. Babysitters didn't exist at that time. We had no relatives around to watch children, so written instructions were left for doing homework plus shopping, cleaning, and cooking, replaced a babysitter, which she couldn't have afforded anyway. I was barely ten years old and in charge.

Our apartment was very basic. No bathroom, no central heat, no hot water, but we had a roof over our heads. Once a week we marched down to the public bath house which I loved to do, because I had my own stall with my very own bath tub. We lived a simple life without a vacuum cleaner or refrigerator and of course no washing machine, not even an electric coffee pot or toaster. But we did have a radio and spend many hours listening to delightful plays in Swabian dialect and *die Kinderstunde*, a special program. I never remembered being bored.

Intrusions

Mutti's sister, Ilse, had fled East Germany as well. In 1949 she and her four children entered the East Berlin subway and got off in free West Berlin. This was still possible at the time. They carried only the clothes on their backs. Inconspicuous items were distributed among the children. Mutti, of course, allowed Tante Ilse to stay with us in Stuttgart for a while. Onkel Fritz, the children's father, worked already in a grocery store in Freiburg close to the Swiss border and was trying to find a place for his large family.

With company overflowing our small apartment, I needed to stay home and help out with my younger cousins. We slept two children to one bed and had pallets on the floor to accommodate everybody. I shared my clothes and my toys gladly, because we cousins loved each other. That's when my brother bonded with Jürgen, venturing out more and getting into his own little mischief.

With our crowded living conditions, I had other youngsters to share life with. As the oldest, I knew my duties toward relatives in need. Therefore, I saw Helga only at school and on our walks to and fro.

When Achim and I left for school in the mornings, my cousins stayed back with their mother. Meanwhile, my Tante Ilse busied herself with picking up the apartment and clothes of six children. She invented cheap but still delicious meals such as cream of Farina with fruits. It was truly a godsend for Mutti, because Ilse was optimistic, had knacks for handling many tasks at once without neglecting her kids, and never seemed grouchy or exhausted. Her eyes were everywhere.

She sympathized with her sister's stress at having been left by her husband. Ilse's situation was so different and her husband was still there. But they had just started out in the West without a place of their own. My cousins' schooling would start later in Freiburg in the southwestern part of Germany, close to France and Switzerland. With their formerly Russian-influenced education in the East, they were facing challenges ahead for their proper placement.

Every day, Barbara stood outside my school waiting for me, all dressed in my clothes and accessories. I had an ugly play-purse, with an exterior like fish scale, which Barbara wore proudly to greet me. I couldn't help but laugh at the sight, and under my breath I said to Helga, "Look over there, that's my cousin, Barbara. How funny to see her dressed like this!"

"Is this your *Bäsle?*" By now, I understood the Swabian word *as meaning cousin*, the High German word for Cousine.

"Yes, Helga, that's the oldest of the bunch. She's pretty ambitious and smart, and she loves to imitate me, the oldest of all of us."

"No wonder," Helga chuckled.

After my aunt and four cousins left Stuttgart, I was

done with dolls and most of my old toys. I found a small doll with real hair and mechanical eyes mutilated by little Doris. She was now blind, and Doris had practiced giving her a new haircut. When I came home, I was disgusted by the sight of my blind doll that suddenly had only stubbles of hair remaining, her blond locks scattered around. Disgruntled, I started packing up and giving away my childhood toys.

New Games Invented

It was time as well, for I had grown into a tomboy, no longer a *Spatz* and engaged in rougher games than Mama Knosp would allow her daughter to do. Helga was delicate; I thought her mother was too protective and kept Helga close to home. For whatever reason, she was never allowed to visit me in our apartment. In fact, Helga told me one day, "Your Mutti doesn't like me, because she always gives me such sideways looks."

"Oh, don't pay attention to my mother. You are playing with me, not with her. Remember, she's a Prussian, and they come across differently to the southern Swabians who are suspicious of northerners," I tried to explain.

We continued our friendship into the new parochial school. When I started my serious swim training, she didn't show any interest. It took much of my time as well. But I offered to teach her swimming. At thirteen, Helga still couldn't swim and I asked Mama Knosp to let me take her to the municipal pool. Over one summer's time, I managed to convince her to jump into the water without fear and paddle across the side of the pool. For years to come, Helga told everybody that her girlfriend, Mani, taught her to swim and do other athletic things which included jumping off the swing and repeatedly rolling down her front yard. It seemed to me that

Helga was satisfied with one friend at a time.

"She was my PE teacher, and good at it," years later Helga would say, "She also helped me understand stuff at school. But her mother was something else - a fine lady who didn't bother to take interest in Mani's dreams." Helga would rarely mention my mother or brother, but she enjoyed my amusing younger cousins who spoke yet another dialect from the Berlin area. She needed only one friend, nobody else. Helga and I were very close, and I usually visited her in the afternoons.

Helga's house was located up the hill where the vineyards started that stretched up to Degerloch. The climb was too steep for me to peddle. I almost had to push my bike up the street. But returning home, downward all the way, I rode with a vicious velocity that would have prompted a reasonable person to apply brakes. In my case, however, the brakes were rarely used except shortly before turning right into our street. We lived on Dornhaldenstraße and across where all the American vehicles were parked along the factory's side. An army of angels must have been busy protecting me from harm. I could have landed smack on top of any of the American cars, but instead I rode razor-sharp past them. Luckily, nobody opened a car door while I passed.

I played more civilized games in our courtyard. Girls preferred playing ball, and we had a game invented called *"Zehnerle,"* involving the number ten, and counting down to one. Helga never joined us since Mama Knosp didn't allow her out of her sight.

The rules of the game were easy. Ten throwing efforts to bounce and catch the ball started each game. We bounced the ball against a solid house wall. After successful catches, the player moved to the next task, throwing the ball nine times, doing some turning, clapping hands, or bouncing with the forehead. The rules could be changed by a democratic vote. When the number one was successfully reached with all its requirements observed, the winner was hailed. This game kept us busy for hours. Our perfect wall, one without windows, was located between the apartment house and the business where Mutti worked.

We had only one little mishap with the ball. I had to retrieve it from a deep shaft. Before the war, the Esüdro Company had received coal deliveries which were dumped into open shafts. Three of them stood side by side in our courtyard, surrounded by a flimsy chain-link-fence. I was always the one to climb into the shaft to retrieve our ball.

There was no fifteen foot ladder available. I could have become the first "Spider Woman" of Germany. The kids watched me slide down to stand on the bottom of the pit. I pressed my back against one wall while my feet stemmed into the other wall's side, and I shimmied inch by inch upward to where a three inch ledge gave support. No other girl ever tried to imitate me, but a few guys from the gang showed off after carefully studying my girl-act. They proved they could do it too.

Another exercise was our iron pole for rug beating. The pole hung fastened on both ends with iron chains. They could be lowered to load and unload heavy carpets. The rug beating was actually fun as long as one didn't mind the dust flying and carrying the rug up and down the stairs. But when not in use for rug beating, we created a gym. We hung heads down, swinging back and forth with glee. Nobody got hurt, but our landlord found it objectionable. He worried not about the children getting hurt, but about his rusty contraption breaking.

153

Mr. Bergmann, our landlord, became my next rescue person. He occupied a luxurious apartment above us, a combination of two apartments of our size. It had a comfortable bathroom, with a tub and boiler for hot water preparation. We considered him rich and his daughters privileged. The younger girl, Ursula played piano every afternoon, which she hated.

But when at home, I listened to her pounding the keys and wished I could change places with her. Sometimes, she was allowed out in the courtyard where both of her parents could observe us from the kitchen balcony. That was how they learned how we abused the rug-pole which had to be stopped immediately. No hanging and swinging kids for heaven sake. It was no surprise, when I heard a roaring man's bass. "Dammed, dammed and dammed!" Mr. Bergmann stood shaking his index finger at us and then he turned to Ursula with an outstretched arm, rescuing her from the street urchins. The landlord's expression turned a vicious hissing, "What the war has left untouched, you kids can destroy it all in one afternoon!"

With noticeable arrogance and disgust, he addressed the children assembled in his courtyard. "No more swinging, you understand, and only children of this house are allowed. The rest of you: Out, and fast! If I catch any of you over here…" he trailed off, but the threat was unmistakable.

That unpleasant incidence pretty much concluded our courtyard games. It shut down all our ballgames, the beloved Zehnerle, and my climbing the coal-shaft. Thanks to Mr. Bergmann, he probably protected me from myself. Later, when boys approached me to retrieve their soccer ball, I denied them by saying, "you better learn to take care of your game yourself."

Mr. Schneefuß was a tenant way up on the fifth floor who knew me well. It was evident to him how unsupervised I was. He was a widower with two daughters, both older than I, and he took his responsibilities serious. Mr. Schneefuß was a former champion diver, a fireman by profession, and a swim coach at night for the *Schwimmer Bund Schwaben.*

I received his invitation for a try-out. With every passing day, swimming sounded better to me. Mr. Schneefuß became my second father, a tough coach who instilled in me the ambition and the ability to endure long hours and endless laps without a break. I loved the challenge and was promised a swimming career.

I was only eleven-years old, and without an identity. I probably didn't care in 1949, but Mr. Schneefuß channeled my physical ability appropriately and instilled in me tenacity for every task at hand. Unspoken love and respect marked our relationship. Inadvertently, he prevented me from having probable and severe accidents.

From Volksschule to the Gymnasium

The last year in Lerchenrainschule, I had an unpleasant encounter that hurt me more than falling off a bike would have. Plans had been made that Helga and I would enter a parochial school for girls, a school preparing us for a secondary education. We had already passed our entrance exams and waited for the end of the school year so we could switch over.

During that last year, a specialized teacher, Fräulein Hartmann, was given one hour a day to teach us beginning English. All excited, I was ready. But to my vexation, we had to practice certain sounds such as the "th"-sound and the rolling "r"-sound which she claimed to be prerequisites to

155

English. The first sound was manageable, but the rolling "r" gave me trouble. Miss Hartmann had standard practice exercises to say repeatedly "fri, fra, fro…" and once more "fri, fra, fro" ad nauseas.

I never passed this first English lesson. So I found myself with other slow English learners. I was put in the group of dummies who continued practicing "fri, fra, fro." I should have been discouraged, but in reality I was a good student, just mostly bored with whatever we had to learn by rote. But with the assurance of leaving this school pretty soon and saying goodbye to Miss Hartmann, "fri, fra, fro," comforted me immensely.

Our main teacher was an attractive blonde about thirty years old. I admired the pumps she wore that made clicking staccato noises. She also wore beautiful orangey lipstick and looked prettier than most other teachers. Her name is erased from my mind, because she committed the unspeakable sin of slapping me smack across the face when I interrupted her lecture with a private whispered conversation with a class mate. I didn't tell my mother. She had a ready hand herself and would have smacked me yet another time. My feelings were hurt, and I blocked out her name forever.

I reasoned that she was mean and took unfair advantage of me. Before I knew better, I volunteered to walk to her home one day to fetch books or folders she had forgotten. It didn't matter to her that I missed two hours of class. This walk was almost four miles from the school house which, of course, I walked both ways. I found the assignment enlightening since I was able to meet the teacher's landlady, an eighty-some-year old woman, who was surprised to see a nine-year-old walk all this way from the school to carry teaching materials back to her teacher. But I felt needed, grown-up and honored to be trustworthy. Considering all those events between 1946 and 1948 and roaming without supervision, it was incredible that I grew up unharmed.

Another remarkable influence in my life was the new school for girls. The *Gymnasium* for "higher daughters" required a fresh outlook with studious intentions. Since it was a Protestant school, weekly services and increased religious instructions became mandatory. Girls in proper dresses, very modest, sat like proper ladies at their desks. I fell right into place, because getting away from Fräulein Hartmann's "fri, fra, fro" and the blonde's corporal punishment, directed my young life into a bright directions. I went places where the sun never planned to set.

The old ladies, our teachers, all had PhD's degrees. They loved their students like daughters. After correcting my talking in class, I met all the necessary qualifications and became a pet to two teachers. I didn't tell anybody, because I didn't want to have jealous friends talking behind my back.

The teaching took us far beyond the dreaded "fri, fra, fro." The new, plastic-covered English book was a treasure. The pictures of the Golden Gate and Statue of Liberty jumped off the page and lodged themselves into my brain. In fact, they called often: "Remember me. Come and see me."

Mutti's New Life

The next lucky event came with Mutti's new job. A woman in our apartment building arranged for my mother to work as a receptionist, typist and overall Girl-Friday. The office was right behind our house, only divided by a courtyard.

Esüdro was a wholesale business handling all kinds of drugstore needs. From Mutti's workplace she could easily see our kitchen's balcony. Sometimes, we stood under her office's window and called 'till she heard us and peeked out to see if it was an emergency. Mostly, however, she'd wave us off, communicating she didn't have time to listen.

Mutti did well as a working woman. Herr Petzold, her short and severe-looking boss, liked her. Soon, she became the greeter, because of her beautiful sounding High German and her pleasant telephone voice. Every representative selling their companies' products wanted to talk to the melodious lady.

Mr. Petzold was smitten with my mother. His attention to Mutti didn't escape me. Loaded with delicious goodies, he would sneak across the courtyard after office hours to visit her. I didn't know much about him. I certainly didn't like him. But, having the left over grapes and cheese they had shared the night before made his appearance a bit more palatable. However, these clandestine evening visitations, after our bedtime, rang an alarm in my head.

At dusk, our landlord locked the backdoor of the building. From the kitchen's balcony, my mother exchanged a flashlight signal with her boss. After the flickering she would rush down one floor and unlock the backdoor. I could see the light signals from our bedroom window which also faced the courtyard.

Their little system was easily decoded. One evening, I had the idea of closing the back door, after my mother had opened it for her evening guest. I tried to wake up Achim to make him my accomplice. But, indignantly he grumbled in a way that let me know that he didn't want to be disturbed.

This wasn't unusual, my brother refused to participate in my schemes. His preference was to follow the path of least resistance. Thus, we continued with different interests throughout our childhood, youth and adulthood, as well.

My evening activities, designed to discourage Mr. Petzold's rendezvous didn't last very long. Ms. Wűst, his secretary, became aware of the liaison and she turned against the attractive single mother and divorcee. Mutti also found out that her boss wasn't popular with us either. The relationship unraveled as another man entered our lives for a spell.

Mr. Mayer was a jovial representative of car cleaning products. He tried to include us kids in their dates. He had honest intentions, and 1 liked him. The man delighted in children, and courted my mother with sincerity. I was impressed with him. He was obviously ready to make a commitment to all of us.

Like a family, we took fun weekend excursions. One time, we watched the famous *"Solitűde Car Race,"* which in those days was quite an excitement. Cars, absent from our lives during the war years, found their way back into man's possessions. Mr. Mayer owned a little beat-up Opel, and we always climbed into it with adventurous delight. Looking back, the man reminded me of a good natured fellow, but he lacked our family's sophistication. As an eleven-year-old I wasn't able to discern this, but apparently, Mutti did.

My mother hadn't quite adjusted to our new lower standard of living. Socializing with Mr. Mayer wouldn't have received Omi's approval. My father's family was snobs, I concluded, once I had lived long enough with common folks to notice the difference. It didn't seem to matter that our upper class father had divorced his beautiful wife and left his children unsupervised in poor circumstances. My mother had been less fortunate but had been inducted into upper middle class by virtue of her marriage. She was determined to remain there, even if we lived in pitiful conditions.

Our grandparents remained in East Germany, and we had little contact. Communication problems arose between East and West. Mail was censored or undelivered when the communist regime decided to clamp down. We never had a phone while living in Stuttgart, and my grandparents couldn't use theirs anymore because their house had been turned into a daycare center. Their living space was reduced to the upstairs rooms which lacked a telephone.

Nevertheless, my grandparents' opinions remained a measuring stick for our life. A slow but steady correspondence compensated for the lack of physical closeness we had enjoyed before the end of the war. Everybody left in East Germany tried hard to keep in contact with us in the West.

Mutti made us write to the grandparents. She required us to give plenty of substance and details in our writings. A legible handwriting was a must and occasionally drew seasonal illustrations on the margins of the letters. 'How are you? We are fine and love you, goodbye', didn't cut lt. Ex-Daughter-in-Law and grandchildren were expected to meet prewar social guidelines.

"Details, kids, details," Mutti demanded. "Your Omi and Opa have been very good to us. They sent us remnants of cloth so we could barter for groceries. They want to know exactly what you are doing. They want to know about school, friends and activities. The more the better! Write, write, and write." Mutti was morally supported by her in-laws who worked behind the scenes to correct the wrongs their son had done. But their influence came too late. In the end, they had to accept their son for who he was.

Writing it Down

At an early age I developed an appreciation for writing. It was drilled into me at first, then it was re-enforced, and I started putting ideas and experiences on paper. I could describe, for instance, how a little sparrow on our window sill fluffed up and hopped looking for some bread crumbs. I told Omi what I saw and felt, and she commented back in writing how much she loved my letters. They held exaggeration or perceived nonsense, but Omi said nothing about them.

Some of Omi's letters I found buried in a box in the attic box showed her ability for writing prose and poetry. She spoke and wrote with invented words. They accompanied me through life, especially when Mutti was wrapped in her personal relationships. She created a stifling silence that excluded us children totally. She was discontent and bitter about her lot in life. But, my Omi made all the difference.

Thanks to my mother forcing writing exercises at the dining-table, I excelled in school, especially in the language arts, visual arts, and singing. I could give endless accounts of school outings and excursions, and my essays showed up on display boards, adorned by cute drawings. I thought I was a blossoming artist; however, this ability was never further developed. Instead, I wanted to learn to read music and play the piano.

"Be happy you can fill your stomach with food and have a roof over your head," Mutti's pragmatic discouragements kept me from dreaming. I felt guilty when I wished for things.

"Do your schoolwork. Get an education. The rest will come," She lectured.

With this in mind, I entered Möricke *Oberschule* at the age of ten and after fifth grade in Volksschule, at which time an appropriate age adjustment was made since, according to the Gymnasium's principal told my mother that I was too young and immature and should wait another year before entering Möricke Oberschule. I felt that I was placed correctly and thrived. The school was named after Möricke, a regional writer and poet. This Swabian writer made a lasting impression on me.

"Knowledge and a good education are priceless, children." My mother said quite convincingly. "Remember this. Nobody can take it from you." Her remarks became my mantra.

Mutti was the enforcer, but hardly ever participated in school activities. She was depressed, slept excessively on most weekends, and left us to our own devices. She couldn't cope with life, much less raising two children by herself. Carrying all the responsibilities overwhelmed her. Therefore, she kept us busy and expected the best grades. We owed it to her.

But with all the demands and expectations, I longed for recognition and some motherly reassurance. Mutti wasn't the person to dispense tender feelings.

Sometimes, if I eavesdropped, I learned what my mother thought about me. Even though I doubted her praise, I still wanted to hear it. I heard her say, "Mani tells stories. The girl has quite an imagination. I struggle to keep her supplied with paper, and colored pencils." Sighing a bit, she went on. "She's a tomboy and she rough-houses with the boys in the neighborhood. They admire her daring tumbles and climbs. She's not very lady-like."

Mutti hardly ever befriended women, but when she happened to get into a conversation she'd take over. This usually happened when she attended a rare school activity.

Not allowing any response from her partner, I overheard her talking about me: "I have to admit, her teachers complain about too much talking, but they like her. She isn't like anybody else in the family. I do wonder." Why wasn't my mother aware that her monologue wasn't a conversation? I'd see the other woman gazing into space, and Mutti continuing, barely taking a breath. "She's demanding. Wants music lessons I cannot afford. She keeps on begging. What am I supposed to do?" Mutti revealed much too much, which embarrassed me. For the most part, I definitely was not the topic of her conversation. Did I have any outstanding talents or beauty? I wasn't sure.

I decided that I was a daughter with some redeeming value in spite of my parents' break-up, my mother's financial struggles, and the years of hostility between them. I took on her burden. It felt heavy as if I were walking with an artificial leg. I limped along, because I had to, but couldn't change anything.

The fact remained, Achim and I needed love. I suppose much of his dislike for me must have resulted from our early life in Stuttgart. At times I thought that he had become so close to Mutti during his asthmatic episodes five years earlier, and felt rejected and deserted when Mutti started working and left him under my care. As the older sibling, I was accountable for all chores and responsible for our conduct. Unfortunately, his orders came from a demanding older sister, not from a loving mother. Most likely, my brother felt depressed like Mutti and at times was unable to cope with his feelings.

Mutti remained attractive as the number of her suitors bore witness. That was an impressive fact considering the lack of available men in post war times. The ratio of single men to single women was about seven eligible women to one man. However, my mother managed, without trying very hard, to attract quite a few.

The last man, Theo Bauer, was a true keeper. He had an unusual history in that he was different. He never served in the military, but had been imprisoned in India as a German civilian POW. At the foothills of the Himalayas, he was imprisoned for close to seven years. He had previously lived in the South East Indies, a colony of Holland, when German troops marched into the Netherlands. These islands are now independent Indonesia, during those earlier colonial times, Europeans operated businesses there.

Theo managed his deceased father's import-export business. For that reason, he was never drafted into the German military. But the long years of incarceration made him a special kind of war victim. He had lived in a men's only concentration camp. There were no gas chambers and no threat of annihilation. Nevertheless, it was a prison.

Nothing was recorded about his years of imprisonment. I do know he lost his freedom, his wife, and a lucrative business. He was born on the island of Celebes where one day he enjoyed a comfortable house with servants and the next he was hauled away, never to see his home again. He returned to Germany after the war in 1948, with twenty Mark to his name, a Red Cross soap box with cigarettes and toiletries, and his mother's new address. Their family house in Stuttgart was bombed out, but he was able to find some of their Asian art "evacuated" to the Black Forest area. Moroccan soldiers, under French commands, found the cache of art and sliced furniture and articles with the Dutch East Indies sabers they found, acting like adolescent vandals and leaving a trail of destruction behind. Another and quite extensive weapons collection from Sumatra, Celebes and New Zealand had been donated earlier by the Bauer family to the city of Stuttgart and were burned to cinder in the museum during one of the many air raids.

Fortunately for both Theo Bauer and Mutti, they met through a strange activity created to ease daily living. Bartering all kinds of goods around and before 1948 was normal. Strangers from all walks of life met and exchanged commodities. Somebody knew somebody who wanted to give fabrics for coffee, cigarettes, milk and butter, or exchange an antique chair for a baby carriage. Theo had a cousin who introduced my mother to him. This cousin in turn, was an old school friend of Aunt Elisabeth's in Central East Germany.

After the war people were shuffled around by forces beyond their control. A positive outgrowth of this mixing up of people was eliminating prejudices between the North and the South, East or West. Germans from all different regions met in new places grasping desirable cigarettes or a cup of coffee.

Naturally, suspicious of men after the divorce, and reserved to a fault, Mutti accepted this personal invitation to trade with Theo Bauer. This chance meeting was like predestination.

Vati and Family Move to Mannheim

In the following years, we had more but shorter visits with Vati in Mannheim. He and his family had moved there during my baby brother, Joe's first year.

This house was spacious as well, had high ceilings, and plenty of wall space to accommodate the mostly life-size paintings of our ancestors which Vati had managed to move from East Germany to the West. The communist regime didn't consider such art as the state's cultural heritage and released them. I'm sure Vati didn't spare any expenses for transportation and red-tape-fees.

Another quite different painting on display was a biblical rendition which appeared a bit risqué to my young eyes. Vati loved ornate Chippendale furniture which distracted from the questionable art work. Vati and Else created a new-rich ambiance and it appeared to me it was an attempt to revive his parents life style that vanished after WWII. Since the end of the war, Vati had been lucky to sell his business abilities and foreign language expertise to the American occupational forces and soon thereafter to the new emerging international companies. Thus he climbed once more to upper middle class status, faster than most other Germans did during this time.

Joachim Richard Hunger was Vati's full name. He was about 5'8" tall, bald with hazel eyes and a prominent nose. Actually, he appeared statuesque, and his eyes were those of my beloved Omi. This was the only similarity which made us look like family.

My brother and I never bonded with our father, mainly due to his absences during the war. I remembered one week when he came home to recuperate and take family photos. Vati must have felt uncomfortable with us kids. One such moment was while he was visiting with us in Mannheim and he took out his antique violin. A *Stradivari* it was not, but he treated it like it was. Then he lifted his right arm, hesitated a moment to make eye contact with us, as to elicit certain expectations for the virtuoso. Achim, our half-brother, Joe, and I sat next to each other on a settee. We were arranged like organ pipes and sat like salt pillars in anticipation of Vati's musical presentation. But should we really applaud, I wondered. I felt more like laughing. I had to bite my lips. The scratchy notes from the violin could have sent a cat screaming. The embarrassing moment passed when my father broke off his concerto. We applauded enthusiastically. The relief of escaping Vati's violin torture was written all over our faces as Vati finished his performance he proceeded to address his older son.

"Achim, when you are old enough, I will pass this valuable violin on to you."

"Thanks, Vati," Achim responded unconvincingly.

I wondered why Vati wouldn't leave this expensive violin to his second son, Joe. The sweet little boy was everybody's pet, and Achim had never displayed musical interest. I was not considered, and it never bothered me. I wished for a piano, and that was not up for discussion. In fact, money spent for Achim and I was never a positive discussion and usually lead to a litany of reasons why Vati couldn't indulge us, or worse. Almost unattainable conditions were attached to our wishes.

During the virtuoso's performance, my eyes wandered around the room. I studied Vati's paintings. I peeked at the monstrosity of a biblical rendition of John the Baptist's head on a silver platter, blood still oozing while a naked Salome danced in front of her stepfather, Herod Antipas. Helmeted Roman soldiers filled the background while Salome was presented with this gift. My fascination went unnoticed; I continued my observation of Salome's fluttering veil and of the artist's talent in obscuring her nakedness. Nudity was accepted in Europe, and some German parents displayed such art regardless of their children's age. My father mentioned how priceless this oil painting was. Mutti, by now divorced from Vati, was of course unable to experience my father's new lifestyle. I couldn't help wondering how she would have responded. "Gaudy. *Mein Gott, so ein Schinken!"* In English: what tasteless art. "Whose influence is this, for heaven sake?"

I recalled that Omi told us that Vati had problems learning Greek. Apparently, Vati overcame these initial struggles, practically outdoing anybody else. In fact, he was a gifted linguist and could manipulate long dissertations in speech or on paper. His writing was also impeccable, however lacking in creativity. If need be, he pulled out a law book from a plethora of reference books, to prove a specific point to whoever was willing to listen. If violin playing wasn't his strong suit, he impressed me when he conversed in French, Spanish, English, and Italian. I was amazed by the way he picked up enough vocabulary to make sense in Polish and Russian. His Latin and Greek knowledge prepared him well. No one could have convinced him what a flop his violin playing was.

My father emulated his uncle. Over the years, Vati became embattled with his bosses and other family members. His scathing letters about any given subject, and his sarcastic remarks would hurt for years. He possessed such extraordinary abilities but used them as a channel to vent resentment and hatred.

The expansive house where Vati lived was located across the beautiful Luisenpark. The neighborhood was not bomb-damaged for the most part. I had the distinct feeling that Vati was trying to recreate a pre-war life style.

Mannheim had wonderful parks. Luisenpark had ponds with geese and swans, large birch trees, and was interspersed with English gardens. Especially on weekends, the park was busy with Mannheim's citizens. I enjoyed walking there on soft sandy paths, or sit on one of the many benches watching the birds and squirrels.

It was not unusual that I walked around there unaccompanied. I delighted in showing off my little brother in the stroller, and loved the unsupervised freedom. I didn't have to listen to Vati's lectures on how to make better grades, act and look more lady-like, or worse, how immoral my mother was, and how poorly she managed us children, and to top it all, how she dressed me to look like a boy.

The last day of this particular visit remained imprinted in my memory forever. During my last walk through the park, I picked green sprigs with pretty berries along my path and stuck them as decoration on the stroller's outside, between some curlicues of its wicker constructions. These white wicker baby-carriages and strollers were fashionable during the 1950s.

When I returned to the house, it was time to prepare for an almost two hour train ride back to Stuttgart. I kissed my father goodbye and gave the expected "thank you" for all I had received. I had been taken to a hair salon for my first permanent. Vati bought me red shoes and a flower print dress. I thought I looked like a girl.

My mother wasn't able to buy dresses for me. She managed to sew some basic outfits with her treadle Pfaff machine, but the desired elegance for young teens was obviously not of Mutti's concern. "Practicality, practicality," was her favorite explanation for frugal living and modest styling for us youngsters. Homespun was our trademark.

"*Oh, mein Gott.* A kinky permanent," Mutti said when she saw me.

I was a disappointment again. I didn't look right to either one of my parents.

169

Three days later, the dreaded letter arrived. Mutti looked shocked as she read in silence. Then she hesitated for a minute and reread some lines a second time, maybe three times. It took too long to feel right. I was curious to know why Mutti seemed so dismayed. After a long pause, she informed me. "Your father writes." Her voice was icy, and I shivered. When I read the letter myself, I was stunned by Vati's insinuations. They hurt like acid poured over a wound. My father accused my mother for putting me up to kill my little brother, Joe, with poisonous berries I'd placed in the toddler's reach. It didn't make sense at all. I reread and reread like Mutti did earlier, but the accusations resisted entering my mind. I loved my little brother. I would never hurt him. How could Vati be so wrong, so cruel, so out-of-touch! I cried for days.

The ending passage of the infamous letter read something like this:

"Herewith I put you, Hedi, on notice to refrain from influencing your children in a detrimental fashion." Vati signed off his scornful letter with his nickname, Jochen.

"Now you can understand what I went through with this man," Mutti lamented. "He is always accusing somebody of something!"

I carried the guilt of this innocent mistake for too long. Nothing ever happened to my little brother. Joe didn't have a chance to touch the berries, and I never mentioned this episode to him either.

Pastors and Saints

The year Mutti married Theo marked a new period in my pre-adolescent life. I had become familiar with religious instruction and attended a make-shift church since the neighborhood evangelical church had been totally burned out during the war. This neo-Gothic skeleton of a majestic building was the neighborhood's former church. Its stain-glassed windows had exploded and were melted away. Several wooden doors were missing and a swarm of pigeons now roosted in its white sandstone carcass. This was St. Matthew Church, gutted to the core. No sound came from the two bells, silenced by a brutal attack. The clock's hands were stuck at the precise hour and minute when the bombs hit. The suspended time disregarded day and night.

I saw much destruction along the intersection of Schreiberstraße and Böblingerstraße. Humans rushed about like busy ants, but unlike the insects, the humans worried about another tomorrow. The fire-station and a row of apartment houses stood like tall, petrified creatures crying out blank faces, their entrances were blockaded with crossed timber and signs of *Betreten Verboten.* I saw piled up rubbish when I peeked through the slats, and the adjacent church was blocked off for repairs. Rumors circulated that St. Matthew's would be rebuilt.

They said it would take seven years in all. I was hoping that by spring of 1953 our church would be reopened, because my confirmation was scheduled for March. We all looked for new hope, and this cathedral building was a symbol of our anticipation.

Regardless of missing formal facilities, I was enrolled in confirmation class. An old town hall had been converted into a temporary church. The new pastor and his young family moved into a modest apartment nearby. One of their bedrooms was converted into an office where Mutti took me to add my name to the register. Mutti took me to the location of the *Evangelische Kirche's* office. It was within walking distance, right around the corner from the butcher shop.

The congregation adored Pastor Hutjezt. I heard young and old mention him with great reverence, and Mama Knosp talked about him with veneration. It clearly reminded me of pious people looking up to their favorite saint. I was curious to see this Pastor Hutjezt.

Mutti told me that the pastor was a refugee from Romania. When I saw him, I knew he wasn't German. Mutti assured me that he was indeed, because many Germans had lived in the Balkans and were forced from their homes after WWII. He was handsome, dark-haired, a bit like Dr. Howorka, but much nicer and far better looking. He spoke with a mellow Eastern twang, but was so charming and attractive that nobody dared criticize him for not being Swabian or sounding like one.

Soon, I started my confirmation classes in a room filled with boys and girls. I loved our weekly gatherings even with the extra demands of memorizing the Catechism, Bible verses, and hymns. Everybody adored Pastor Hutjezt. Chatting and restless kids didn't seem to annoy him; he was temperate and had a gentle demeanor. I thought he possessed qualities of a living saint. At age twelve, an overwhelming feeling came over me that our pastor was Jesus-like.

Mutti had married Theo Bauer in 1951. We liked him very much, called him Uncle Theo and eventually Papa. Although pleased about Mutti's marriage to Papa Theo, I didn't want to say goodbye to friends, school and familiar surroundings. How dreadful to leave friends, my swim coach, Helga, all the kids from the neighborhood, Fräulein Lächele, and the superb new teachers at Möricke *Oberschule*.

My heart was twisted and squeezed. All I could do was cry, cry, and cry. I cried when I talked to Pastor Hutjetzt about having to move. He hugged me and said, "Child, you don't know what's ahead of you. If God wants you to leave, it will be a blessing to you."

I didn't care to hear this, but his embrace was genuine, and his voice was comforting.

"I'm sure your friend, Helga will report back to me how well you like your new pastor in Mannheim and all your new friends. Just continue on God's path, and you will be blessed."

When St. Matthew Church was reopened for services, Pastor Hutjetzt no longer pastored St. Matthew. After Mutti's marriage and our moving to Mannheim in 1952, his son hanged himself. Pastor Hutjetzt was devastated. He went through the motions of ministering to the old, needy, young, and dying, but never adjusted to his tragic loss. I heard that on one harsh winter day with driving snow and icy wind, he was out on foot to see a dying person from his congregation. Two blocks from his home, a few steps from St. Matthew's, he stepped in front of a streetcar and died instantly. It was another tragic loss.

I was already enrolled in my new confirmation classes in Mannheim when I learned about the accident. Helga wrote to me about Hesslach's news. The shock of Pastor Hutjetzt's untimely death left me with a horrid image of a streetcar in a blustering snowstorm. I was grateful to Pastor Hutjetzt and remembered what he told me. Good surprises did await me in Mannheim; and most of it, I was put into a much safer environment than the one I left behind in post-war Stuttgart.

Living in Mannheim Once More 1952-1958

Mannheim was equally devastated by the war. But by 1952 much had been rebuilt. Hundreds of "Marshall Plan" apartment houses, which were built in a hurry, gave thousands of displaced people a place to live. American General George Marshall was the man who formulated the Marshall Plan. He was the Army chief of staff from 1939 to 1945, U.S. Secretary of State from 1947 to 1949, and Secretary of Defense in 1950. He initiated a recovery program for Europe and supervised the distribution of aid money. It amounted to billions of dollars. Marshall received the Nobel Prize in 1953, honored as the architect of the Marshall Plan.

I saw the Marhall Plan's impact just a few blocks away from the *Mannheimer Bettfedernfabrik* where Papa Theo worked and where we lived. I walked through blocks and blocks of housing projects, giving thousands of folks a roof over their heads. These apartment buildings, blocks of four-story buildings with military conformity and efficient planning, housed uprooted people and gave them adequate living space.

During our time there, our neighborhood increased by the hundreds. I knew many children who lived on these blocks. One could hear a cacophony of German dialects and eastern *Zuwanderer* (immigrant) who made an effort to become *Mannheimer* (Mannheim resident).

I met most of my new friends at our convenient meeting place: The church's name was actually Luther Church, an Evangelical Church, which had escaped war damages and was located on the banks of the Neckar River. This river also ran through Stuttgart and Heidelberg and joined the majestic Rhein River less than a mile from our church.

In the ensuing few years, I walked and rode my bike along the Neckar dam in the church's vicinity. From downtown, on the left side of the Neckar, one could see the church's steeples, a prominent landmark.

Sometimes we met at the youth center. It was also built with Marshall money, and was new and modern. In the afternoons, I went there to meet up with friends. We rode our bikes together and associated with what my parents considered "good boys" from the neighborhood. The boys went to the boys *Gymnasium*. We youngsters grouped together by religion, education and neighborhood. My buddies went to the same church, attended *Gymnasium* and lived within four to five blocks of one another. With all of these common interests, we enjoyed each other's company. Some of us have even remained life-long friends.

Our leading pastor was Pastor Lehman. His wife ran the office. My mother had no inkling she knew him from somewhere else when she registered me with a referral from our former Pastor Hudjezt in Stuttgart.

Our confirmation classes commenced on Wednesdays and sometimes Saturdays as well. In those days, it was common to go to school until noon on Saturdays. Most families didn't own private vehicles and had little money for a weekend travel. We took the streetcar to school and our bikes to confirmation class or visits with our friends.

"The world is so incredibly small, Mani. I knew the pastor years ago," Mutti finally realized. I wished I had witnessed her surprise when she saw the pastor eleven years later.

"Would you believe he's the very same man who baptized both you and Achim?" Mutti added, "He and his wife lived in Switzerland during the war and have just returned to lead Luther Church."

I didn't think that this information was such a big news item and wondered why Mutti was so mysterious about the Lehmans. I thought there was more to it than what she said.

I eventually learned the truth about the pastor's Jewish ancestry and that he had also lived in Gelsenkirchen in 1938. He and his wife had spent the Hitler years in Switzerland. Nobody ever mentioned it, and the pastor kept a low profile due to his clerical modesty which didn't allow any unnecessary attention. Most of all, he didn't want his countrymen to feel guilty. He was German and felt bad about his countrymen's sufferings, which he was spared in Switzerland.

Mutti and Papa Theo became friends with Pastor Lehman. Sometimes, when I came home from school, I found him visiting. He had coffee with Mutti. After visiting and resting for half an hour, the pastor regained enough energy to climb thousands of steps in the "Marshall Plan" apartments. There were no elevators and with four flights in every stairwell, it was an ordeal for the pastor to welcome new folks, listen to their stories, pray with them, extend invitations, and dispense booklets with information about social services. Sometimes people would slam the door in his face. They had many reasons why they were through with church and religion.

The pastor visited his congregation on his old, rusty bike. The post-war territory had doubled in square kilometers and population. The new church was in the planning stages, but meanwhile he and his wife worked both the ministry and the administration. Day after day, he rode his bike, carrying a brown, beat-up satchel that contained his Bible and communion materials. He also handed out information, helping refugees and newcomers adjust, telling them about the new youth center and explaining for the hundredth time where Luther Church was located. Pastor Lehman was in his 50's, gray-haired, wore thick glasses and had seemingly an endless stamina. I thought he ran on spiritual energy only.

Mutti was always glad to see him at Industriestraße 35. The pastor was familiar with opening the heavy factory iron gate. Nobody stopped him. I wasn't privy to their private conversations, but it must have been mutually beneficial. Mutti never revealed much, but I suspected she opened up to the pastor more than anybody else in the world, Papa Theo included.

Mutti related that much to me, "This man is a saint. You'll never see one like him ever again. He was Jewish and loved the German people regardless. His wife insisted on leaving the country, not him. Please, Mani, promise, never to tell anybody about that, and especially not your father. We go way back – and your father doesn't even know that the Lehmans are alive and in Mannheim."

I was pleased that Mutti trusted me with this information, but I couldn't understand why Vati shouldn't know about Pastor Lehman's return. I wondered if it was a form of punishment to deny Vati the pleasure of seeing an old friend.

"I'm so happy he's your *Pfarrer,*" Mutti added. The kids you are running with right now are good kids, for *he* told me so. He will steer you the right way. He knows everything about everybody in the congregation." It felt like Mutti had handed me over to the church and could stop worrying about me now for a spell.

Pastor Lehman helped me make some good social connections. My move from Stuttgart to Mannheim hadn't been easy, because I didn't know who I was, and I didn't handle new social situations too well, or how to make new girlfriends in high school. Besides, the newly acquired Swabian was critiqued here as well.

177

Both Hungers and Bauers Live in Mannheim

Vati was a stickler about observing our obligatory visits with him and wife, Else. The new Hunger-family had moved to Mannheim. During that time, Mutti dated Theo Bauer, soon to be married again. By now, Achim and I had a new step-father and strangely enough, both Hungers and Bauers would wind up in Mannheim.

Vati, Joe and Else lived about six miles from us in their upscale neighborhood next to the park. The area had ornate residences with wrought-iron fences around, similar to the White House in Washington D.C. We saw each other more regularly, a routine, and every second weekend.

At first, we took the streetcar to Vati's, which was a one-hour ride through the center of Mannheim. The fare was promptly reimbursed when we arrived since we had little pocket money. My brother and I decided to hike home and save the 50 cents. This foolishness stopped when we were given permission to take our bikes. The bike ride took only 25 minutes, depending on the traffic. In retrospect I'm horrified to think about the dangers we faced with heavy traffic on busy intersections, crossing the Neckar Bridge with vehicles and careless bicycle riders trying to pass each other.

In the mid-1950s, many of the over 350,000 inhabitants in Mannheim traveled by bike. To us, danger had been climbing in ruins or avoiding unexploded bombs. Maneuvering inner city traffic was easy, like knowing the contents in our pockets. Nothing to it!

"Pay attention and look for the other idiot!" I heard both Mutti and Papa say this many times. My bicycle remained a close friend until I left in 1964. Rain couldn't even keep me from riding. In one hand I'd hold the umbrella, and with the other the handle bar. It was quite a sight, but I didn't think twice. Other modes of transportation were often impractical.

"Just be careful, and be home before night fall," were Mutti's common admonitions. Achim and I celebrated being mobile. I don't know if living in the same city with Papa Theo and Vati was beneficial, and I wondered if my divorced parents would raise "normal children." We did not discuss complex family matters, either questioning Mutti or Vati, or discussing them with outsiders.

Mutti was frugal with household money and saved every penny so they could build a house somewhere outside the industrial fumes and soot. She rationed the "better foods," giving our stepfather the more desirable cuts of meat. My mother clearly goofed the time she created a situation which played right into Else's hands. Else, the infamous second wife squeezed juicy information out of Achim and me.

Else compensated for all the books she never read. She made up for it with her knowledge of the common boulevard press, called *Bildzeitung*, at the German grocery stores. Well informed about the rich and famous, she savored in their reported scandalous behaviors. Never stopping, she pressed for news about our new stepfather and tried to glean information about my mother's private life by bribing us.

For example, I loved smoked ham and Italian Salami, cold cuts we never saw at home. They weren't served to children in our household.

"Shocking," Else said.

Immediately I was allowed to gorge myself in her kitchen with foods I was denied at home. I chewed plenty of kosher pickles and soft boiled eggs in exchange for what I thought were harmless stories about Mutti. Other methods followed and probably influenced my relationship with my own mother. I regretted falling for those bribes. The entanglement with Else was difficult to undo.

When I figured out how I'd been manipulated, I stopped taking her bait. I learned quickly about integrity. Guilt invaded my soul since too much of nasty gossip had stacked up.

"Why would soft boiled eggs be so desirable?" I asked myself. Food for reward had been practiced throughout my childhood. For instance, eating eggs for breakfast was reserved for the breadwinner, our new stepfather. On Sundays only, everybody was allowed to eat a precious soft boiled egg, served in a cup. I never went hungry in those days, but I questioned why my stepfather chose not to correct Mutti.

My Good Buddies

My first and best friends were boys, all approved by the pastor. After school and homework I met up with them, and we rode our bikes back and forth, crisscrossing all the Marshall Plan blocks, to the church and back, miles and miles every day. We rode around up to the point where the Neckar and Rhein joined. Observing the barges go by, we felt happy and free. We exchanged school experiences from the boys *Gymnasium* and compared them with my girls *Gymnasium*.

We rode on our side of the river and saw Ludwigshafen on the other side. Ahead of us stretched an island, formed by the canalized Rhein and the original Old Rhein. I knew every nook, every field, every tree, and every dirt path. In those days we saw nothing but green space. In years of heavy rain the area was flooded, which made the soil very fertile. The boys and I pedaled along the dam and rested at the tip's island.

The wind brushing over us sometimes carried horrid chemical smells from across the river. The Aniline Chemical Company was a major polluter in the 50's, but we didn't know any different. We stretched out to relax, and I talked to my two favorite companions, Siegfried and Dieter. Both of them attended the same confirmation class, though two years my senior. Strange as it might seem, I communicated better with them than I could have with the girls my age.

We did have one walk through the park that I specifically remembered. My new girlfriend Karin was along. She and Siegfried liked each other, and I definitely liked Dieter.

Dieter and I shared experiences of our refugee-background. His father was missing in action and was subsequently declared killed in action. Both our mothers had remarried and formed new families. We had a lot in common and felt a mutual attraction. During our strolls in the park, we couldn't come to grips with our national history. So we berated our elders for what they may have done wrong. We couldn't understand that none of them talked about the war and the persecution of the Jews. Did their generation leave us in the dark? Recent German history had not been discussed, and both of us felt ignorant and left in total darkness.

On this day, Karin and Siegfried walked ahead of Dieter and I. Karin was my new girlfriend, and she liked Siegfried. As we strolled along, Dieter and I fell behind step by step. We must have discussed more serious matters than Karin and Siegfried did, so we stopped along the path, pondering ideas. We also talked about lighter matters and mentioned school activities, teachers, and the latest movies.

Then, I changed the subject, "Do you know, Dieter, "it came out of nowhere, "I got this distinct feeling you'd make a super attorney one day."

Dieter faced me and we stopped once more along our path. "Nobody has told me this before. But I feel, you are right, Manu. I have felt this myself but hadn't verbalized it yet."

I liked the new name, Manu, he gave me. Besides, I noticed that I was developing a crush on Dieter.

During those teenage years, things changed rapidly. Dieter and I never conversed like this again. In fact, Dieter went to London during summer vacation and when he came back, he suddenly showed interests other than running bikes in the late afternoon or going for a stroll in the *Luisenpark*. This change also coincided with entering dancing school in fall when our clique split up, and new groups created different dynamics. It happened. We were young, explored and adjusted.

Studies became more demanding with little time left for seeing friends in the afternoons. The dancing school was very important to both boys and girls attending the *Gymnasium* since it traditionally started the dating of German high school students. No more time to waste. I started to experience teenage-stress, not known to me until then.

Besides, Mannheim had two dance studios. So it was that Dieter and I were separated by dance partners and by two different boys *Gymnasiums*. In short, we started running in different circles. Neither Dieter nor I had made a concerted effort to be together.

I met other classmates of Dieter and Siegfried, especially a boy named Hans who fell for me. I wasn't focused on one guy alone; I liked most of the fellows. That I didn't marry any of them in later life, hinged on the fact that I was kept from going to Heidelberg's University. Youngsters didn't have cars in 1958, and though there was only 20 miles distance between us, our communication stopped and no convenient ways existed to see each even by taking public transportation. We drifted apart.

All of the girls eventually came around and accepted me when I turned more fashion-minded. I annoyed Mutti with frequent request of using her sewing machine to create more stylish outfits.

While in Mannheim

The best thing in my mother's life was her marriage to Theo Bauer. He was a gentleman, well educated, world-traveled, and experienced in business. Theo, short for Theodor, was Mutti's companion for life, very different from Vati. After his long hospitalization and rehab from a ruptured stomach, he needed stability. Mutti nursed him back to health, and their union turned out to be a perfect match for both of them and they knew it.

Through an old school friend's connection, Theo soon found employment. He had been binding old books and doing odd jobs, but couldn't find proper employment especially after his employment in the Dutch East Indies. Potential employers looked at him as overqualified. They couldn't tell if he was right, or maybe a risk, and wondered if he could take orders from lesser qualified people, and fit in. They wanted to know was he not in the military like everybody else. But Theo proved he was still productive and capable of being successful into his 40's and 50's.

His old *Gymnasium* friend knew he had found the right man to head up the sister company in Mannheim. Theo Bauer moved to Mannheim, south of Frankfurt, on the Rhein River. He and my mother married in 1952. Cousin Fritz, a Lutheran pastor, blessed their marriage, which lasted until death.

This second marriage finally brought happiness into Mutti's life. She spoiled her husband, and they adored each other. She made sure Achim and I wouldn't be a burden to Theo and never quit reminding us who our father was, especially when we needed anything.

"Don't bother Papa Theo with this. Go to your father," She would snap. "After all, he's required to look after your needs." Mutti never ceased to inform us whose responsibility we were.

During my adolescent years, a strange rivalry between me and my mother developed. She didn't appreciate my young womanhood. She actually told me to keep a distance from my stepfather, even though there never was a concern about inappropriate conduct between Papa Theo and me. Mutti made sure, just in case, and created a regrettable barrier. By the age of fourteen, at least, I could read my mother's body language quite well. Tightening her lips was an indicator she was displeased, wrinkling her forehead meant she was skeptical, and a prolonged look, short of staring told me that Mutti had great concerns.

Our blended family worked. Thanks to a very large apartment built over the cantina of the factory, we all had privacy. We had separate bedrooms, bathrooms, and a large living room with a spacious kitchen.

My own room was a joy. It was about 20 by 20 feet, with a sleeper couch, a desk, and a freestanding cabinet where I stored all my belongings. Two paintings depicting Mont Martre and Sacre Coeur by Paul Ferón, which Vati had purchased in the 30's while studying in Paris, became mine by default.

Another treasured item was the door to my room. For

the very first time in my young life I could shut out the world whenever I needed. The window enhanced my studies; I could ponder difficult math problems, while letting my eyes wander outside for a moment. I could look up from doing my French and English homework and dream. I studied and rehearsed for tests, regurgitated expositions in history and literature. Once I memorized 35 verses of the *"Glocke,"* a famous poem written by Friedrich Schiller. I also memorized at least 50 well known Protestant hymns dating back to the Reformation.

While Mutti was busy in the kitchen, she could hear my loud reciting in the corridor. Whenever I lost my place and hesitated, Mutti's voice came on, like a light bulb, and prompted me to regain the flow of rhyming words. "Wow, she's smart!" I thought. In her own words she told me: *'sie hörte die Flöhe husten'* (she heard the fleas coughing).

The other amenities in our new home were our wonderful two bathrooms. Steaming hot water came out of the faucets. I indulged in taking bubble baths several times a week and loved laying there up to my neck in the warm water embracing luxury. No restrictions were ever imposed about too much water usage or electric bills.

"You take all the baths you have missed in the past," Papa Theo said. "I know you gave up your swimming training at the Stuttgart city's pool, so at least you can swim in a Mannheim bathtub."

"Imagine what a mess I would make doing the freestyle!" I laughed at the idea.

Papa answered with a wink, "Don't let it run out in the hall. Be sure to use the big mop or your mother will scream."

There wasn't a day I didn't hear Papa Theo laughing and joking. He was a man with a joyful soul. He had been hired as the factory's new manager, turning different kinds of feathers and downs into fluffy pillows and bed covers. The business boomed as Germany grew out of WWII and people needed to replace old furniture and beddings. He was engaging with family, employees, and business associates alike.

The neighborhood we lived in wasn't very attractive, but living in the industrial area of Mannheim in 1951, was doable. Theo's plan was to make enough money first to buy a lot and eventually build his own house. We had escaped our Stuttgart apartment's substandard living arrangements. Everybody in the Bauer-Hunger household was satisfied. In reality, I was overjoyed.

Papa Theo Bauer couldn't adopt us, because my mother insisted on Vati's child support. It also posed some complicated legal questions. I knew in my heart Papa Theo would have loved to call Achim and me his own. He treated us as such in spite of our surname remaining Hunger.

During my high school years, I appreciated our comfortable life with Mutti and Papa Theo. My mother bloomed once more. She had a good and devoted husband who also took delight in *her* children. He spoiled and indulged her. As a capable manager and CEO of *Bettfedernfabrik* Mannheim, Theo Bauer had many social contacts. They added flavor to our lives.

My mother glowed in his success and participated in all formal and informal business events, including socials through the Mannheim Chamber of Commerce, whose membership provided most of my parents' new friends. When parties were given, my mother was a capable hostess, and nobody seemed to be bothered seeing us live in the industrial area of Mannheim. Located inside the business's property, and surrounded by a six foot brick-wall, we lived in a compound. This somewhat isolated and secluded place became a haven for parties on weekends and holidays.

Nobody seemed to notice the odor when an adjacent rubber factory released nasty fumes or when the steel plant across unloaded tons of soot on waiting flatcars. Some railway containers missed catching all the waste when the steel mill's chute unloaded its debris. Instead, the soot floated through the air and polluted our environment. My room's white windowsill with its daily fine black dusting was proof of our industrial environs. Our cleaning lady repeated her bi-weekly chores, washing the windows as well, and the repetition never ended during the six years we lived there.

Every year, for three long weeks, Mutti and Papa Theo went on vacation alone. During this time, I joined youth groups from church. Usually, my brother did other activities. He and I hardly ever shared vacations.

Theo Bauer drove only Mercedes, paid for by the company. Some years he had a burgundy one, some a black one. He also had a chauffeur who prided himself on being part of our family events. In addition to chauffeuring, Herr Ernst found a way into our kitchen where he would put on Mutti's apron, whip cream, cut cakes, and hard bread. He was a kooky bachelor. I remember our factory-living years as fun-filled. Achim and my cousin Jürgen who came sometimes, teased Mr. Ernst. On one of these occasions, the aggravated chauffeur, in the process of washing company vehicles, took the hose and gave the thirteen-year old boys a good washing.

Many of Papa Theo's employees became extended family. My favorite person was the factory's cook, Mrs. Beyer, who ran the cantina. We lived right above it. The cook knew my favorite dishes, and when I came home from school, I immediately checked the day's menu before going up to our apartment.

"Look in the refrigerator, Miss Mani, I have some bread-pudding for you," She would say as she washed her huge aluminum pots in the sink. She never looked up from her chores.

"Say hello to your Frau Mutter."

In the sample room, different kinds of Chinese goose and duck feathers were mixed to achieve a special blend for pillows or coverlets. Huge blowers separated the various qualities of feather. The distance feathers flew before settling down determined their downy quality. Thus, the feathers were caught in chain linked bins according to weight and distance flown. The factory had eight foot drums in which the raw material was washed and bleached. After this procedure, the merchandising of different feathers and downs could start. They called it sampling and displayed boxes with varying qualities for buyers to examine.

I loved to observe the factory procedures. In those days, we had no security or safety measures in place and nobody stopped wandering children, especially not those of Mr. Bauer. God forbid. The workers loved Mr. Bauer.

"*Guten Tag,* Miss Mani, how's it going?

I treasured the freedom of roaming, of course, and I valued the familiarity of Papa Theo's staff. It was fun.

Once a year, the company went on an employee field trip. The business stayed closed for the day, and we headed for the train station, destination unknown. It was a surprise. Everybody knew dinner, music, and entertainment would follow. As teenagers, 14 and 15, we took pleasure in the office staff's indulgence. I guess everybody longed for a piece of Theo Bauer's private life. An amazing discovery it was for me, since I never experienced such close-knit company before.

Flawed Genius

The old type *Gymnasium* in Germany used to be a select high school for students who were destined for academia. Usually, two tracks offered some flexibility in which students interests and ability were considered. The two branches represented a language and a scientific branch and in some cases also business classes in lieu of fine arts.

Normally, everybody went to elementary school for four years. After completion of grade four, one could be tested to determine capability of succeeding in the *Gymnasium.* Whoever remained in *Volksschule,* would graduate at the age of fourteen. Then, those students would continue their training in a variety of trade schools.

When entering *Gymnasium,* in contrast, a student faced eight more years of math and science or foreign languages before passing rigorous testing for the *Abitur.* This was the last exam to qualify students for entrance to any university in their major fields of study. This was without accumulating credits for basic courses, like is customary in the USA.

This very German high school system in which I was educated used to count grade levels in a Latin-inspired fashion. Thus, I entered in grade *Sexta,* progressed to *Quinta, then Quarta, Untertertia, Obertertia, Obersekunda, Unterprima,* and graduated after *Oberprima* with the *Abitur,* the official ticket for the university.

The foreign language branch in those days included Latin as well. My immature thinking led me to reject the language branch. "Mutti, I don't like Latin, I want to study modern things and subjects which are alive." The statement was sufficient for my mother, and she promptly entered me in

189

the math and science branch of the *Gymnasium*.

As a child, I memorized Latin poems, and enjoyed Onkel Dietz's instructions. Why did I make such a dumb decision then? I think Mutti wanted me to be educated and learn general knowledge, not necessarily trigonometry, chemistry, and physics, to keep me in school and out of trouble.

It was definitely not a good plan! I struggled with science and specifically with higher math. My preference was clearly the liberal arts. I did not realize the usefulness of Latin and what a magnificent vocabulary builder it represented for many languages, not only English, French and Spanish. But I disliked the outdated system of rote learning and regurgitating nothing but *Klassiker*. As so often in my life, I lacked the ability to make critical decisions. Nevertheless, I received a good education.

Dr. Müller was a single man his 30's who had served in the war. He returned and found himself homeless since Silesia had become Poland after 1945. At Heidelberg University, as a legitimate refugee, he found a paid-for place to continue his studies in history and education. While studying, he had the opportunity through an exchange program to spend one year in the United States.

He arrived on the scene and I concluded I had been misplaced; my abilities did not lay in science or math. In my heart I knew better. But as a teenager in an all girls' *Gymnasium,* I had both puberty and inexperience as my enemies. I needed encouragement and Mutti to take me on occasions to the public library. I was unsure of its location and was afraid to wander around a large building and afraid to ask for help. We had to do these things on our own since the school building was shared with another Liselotte Gymnasium that had been destroyed during the war and was under new construction. Extra curricula were taught outside the schoolhouse. My communication with Mutti wasn't easy and with too much homework and chores I didn't feel like explaining our extra requirements at school. Mutti took her afternoon naps and read, and I didn't want to bother her.

I was 16 years old and in *Untertertia* grade of Elisabeth Gymnasium in Mannheim. Compared to other girls, I was quite naïve and on the cusp of exploding into full womanhood.

Nutritional shortages caused a stunted growth during the post-war years. I was the shortest girl when we lined up for PE. How could I pursue my swimming career in free style? Competitions were tough and any Olympic aspirations were clearly out of the question. My physical strength and powerful leg and arm strokes still couldn't compensate for my height. I looked at the giant girls around me. I felt inadequate and my beloved swimming coach was in Stuttgart, and I couldn't call him to discuss my feelings.

Fortunately, after moving to Mannheim, my life was channeled in a new direction. I didn't waste any time at the pool and Mr. Schneefuß's influence faded with time. My new circumstance required a new mindset, and I plunged into my school studies. My parents didn't have to nudge me in this direction. I had an instinctive desire to carve out a niche at Mannheim's high school. Like all the rest of teenagers, I wanted to fit in.

During this time, I worked once again on a new dialect, dropping Schwäbisch for good, and substituting it with *Hochdeutsch* spoken throughout Germany.

My previous homeroom teacher, respectfully called *Professor* Ahlers, had suddenly died. A new teacher was anxiously expected. All kinds of rumors circulated about who this mystery person would be.

As it happened, Papa Theo had contacts and privileged information. One of Papa Theo's old school friends was a history professor at the Heidelberg University.

From Papa Theo I learned that a student of his old friend was coming to Mannheim to teach at the Elisabeth Gymnasium.

"Papa, I bet he will be our new teacher." I got excited. Pressing on, I asked, "Do you happen to know his name?"

"No, Mani, and I suggest you keep it quiet for now. I could be wrong."

But I was convinced Papa Theo was correct. How exciting for me, I had inside information. Wow! I was so sure. Immediately, the information went to all my girlfriends, conveniently forgetting Papa Theo's remark to be quiet.

I was right. The girls saw him climbing the open staircase. With youthful exuberance, he took two steps at once. Over six feet tall, this handsome dark-haired man in his early thirties came strutting down the long hallway. Our classroom was on the fifth and last floor of the building. Eventually he came close, walking with long strides. Up to then, I had never seen such a tall German man, especially one with such impressive long legs.

"He is coming!" A girl hollered. "You all sit down and shut up!" Like a gaggle of geese, the girls hurried to their assigned seats, straightened themselves, tucked blouses into skirts, sat straight with a charming demeanor, and automatically arranged their supplies on their desks as to give a first impression of orderliness.

Dr. Müller practically flew into the room with his huge stride. He tossed his books onto the teacher's desk. They stopped just before tumbling over the edge. He had a square head with black sparkling eyes, and thick bushy black hair. A new wind blew through the corridors of old Elisabeth Gymnasium.

The customary greeting from the students to teacher was to stand until acknowledged. We heard him say: *"Alle hinsetzen!"* This routine was repeated for two years without fail, for he was never absent and never sick.

He taught us German, geography and, of course, history. He also gave us English lessons until a new female teacher took over. There was hardly a dull moment, and he held us mesmerized with expressions we heard for the very first time. We laughed often, cursed at the demanding homework, but seemed to learn through osmosis. At least, that was how it felt. His youthful energy was catching, and none of us wanted to disappoint him.

We made goo-goo eyes at him and whispered about his appearance. The rafters crackled with sexual tension. *Everything* about him was amazing. Playing hooky for one day was unthinkable, none of the girls wanted to be absent. The girl in front of me was so enamored with him that she blushed and stuttered when he called her to answer a question.

Our lady principal, Dr. Graves, seemed less pleased with Dr. Müller. One day it dawned on me that the old school's tradition had crumbled with Dr. Müller's arrival. The very old male teachers, retired after the war, made room for the female teachers.

Our principal was fiftyish, not much over five feet in height. She needed to tilt her head to look up to the new male-teacher as if admiring the Tower of Pisa. What a sight! We girls had our pre-soap-opera, before they ever became popular in Germany.

Dr. Müller displayed playfulness. Like a boisterous boy, he danced in front of us and elicited feelings that caused the walls to tremble with sparkling electricity.

Up on the fifth floor, Frau Principal didn't notice the new sexual revolution invading her school. An awareness of something forbidden had entered the respected walls of Elisabeth Gymnasium. My classmates groomed themselves, and I saw ballerina shoes and bunchy petticoats under wide skirts. We called them *Glockenrock* (bells skirt). German fashion excluded the American poodle skirts, but the girls did their best to imitate whatever the Hollywood movies showed. I was not able to keep up until I learned to sew a bit – again Mutti was resisting all "this fashionable new nonsense." But most of my classmates started changing into little Doris Day-images. The formerly forbidden lipstick showed up on pursed teenage lips, and I quickly ran to the new Woolworth store to find a cheap lipstick that, of course, I hid from Mutti.

"People, we will have a test on this material on Friday," I can still hear him roaring. "If you are not prepared, there will be loud crying and gnashing of teeth!" Wow, what language in front of young ladies! "And if it's not quiet in here right now, you'll get another assignment to keep you busy every afternoon 'till the end of the school year."

One time I talked, or actually, whispered during one of his lectures. A long index finger suddenly shot out of his sleeves and pointed at me. My heart was pierced by a sword. It felt as if my eyeballs were punched out. With a broad and almost sadistic grin he announced that I had to draw a picture of Japan including all of its islands as punishment for talking. Naturally, I had no idea how many bays and islands Japan had.

"You will also use the correct colors for rivers, valleys and mountains. Is this clear, *junges Fräulein?*" It was clear to me and took me hours of drawing time. Tracing paper was definitely not allowed.

Needless to say, I learned geography very well. If I'd kept all the maps I drew for talking in class, I'd have a complete world atlas. Assuredly, I was not ill behaved. Discipline had never been an issue in the *Gymnasium*. If a student didn't fit in with either behavior or grades, the student was simply expelled, and the parents had to find a new school. In our class, however, an inappropriate whisper to a classmate, and *wham,* you got it! We accepted strict rules because attending this type of school was a privilege, not a right. The students knew it, and our parents knew it, too.

Reading and acting out Shakespeare's plays was never one of my favorite activities. We had to read King Lear, with parts assigned to different people. Macbeth was another play we read. I liked it better when performed on stage.

Our recitations sounded boring to Dr. Müller. He bellowed with a commanding voice *"Halt!* We are not squeaking like little mice."* So he demonstrated, and the class rolled with laughter. Shakespeare would have been proud of him. Another loud command of "Ruhe" followed! And we went immediately back to work. No delays, this teacher was efficient with time, and most of all, he had us well trained.

He had us totally under his academic control. As impressionable teenage girls, we adored him, and I definitely admired his knowledge, intellect, and life experience. He told us about the year spent in the United States as an exchange student-teacher which made me envious with yearning, another hint as to my then unknown destiny. Interspersed with subject matter, we learned what America was all about. At the time, I didn't question anything he espoused.

It was during this time that Dr. Müller's students were

required to do a research paper. After school dismissal in the early afternoon, I had difficulties getting back to the downtown public library to research a topic for my essay. I had three months to complete. Dr. Müller mentioned that information through correspondence, including mail from East German relatives, would satisfy his requirements.

It was summer 1955. I was delighted, because I felt cut off from old family-stories and facts about our estate in Schosdorf. I asked my aunt Annemarie to send me as much information, old letters and pictures to combine the contents it in my research. My research topic was our estate in Schosdorf. The byproduct of this research became my Omi's life. Aunt Annemarie had been my grandparents' caretaker since she fled Silesia and lived with them in the upstairs' rooms while the complete first floor was turned into a state-run daycare center.

Opa was employed by the new communist regime to run the factory, now the state's confiscated property. He worked there for less than two years and saw his factory mismanaged, machinery dismantled and sent to Russia. Annemarie became the paid gardener and groundkeeper for the park and surrounding property. Opa, Omi, and Tante Annemarie's lifestyle was lowered to the level of a common man or woman from the village. My grandparents had watched as many of their household items and precious Meissen Porcelain were taken by Russian officers. Anything on display, like paintings and stained-glassed inserts in windows and doors were removed.

As the granddaughter and niece of Tante Annemarie, I felt the urge to preserve my ancestral connections. Therefore, I delved into recording old stories. Little did I know where life would lead me; I needed a written document to that effect.

My Omi (1886-1967)

Omi had a special touch and became my hero growing up. After moving from Mannheim to Döbeln, Saxony, we were a two-hour train ride away from the grandparents' home. Our time was equally balanced between Döbeln and Olbersdorf. This location was exactly on the Neisse River which later became Germany's east border at the end of the war.

Holidays and summer time were spent part time in Olbersdorf and several months in Schosdorf. The remote village Schosdorf where the farm was located lay along the train line. We used horse and buggy to travel a short distance since cars had vanished from the landscape. Mutti worried that too much time with children might be overwhelming for Omi. However, I felt welcome all the time. Omi and I loved each other and couldn't stay apart for long. Throughout my life, I thought of her with deep affection and appreciation. She was unique, truly a nineteen-century lady and was adored by everybody in her family.

What lovely girl would not be flattered to get the attention of a king? Born in 1886 in the small German kingdom of Saxony, my Omi grew up to be a young lady possessing a beauty of such magnitude; no gallant man hesitated to take a second look. Neither did the last king of Saxony, whose habits were to mingle occasionally with the common people in the metropolis of Dresden. It must have been around the year 1902, and this girl went shopping accompanied by her mother.

They strolled along *Brühlsche Terrasse*, a gardened promenade above the Elbe, overlooking the river's bend in one direction and to the other one the city's sky line. If you wanted to see people and be seen, this was a popular place in Dresden.

Unexpectedly this day, King Frederick Augustus III, appeared with his entourage and slowed his pace. He stared at the stunning young lady with open admiration. Caught in slight embarrassment, the king greeted my great-grand-mother and daughter. With an elegant backwards movement he swung his hat and bowed like a subject not like the king. Very much acquainted with proper etiquette, he quickly redirected his attention to his group of people.

After the encounter with the king, my Omi Leupold, sixteen-year-old, turned around to catch another glimpse as she passed Frederick Augustus. At the very same time, the king also sneaked another look at Omi. Frida chastised her daughter for her unladylike behavior. Over the years, my future great-grand-mother, Frida, told everybody who would listen to her how attractive her daughter, Ilse appeared to the king.

Omi was the youngest child and only daughter, her parents pampered and spoiled her. She grew up fast to take over family responsibilities when her father died before either of her two older and surviving younger brothers could run the business: manufacturing cords and sacks made out of hemp.

Hired people managed the Leupold's small factory under the watchful eyes of a strict and ambitious Mrs. Frida Leupold. To her dismay, the oldest son became a lawyer, and so Omi's brother, Werner was left to do the job. Unfortunately, he died in his mid-20 of a brain tumor, leaving Omi with her determined mother to run the family business.

A practical solution surfaced. A capable young man was employed at the factory and worked to the satisfaction of Frida Leupold. Mr. Richard Hunger was an eligible bachelor and charming. Omi obviously liked Richard, which pleased Mother Fida. With some coaching, Omi agreed to marry Richard, almost fifteen years her senior. At that time she was only 16 years old and was still mother's spoiled little girl.

In spite of Ilse Leupold's immaturity, the marriage became a happy solution to the continuation of the fabrication of cords and sacks.

Obviously, Omi was rushed into marriage and motherhood. A girl and a boy were born before she turned 21. My grandmother preferred to jump and bounce around house and yard, catch butterflies or sit under a shady tree than to be reminded of her obligations as home-maker and mother. Reality forced her back to attend to her duties. In spite of her young age, and with some prodding from her mother, Omi eventually managed to play her role well.

This young family's life didn't last very long. Tragedy struck again and took Richard's life. In later years, my grandmother referred to his disease as heart asthma. Richard Hunger, my grandfather, made his young wife a widow at the age of 23, and she raised two small children by herself.

Under pressure, my great-grandmother had to make another business decision. She decided to liquidate the cord business and divide the money among her surviving children. The plan included Omi and her children, Vati and Tante Annemarie. Urmi, a nickname for my great-grandmother, and her only surviving son, Eberhard, who became an attorney, were financially secure during their life time.

Omi was not a widow for very long; for Albert Wagner, the wealthiest man in town also lost his spouse. The one-year-mourning period passed, and he asked the most beautiful girl in town to become his wife. Omi accepted the proposal, probably strongly encouraged again by her mother.

Thus, Mr. Wagner's only daughter from his first marriage found a new and loving mother and two siblings, Annemarie and Joachim. I knew Mr. Wagner solely as Opa.

Omi turned the two-story, stately Wagner house into a plush mansion. To me it was always a castle. A royal flair surrounded her. Coming down the cherry-red carpeted stairs into a spacious entry hall, she was as radiant as the huge chandeliers hanging from a high ceiling above, and sparkling with brightness. A fragrance of lavender surrounded her, and she wore dresses of pleasing smoothness, mellow colors that gently draped her slender figure of a lady in her fifties. Her premature white hair, silky, soft, and fine, was neatly arranged on top of her head like a baroque ornament, pinned down in an orderly array and covered with a white net. With a demur smile, her face shone with warmth, and her greenish-brown eyes spoke of hidden wonders.

Everything of her appearance was in harmony. Fashionable colors enhanced her personality, jewelry and accessories added to her charm. Still, as an aging grandmother, she remained an unblemished youthful picture.

Over the years, with exaggerated attention to details, she became tired. She found increasingly less time to leave her home. Her friends wondered and saw her less. Even Opa started going on business trips alone. To send her regrets, she wrote apologetic letters why she wasn't able to meet. Several maids assisted her, but Omi wasted time with rearranging pictures and re-dusting furniture. Her friends accepted the fact that Ilse Wagner had turned into a hermit.

But at home she was the queen. In her castle she played the piano, entertained her husband's friends, wrote and read poetry and communicated with the outside world with lovely sounding letters. Omi described how spring time

200

arrived outside her bedroom window. The outside world had lost its luster.

Another hobby was collecting precious Meissen porcelain, pictures and exquisite linen. Opa indulged her with money, so she could create a pleasing home. No matter how much she spent on luxuries, she was assured of her husband's love and admiration. Friends and family adored her, occasionally smiling at her eccentricities.

My early memories of the house were of happiness and security. Omi touched me with her tender hands, brushed my hair with gentle strokes and massaged my tired, restless feet after hours of romping around the huge house. As she held me close, I could hear her soft voice escaping from deep inside and lulling me with her stories into cozy dreams. I had no need for any fairy tale queen, for the most favorite queen of all held me on her lap.

When my father was a young student, he struggled with Greek. Omi searched for a tutor and found a monk. One day, she engaged him in a spiritual conversation. She inquired about his life's ambitions and learned about his life's dream to visit Rome one day. He longed to see the Eternal City, Rome. In addition he desired an audience with the Pope.

What an opportunity to enlighten a monk's life! Without any hesitation, and without consulting her husband first, Omi planned to send the monk to Rome, all expenses paid. Omi had a good excuse. She explained the concept of sainthood of all believers, which was binding for all Christians.

When Opa found out, he was not pleased with his wife's capricious albeit generous behavior. He felt charity to the Catholic Church was foolish when they were Lutheran. That was when Opa decided to limit his wife's spending. At least, he tried.

In the end, Omi was already a more liberated woman than her mother had been. She showed early rebellion against a stifling upbringing, but again succumbed to a comfortable lifestyle, because she was tricked into a romantic alliance with that benefitted the family business. My grandfather Hunger was already employed by the Leupolds, was a capable factory manager and why not marry him? Urmi heralded him as a suitable husband for Omi soon after her husband's sudden death. Omi at 16, madly in love with her third cousin, Max Teichmann had to be swayed. Urmi convinced her daughter to do the right thing and forget Max.

Omi had her idiosyncrasies. I saw her take a handkerchief from Opa's pocket and gave it to the maid for re-ironing. But those peculiarities never bothered me. I was a child and had all her love and care; she was perfect in my eyes. All my paternal relatives by the names of Teichmann, Leupold, Hunger, or Wagner I observed during the early 1940's were ninetieth-century people. I'm still amazed to know I was there to appreciate this experience.

I thought that Omi compensated for what she lacked in life. Since she lost her first husband in her 20's, she remarried and was happy in her second marriage to Opa Wagner. Without financial worries and other challenges in prewar Germany, she was the gentle ruler and organizer of the household. Her acquired compulsion struck me as strange when she examined the grandchildren for clean finger nails and hands, washed necks and ears and checked for spotless clothing before they could join the dinner table.

Since we usually stayed miles apart from each other, every visit became a highlight that I never forgot. Even in old age when she was skinny and wrinkly, she made sure that her make-up was applied with care and her silver hair was neatly put up and hidden under an almost invisible net to hold her coiffure for the day. "You owe it to the people around to look attractive.

And if nothing else, my child, it makes you feel so much better when you catch your image in the mirror." She snickered and continued, "I also hate to scare myself."

More High School Activities

The years 1954 and 1955 passed fast. Dr. Müller kept us busy. I was glad and excited to finish my research paper by Christmas 1955. The packages from East-Germany containing old letters from my great-great-grandparents and Annemarie's additional biographical stories delighted me. I knew that one day I would use the documents to pass them on to my children.

The Gymnasium's requirement kept me very busy. In fact, I never remembered a dull moment including other teachers than our homeroom teacher, Dr. Müller. Our PE teacher in those days was a stern old lady by the name of Dr. Ernst. She was equally bewildered with the arrival of this new male teacher. She complained with visible disdain, "Your Dr. Müller" never seems to be wrong. "Dr. Müller, here, and Dr. Müller, there!" She threw up her skinny, wrinkled arms in despair. "Can anybody tell me what happened to our school?" Dr. Ernst concluded with a sigh, clearly resigned to a new way of life.

Our school owned a recreational house in the Oldenwald, an idyllic hilly country along the Neckar River's valley, and once a year the whole class, accompanied by two teachers, was eligible to spend one week at this lovely vacation spot. At least four hours of formal instruction was required. But otherwise we considered our stay a holiday.

Dr. Ernst and Dr. Műller, midget and giant, formed an unequal pair of chaperones for teenage girls. Poor Mrs. Ernst wasn't thrilled. She trotted with her head hanging low, while her male counterpart, tall and erect, strutted with more confidence than a bull fighter entering the arena. We noticed their differences, but accepted our fate, considering the alternative of remaining in Mannheim and trudging daily to the school house.

The school's home was a wooden structure with three levels. A married couple ran the kitchen on the first floor, adjacent to the mess hall, which also served as a class room. The old piano, upright and on wheels, stood sideways in the dining area.

The girls were divided between two sleeping areas and shared one washroom and bathroom on each floor. Our meals were cafeteria style, forget the delicious wine sauces Mutti prepared at home, but were edible. On Sundays, we were served hot chocolate with fresh white, sweet bread, which we considered a special treat.

The village where the house stood was called Buchklingen. It was remote, bypassed by regular traffic. 30 miles away from my house in Mannheim was no huge distance, but still we found ourselves in the quiet countryside surrounded by rolling hills. It seemed so far away from the busy bustle of half a million people in Mannheim. We enjoyed the quaint hiking paths and kilometers of daily walking, which wasn't unusual for German youngsters, still unaccustomed to being hauled around by cars. We walked everywhere a streetcar was unavailable. Nobody complained or grumbled. Instead, we sang, laughed, and talked for hours on end and felt happy.

Searching the Ruins

This particular year at Buchklingen with Dr. Müller as leader turned out differently than anticipated. We had chosen early spring as our time for the retreat, and the snow had not quite melted. Some white patches on the hill sides were still visible which the skiers among us welcomed. Even though swimming was my métier, other sports interested me as well.

At 6 a.m., we heard Dr. Müller hollering from outside the front door. Like being called for reveille, sleepy and muttering wild-haired girls, all bundled up, had to run along the side of the road. Breakfast was our reward after washing up in the community bathroom.

The converted farmhouse had the bathrooms added on to the back, resembling a glass enclosed veranda. Pipes ran along three sides of the lower walls, supporting twelve old fashioned metal bowls, with mostly cold running water. Sometimes, if you cared to get up at 5 a.m., the water at least felt lukewarm. Showers remained a far off dream. Therefore, sponge baths sufficed.

Nighttime was for primping, luxuriating with filing and cutting nails, creaming my face, and sharing the space with only my close girlfriend.

One night, I turned around and leaned against the row of connected sinks in order to face my friend Karin. We discussed important events, and I got carried away in my fingernail filing, which caused me to apply more pressure on the sink than intended.

Whoosh! Some steamy water hit the back of my legs.

"Manu, you broke the pipe!" Karin screamed and ran in the hallway and shouted even louder. "Help, Help!" Wringing her hands, she acted like a mother helplessly watching her child drown.

It was the wrong thing to do with a bunch of young

girls! Girls in long night gowns, hair pinned up or hanging in strands, appeared, one after another, gawking and joining the chorus of screaming, "Help!"

"What in the hell is going on up there?" A thunder-and-lightning voice shouted from below. Gosh, he used the hell word too. Our teacher took three steps at once, pulling himself along on the handrail. The old wooden stairs creaked painfully with this forceful ascent. It threatened to break any minute. The whole rickety stairwell shook. Dr. Müller rushed into the middle of a hysterical, ghastly looking group of girls trying to inspect the disaster.

I was the culprit. In the middle of my private hideout, I found myself the center of unwanted attention.

"I tell you!" Müller screamed, "Wherever this Hunger sits down, no grass will ever grow again!" He swiftly turned around, almost knocking two girls down. Dr. Müller descended the stairs in the same manner he had come up, almost flying.

Dr. Müller searched for the home parents so they could shut off the water, and the next day, I was asked to call Papa Theo's office at the *Bettfedernfabrik*.

Papa Theo listened to my intermittent crying. "What did you break? Now, slow down and stop crying. Tell me again. Where did you sit down?"

After some clarification, he assured me his liability insurance would take care of the damage. "No reason to cry. Enjoy your stay. You didn't do it on purpose. I will come out tonight and talk to the administrator. Your mother can find out later when I bring her along. No reason to get her riled up." Papa Theo paused a moment and added, "I better bring the factory's plumber along as well."

That night, my sleep was restless. I thought my

teacher's remarks were rude and hurtful. How impertinent to call me by my last name, for one thing, and then to make the "grass" remark. I had to let him know. So I mulled all night over how to approach him the next morning. If I could corner him alone, I'd express my feelings, I decided. Almost trembling, but feeling rectified, I approached my teacher the following morning.

"Dr. Müller, I didn't intend to break anything, and my father will definitely pay for the damage. He'll be here tonight with the plumber. I am very sorry."

I had more to say and clenched my hands to keep them from shaking. "You hurt my feelings by screaming at me in front of my classmates. It was humiliating."

He towered over me like a giant. "Well done, Manuela. I am sorry, and I do apologize for my harsh words."

"Thanks," I said in a whisper tone. Our conversation was over, and I walked away feeling I had grown two inches.

Before the week's end, I got "slapped" yet one more time. One afternoon the class split up. The skiers in my chosen group planned their own outing. The rest of the girls went with our PE teacher, Dr. Ernst. Herr Dr. Müller decided to join the skiers.

I was happy to find another chance to ski. Dressed in black pants and black heavy jacket, I thought I looked great.

Mutti had bought both items at C&A for Christmas. This department store in Mannheim was moderately priced, but fashionable. I wasn't spoiled, not since my early childhood with Omi, and as far as I was concerned, anything coming from a department store was super. Most of the time, my mother hired a seamstress who made dull and outdated garments, which I deplored.

On the slopes in Buchklingen, I came down the hill

with power and strength. Exhilarated by the steep descent, snow spraying, my nose red from the whooshing wind, I felt comfortable, and in charge, especially since Dr. Müller had given me the courtesy of apologizing. My poles flung around me with a warning to get out of my way. As I slowed down and prepared to stop, I maneuvered to avoid another skier who had followed me too closely. My teacher stood there, his mouth cupped with two hands as to amplify already loud voice.

"Here comes the Bomber from Morocco!"

"Yeah, yeah!" I heard applause.

I cannot recall my immediate reaction. However, my inner warning lights flicked on. And sure enough, another nickname was coined. From then on, and for a long time thereafter, the Bomber from Morocco became my coat of arms. How I hated this name! But I ignored it and didn't let anyone know it bothered me. The approach worked, and the initial insult lifted like fog after the morning dawn.

At this time, I noticed a change. I desired to be pretty, and more than sneaking a lip stick once in a while. Any symbol of physical strength seemed unfeminine and undesirable. The consciousness of my young womanhood appeared to me like a mermaid emerging from a magic pond. This significant moment on the ski slopes burned into my awareness when I morphed from tomboy into a young lady. My perceived strength and daredevil forces gave away to far more daintiness. It felt like a lightning strike.

Dancing School would open in fall, and I was ready. I planned to join my female classmates and did well with the boys from Hölderlin Gymnasium. These were the guys I had previously hung out with, ran bikes with along the island of the Old Rhein, they would be amazed. I had my old buddies close by and never worried about dance partners.

The Italian Vacation

As a teenager, I needed a father figure. My natural one was four-hours away by train. I never had privacy to call him. Local phones calls were not free. Mutti didn't want me to make calls. Period. Papa Theo, so absorbed with his new life and wife, didn't realize that Mutti distanced me from him. The rejection from both parents was painful. I grew angry.

But not having been around my father much, I forgot the negatives. I agreed to go on a vacation with his new family. It was summer of 1954, a new camping craze held Germans captive. People flocked to Italy, the Riviera and Adriatic Sea. I was invited to travel with Vati, Else, and Joe, tent and all, off to Italy.

When my mother learned about my invitation, she was quite unhappy. "Why just you? Is your brother a step-child? Your father always gives you preferential treatment. I kept my mouth shut, since I couldn't argue. I preferred to swallow my disagreeable statements. I didn't think my brother had much interest in going on a camping trip to play with a baby brother Joe.

"Well, Mutti, do you want me to tell Vati 'no'?" I asked her.

"No, that's not the point. The point is you are always the favorite one. Omi did the same. She favored you as well."

I was surprised to hear this. Wasn't I an unwanted child? How did I get the status of favored one? My parents were so confusing.

Maybe my mother was correct, but in this case I was needed as a babysitter for four-year-old Joe. I was a young girl and well trained in household chores. As the oldest, I had responsibilities and knew, without having to be told, how to make myself useful. What I didn't know, was that my father had bought expensive photography equipment to take on the trip. He intended to capture the whole Italy experience, and I was destined to be his assistant.

So I became the caddy for lenses and tripods. I sat patiently while he took shots of St. Marcus Cathedral in Venice. Winding our way through crowded little streets, I watched his back so nobody would steal his dangling camera or several telephoto lenses attached in leather cases. I smelled the canal, peeked into window displays and longed to be able to stop for a minute to admire all the gorgeous jewelry on display.

"Don't fall behind, girl. Tante Else is watching Joe. I rely on you walking right behind me. There're more pickpockets in Venice than in Mannheim."

"Yes, Vati, I am. I watch your *Po*" (butt). He never heard it, or he chose to ignore me.

My mother claimed I had the Hunger butt, meaning my derriere was large. During my memorable Italy vacation, I did see the original Hunger butt, moving steadily in front of me. It was not very encouraging.

I saw Venice at home when Vati's slides were shown on the white screen. While in Italy, I was so busy watching Vati's damned cameras and backside that I saw little else. I envied my brother staying back in Mannheim and doing whatever he wanted to do.

When we made it to the beach we found our reserved lot. The location was close to the city of Rimini. The Adriatic Sea laid glassy blue in front of us, and the sandy beach was inviting.

I lifted one foot, then the other and watched the silky

sand run between my toes. Playing among hundreds of German folk, I wished they all would disappear and go home. We were in Italy, and I had to endure a German invasion! I wanted to enjoy an empty beach with only a few people in the distance. I stood taking in the salty air and looked across the water, when I recognized an island.

"Look, Vati, is that San Marino over there? I remember you told us it was the smallest republic in the world."

"Smart girl, you paid attention. One of their major businesses is printing new postal stamps faster than you can buy them. A picturesque place, they say."

"Would you believe I have some postal stamps from there? It's good to know where the island is located," I told Vati.

But he had already lost interest in engaging in further chitchat. He had a job to do before night fall. He was creating the tent according to exact guidelines. I held stakes and hammer, and Vati constructed our gray tent with its zippered door. Our tent measured maybe 6 by 7 feet. It was supposed to sleep three adults and one small child. In front of the tent there was an extension, an awning which easily snapped together and spanned a generous 10 by 6 feet, supported by four poles. My father had a system for doing this. He labored and sweated, and I kept little Joe out of his way.

Else ran back and forth unpacking the car. She carried air mattresses and blankets, a few kitchen utensils, and shopping bags full of clothes. The items were wildly strewn about. It appeared they had been dumped out of a laundry basket.

"This is not like home, but we cannot afford fancy vacations right now." Here again was Vati's unnecessary remark about his finances.

What a shame, I thought to myself. Why bring up a shortage of money when you are having a good time camping in Italy?

I held my primitive box camera and shot a picture of Vati. By now, he sat in the back of the tent, admiring his finished construction. He looked small and out of place. Over the years I have examined this snapshot, and each time I come to the conclusion that the business man clad in a dark suit looked more like a poor peasant in this picture.

We stayed at the Rimini beach site for a week. Strolling among hundreds of tents was entertaining and also made me useful as an informer about available shower stalls. Since the showers were shared by so many campers, the timing of our personal hygiene was most important.

Else was constantly washing clothes by hand. I carried buckets of water to her so she could rinse her laundry right in front of the tent. The rest of the family loved our time under the showers in the public bathhouses. This was new to me, because at home we didn't have shower stalls, only sinks and tubs.

Fetching water, I made many trips and noticed new people arriving at the campground. To my surprise, I spotted a single tent a few meters away from ours. It looked like a midget's habitation. It was so small. But then I noticed that a young man had come to stay in it for the weekend. I knew he was Italian, maybe to observe Germans. I figured I'd better watch out for him. My father warned me that Italian men love to pinch pretty girls' butts.

"Manuelita, you better be careful when you do your usual exploring. Got it?"

I loved when Vati called me Manuelita. The sweet

nickname sounded lovely to my ears. Apparently he was in a relaxed mood. He only seemed to worry about Italian men pinching me, or his wife not cooking a fancy breakfast.

"Beachtime, folks!" Vati suddenly announced.

How exciting, I was going to be able to swim by myself. Not to scare my father, I told him: "I'm swimming a bit farther today. The current looks calm, no waves and no sharks. Is it okay with you?"

Here, at the beach was a perfect time to think of my coach. He had been like a father to me. I missed him. I missed the physical challenge of swimming.

Suddenly, an energetic wave of fighting spirit took over me. I hit the water's surface like I was fighting off an opponent in the adjacent lane. Lifting my head to the left, I spotted the fortress of San Marino, and then I turned my head to the right and saw water crystals refracting the spectrum of the rainbow. A great feeling.

I felt I was back to Stuttgart. I was once more training with Mr. Schneefuß. "This girl will swim in the next Olympics in Melbourne in 1956. Mark my words. Since we live in the same apartment house, I will personally see to it, and I shall take her under my wings. Is this all right with you, Mrs. Hunger?" I thought about his words as I swam.

As I lifted my head another time, I heard a familiar name called. "How many Manuels do they have around here at Rimini's beach?" I wondered as I kept going. A shot of saltwater burned my eyes, and I halted my swimming. I faced the shore line. The people there appeared as tiny glass beads on a stick pin.

I thought, "Well, I guess, I better make it back, or my father will be upset. This time, I'll coast along. I can ride the waves. Easy does it. Easy does it. Remember, you don't have to win any more."

To my surprise, I returned to the exact spot where I had entered the water.

Vati stood awestruck and said, "Manuelita, you little devil, where did you learn to swim like this?"

Swim like this! How come, he never listened? That was my life in Stuttgart. My dream was to become a champion swimmer. And Vati never took notice until now.

"Mister, you ought to enter your daughter in a competition of some kind," a bystander advised Vati.

Vati didn't seem to hear or care. The conversations at the beach swirled, and it was Vati that became the center of attention. Yes, he was my father, he declared, and yes he was proud of my athletic abilities.

What a lie, I thought. I know he wants me dolled up with long curly hair in frilly dresses. I felt both sad and angry.

Meanwhile, Vati bathed in his unexpected spotlight. But the scene only brought pain as I remembered the loss of my fatherly trainer back in Stuttgart.

Fortunately, the day ended on a pleasant note. We sat outside of our tent as the sun set, eating canned hotdogs with bread and sipping lukewarm red wine.

Germans are pretty relaxed about allowing teenager to drink alcoholic beverages. Before WWI, children became adults at 14, at which point most of them had left *Volksschule* and learned a trade. The olden days carried into 1953, and I was considered a grownup that could have a glass of wine occasionally.

After supper, little Joe was wrapped into a blanket and went to sleep. The older folks continued savoring the evening night outside Rimini. The murmur of hundreds of camping neighbors died down. I felt at peace with myself and our camp's surroundings. I heard waves breaking, a perfect lullaby for me.

As the week was winding down, I still needed to explore the dunes. Vati said they weren't any different from what we had along the North Sea in Germany.

"Go ahead and see. But do not wander off. Make sure you always see the beach. You may get lost wandering inside the dunes. They all look alike."

I walked past rows of tents. Clad in a one-piece swimsuit, bright red and with white chrysanthemums, I walked barefoot and slid through the sand, up the path that winded slowly out of sight.

Vati was right; there was nothing extraordinary to see. Dunes were like those in Germany. But I was still curious where the path would lead and I went a few more meters around the bend. A couple more steps wouldn't get me lost, I thought.

No sooner had I passed Vati's designated boundary than I was face to face with a handsome Italian man. What now? My father's warning rang in my head. The stranger came closer which made me step aside to let him pass. His intentions remained unclear to me. But he wasn't about to pass me. Instead, he stopped, sized me up – head to toes, and toes to head.

"Hallo, beautiful thing!"

"Mister, I only speak German or English," I informed him politely.

"*Bene, bene*, English is fine."

I stood there like an idiot, but daring enough to carry on a conversation. Some feelings of foreboding crept up my spine, indefinable, but I couldn't find the right vocabulary to tell him, "Get lost!" We were trained to be polite.

He must have noticed how befuddled I was, and felt encouraged to come closer to touch me. However, my swift move prevented him from pulling me over to the high dune grass. Before I could react, he pulled off his swim trunks, more bikini-like as was fashionable all over Europe. With expert hands he exposed everything he had.

Panic gripped me. Up to this moment, I hadn't seen a naked man. It wasn't supposed to be like this. Wait just a minute, Mister!" I became instantly brave and kicked his hairy legs. My foot hurt with the impact. Noticing very little else, my flight instincts kicked in, and I was on the move. Rabbit-like, with a jerky sudden turn, I got away.

"Please stop! I am sorry," he hollered behind me.

I checked over my shoulder and saw that he had already pulled up his pants. When I reached the path's bend, I could clearly see the beach and felt safe again. The campsite was in plain view which gave me a secure feeling like an approaching Coast Guard boat helping a distressed person hanging on driftwood.

Reassured, I stopped at the embankment and hollered back at the man: "My father speaks Italian, and our tent is right there," I pointed in the general direction. "I will tell him, and he will have you put in jail."

To my surprise, the Italian man answered.

"Promise not to tell anybody."

Whatever he had to say, I didn't care. I knew one thing: he had tried to do more than pinch my bottom. "Calm down, calm down, you cannot involve Vati in this incident," I told myself. He is likely to round up the whole Rimini police force and spoil our vacation. I refused to become the center of attention with Vati ranting and raving.

By the time I reached our tent I was relaxed and

resolved to say nothing. Vati never learned about the ugly scene. I was tired of his litigious mindset. Yes, I was stunned and dumbfounded, but the encounter with the man's salacious approach taught me how a potential Casanova, Italian or otherwise, acted.

The week's camping grew closer to its end. It was Friday and some folks packed up, and some started arriving. We had gone to bed after a glass of Chianti. We zipped up our fake front door and settled onto our wobbly air-mattresses.

Saturday morning arrived at the camp ground as the light wafted through the flaps of our tent, and I heard Vati's voice. Quickly, I pulled on a shift and crawled out of our makeshift habitation. Between our neighbors, five feet away, was that tiny tent, reminding me of a doghouse, obviously invading our space.

Lo and behold, Vati stood with a young man chatting away, but not in German. At first I thought my father was talking to the Casanova. But he was merely using his Romance languages in conversing with another man. On a closer look, the fellow appeared neither to be Italian, Spanish nor German, but looked disheveled and more like he was pulled out of bed without much sleep.

"Ravenna…camping…Rimini."

Well, he must have come for the weekend to rest here. But why would he place himself so close to us? I was sure Vati had the whole scoop on him already.

While chatting with the man, my father had extracted facts about his background. His name was Emmanuel. They talked for hours, like family, sharing simple foods between our tents. By then I figured out that he was just another Italian man, working as an Olivetti representative, but of some prestigious descent.

In retrospect, I missed the significance of our meeting; he didn't strike me as special. He had a balding head and was of short statue, only 5-foot-4. At the age of 26 or 28, the fellow seemed too old for me, definitely not a Dieter on a racy white bike. While lying there, I imagined Dieter racing his sporty white bicycle dangerously side by side with the streetcar and waving nonchalantly at the girls waiting on the platform.

But my father questioned the man relentlessly and the man seemed to indulge Vati. I could make out some of their conversation, but overall I missed the highlights. I was relieved that the young man looked nondescript and harmless. This new acquaintance, Emmanuel, remained complacent and good natured and endured Vati's inquisition.

"What's all the excitement with this Italian?" I asked Else who was busy dressing little Joe and tidying up blankets and toys.

"Who knows your father mentioned taking him out tonight. Good, I won't have to cook." She dismissed the subject.

Going downtown sounded like fun to me. I looked forward to a diversion from tent-city living. People sat outside the restaurants and chatted, an enjoyable outing in a happy Italian setting. I heard well known songs like *"Arrivederci Roma"* and *"Marina, Marina, Marina."* The music magically transformed my mood. I felt happy and also picked up some Italian vocabulary. Already able to say *"buona sera"* and *"buon giorno,"* and with a linguist as a father, I simply had to tune in, and *voila*, was soon able to understand simple phrases.

I couldn't remember how I looked that evening. We didn't have a full-length mirror. But knowing that I was well proportioned, with a wide chest, strong muscular arms and legs from swim training, wearing a simple sun dress over a well tanned body, must have highlighted my features. That distracted from my messy salt-water-ravished hairdo. Old photos bore witness that I looked like eighteen rather than fifteen, but I wasn't up to impressing an Italian tent neighbor.

Emmanuel and I, Manuela, sat next to each other at an outside restaurant. We didn't take much notice of one another. Or maybe, I was the oblivious one, for my eyes scanned the busy street with honking *Vespas*, whose drivers blew their horns, greeted friends along the street.

With increased consumption of Chianti wine, my head buzzed, and Vati had to repeat his most important news twice.

"Emmanuel is a grandson of the last king." He tried to convey this in an elevated but still whispered tone. The message was, "Wake up girl, here's your chance."

"Is this so?" was all I could say. My yawn told Vati that his spectacular revelation was meaningless to me. I was again in my dreamy fog about Dieter back in Mannheim.

"Manuelita, listen child!" Vati waved his hand in front of my face. "His grandfather was the last *king* of Italy, the one who abdicated." Vati's voice increased emphatically. Even Else noticed and popped her violet eyes wide open. Her attempts to motion attention to me failed as well. I was a dreamy teenager. Royalty didn't impress me at all.

"Really? Humm." I said something just to be polite. But the weird sign language conversation across the table didn't intrigue me in the least. My father was obviously embarrassed about my lack of interest. Did he expect me to say "Your Highness," or was I to curtsy?

I perked up when four eyes shot daggers across the table. What did I do wrong? Guilt broke my trance, and I paid attention to the new "revelation" about Emmanuel.

219

Umberto I and Umberto II... Princess of Savoy ... names rushed by, not meaning much at that time. Yes, he worked at the Olivetti Company, but he was a real prince.

The spaghetti dinner was served. It was a relief. The pasta was the perfect food to fill my belly and stopped me from worrying about outdated customs and paying homage to a stranger. The southern lights and sounds tricked my senses into thinking that I was eating a real gourmet dinner.

I was still slow on the uptake and my mind stayed foggy about Vati's excitement. Obviously, the young prince had more realistic aspirations than falling in love with a strong-built fifteen-year-old with a crush on a German high school boy. Neither rich nor famous, the Hunger Family couldn't have helped the prince revive his ancestors' lineage to new fame. Thus, no Grace Kelly romance evolved, only a consolatory *"arrividerci"* to a former royal, an impoverished prince.

When recalling this story in later years, I concluded that Vati lived in a dream world. I remembered how he turned melancholy with the memory of a daughter who was too naïve and inattentive. He found much pleasure in impressing his friends with how I ignored the grandson of the last Italian king. It was most endearing to him. He retold the Italian event like depicting one of those romantic European movies from the 50's.

Since the lives of the Hungers and Bauers intersected in Mannheim, I saw Tante Else's son, Heinz frequently. Else would call each time he came to town. I remembered those visits as entertaining and pleasant. Heinz was handed plenty of money, privileges Achim and I didn't share; but Heinz was a generous young man and loved inviting me to musicals touring through Germany and specifically Mannheim.

Recalling the past, I do wonder, why Achim never came along.

On one occasion, Heinz and I went to a dance party, and Else pinned a very expensive diamond broche on my blood red brocade dress. I was afraid of losing it. But she insisted, and I did hand her back the broche after the dance which all along had made me feel very self-conscious. "This could be yours one day," she said. I never considered my time with Heinz as dating.

Gradually, a new routine and acceptance of each other had developed. However, Mutti and Else hated each other and showed it with disagreeable verbal statements, very detrimental to children. But on the surface, we tiptoed around dislikes and delicate issues without letting our guards down. Confused by emotional feelings, Achim and I endured them. I believe if Heinz had been around more, a lasting relationship could have developed. Heinz went to trade-school and later took over his uncle's lucrative electric company in Pforzheim.

Else suggested in round-about ways that Heinz and I would make a good couple. Though we liked each other, we had different ideas about dating. I graduated in 1958 from a Mannheim *Gymnasium*. And truthfully, I had been more interested in the local boys from the *Gymnasium* and dancing school. Vati moved his family once more in 1961 to Düsseldorf. Though a new family unit was formed with Heinz, Achim, and Joe, but eventually we only would have occasional contacts.

Coming of Age

Dating and the *sweet sixteen,* was different in Germany. Dancing school was a must for high school students, and the dating game was part of it. Fortunately, my mother went along with this custom. Yet, when one set of rules were obsolete, she retained her control by making new rules.

In our dancing school the boys were usually two years older than the girls. They were almost 18 and we girls would turn 16 during that year. We all tried to look our best. I imagined my first ballroom dress and my first pumps for this special evening. I couldn't wait to make the purchases.

I wanted a pair of silver shoes with solid but higher than normal heels. My feet hadn't grown any larger since my dreadful *Elefanten* experience in Stuttgart.

Though shorter than my class mates, I fit in well. The boys liked me, never a doubt about it, maybe because I was a buddy to them and acted naturally without pretense or contrite sophistication.

My wardrobe had to be upgraded. And in my preoccupation with dancing school and an upcoming ball, I pestered my mother. I told her while we were busy in the kitchen, "Mutti, I need some yards of white satin for my dress." Her preparing a meal, cutting parsley, losing half of it while carrying the board to the stove, was obviously more important than a teenager's begging. "Mutti, I repeated, "I need yardage for my ballroom dress."

"Hum, I hear need, need, and need all the time. Papa is right when he calls you "Miss Need." Mutti never stopped her activity, never looked at me. She focused on preparing her meal. After an endless moment she said, "We'll hire Miss Wendel for one day to whip it up."

I didn't like the meaning.

"No whipping up, Mutti, please, I have my own ideas."

"Wait, I need to go downtown next week. Don't be so impulsive. Everything you want is right now." Mutti reached for more parsley, and more of it dropped on the floor.

As we planned for the upcoming ball, Mutti and I negotiated back and forth. The dress turned out okay, too plain for my taste, but if I draped it with Omi's old *Brüssel* silk stole, the dress could be saved.

"You checked through our attic's stowaway boxes, didn't you?" Mutti questioned me when she saw the stole.

I designed my satin dress on paper and added all kinds of accessories. Mutti stopped all such nonsense, as she called it, but offered to let me pierce my ears instead. We labored and discussed my evening dress and Mutti showed increasing leniency. It wasn't that I'd acquired a décolleté or diamond studded sandals. My sweet sixteen's experience had arrived.

The ballroom affair came and went. The group picture depicts all participants plus Mr. & Mrs. Lamadée, the dance instructors. Over 50 years later, I still see that no luster was wasted on me. My short dark hair was too boyish, and I needed more stylish shoes, some with an elegant heel. I did like Omi's lace stole, which softened my overall appearance.

At the ball, the boys acted like gentlemen. None of them noticed my fashion shortcomings. My dance partner had to fight off the boys and stood with droopy head on the dance floor while I swirled around with other young men. Naughty it was. But after a few dances, I returned to Werner, apologetically smiling like it wasn't my fault.

We danced until midnight, hardly took a break and especially enjoying the Vienna waltz. For most of the evening, we danced to Big Band music, our favorite music of the day. Could I ever find better dance partners? I wondered. The evening ended, Werner and I said our goodnights. He remained the best Vienna waltz partner ever, but I never told him. My social skills hadn't reached their zenith yet.

I never saw Werner again, but some of the previous dance students continued meeting at the Lamadee's studio every Sunday afternoon. We paid DM 2 or about 50 cents as entrance fee, and stacks of shiny black records entertained us until about 5 p.m. Mr. and Mrs. Lamadee watched for proper behavior. I was happy and practiced new dances with new friends. Hans was one of them, and soon we danced exclusively with each other. We dated for close to four years.

My neighborhood buddies Dieter and Siegfried were still around, but Hans pushed everybody away from me. Strangely enough, my buddies told me, "Hey, Manu, you're a happy person, why do you hang out with a grouch?" I believed anything Hans said, for he was the class genius. Most importantly, Mutti approved of him which made life easier with Mutti.

My mother and Papa Theo had a talk with Hans. They explained the nature and limits of our dating.

I was shocked and embarrassed when I heard Mutti say, "She's not good in Math, and if you care to come once a week to tutor, that would be acceptable to us. Otherwise, you can see her on weekends, no phone calls in between, except for Fridays when you can make plans for the weekend."

She couldn't have been more precise. Needless to say, Hans pedaled over on his bike to tutor me. I grew tired of math and increased my hate for the subject, although the arrangement of seeing each other was wonderful. In similar fashion, we enjoyed our orchestrated dates, our dancing, or our staying-at-home times.

The Wunds, Hans's parents, loved me like a daughter. They trusted us alone at home when they went out to the movies. I listened to Hans's violin playing and was in rapture with his romantic repertoire and expertise. Classical music was all I knew growing up since we had no choice in what music we could hear at home. We didn't own a TV, and the radio played only in the kitchen to entertain Mutti while she cooked and I did dishes.

At times, Hans and I went on excursions. We rode bikes to Heidelberg, or took cheap trips on the local train along the Bergstraße. In the neighborhood of Käfertal where Heinz lived, we walked every street. Its ancient "downtown" area was a quaint little village with narrow, winding streets. I enjoyed walking arm in arm with him, saying "Hello" to passersby and window shopping during the holidays. I remember these earlier days as serene, unencumbered and content. We were very resourceful with our time spent alone, but I didn't realize how I'd cut myself off from my other friends.

Sometimes, Mother Wund wanted to chat with me on their balcony and drink a *Saft* (juice) she made from berries. She thought of errands for her son to do so we would have privacy. Hans was their only child and a prodigy more than they could handle. They had no formal education, and Hans educated them on topics of the day. I found it painful hearing him lecture them for I loved his parents, honest and dignified folk. Hans seemed ashamed of them.

On weekends, Father Wund played with a band to supplement the family's income. He invited us to join him at the dance hall, but Hans tried very hard to avoid him. We only went one time to see and hear Hans's father. The venue was held in Ludwigshafen, a city across the Rhein River. We indulged Mr. Wund Sr., according to Hans, and Mr. Wund was happy to show off his tall, blond, handsome son and girlfriend.

"This is my son and hopefully his future wife,

Manuela. She still needs to graduate from the *Gymnasium*." I perked up my ears when he said "future wife." Was I really to be married?

The worst problem at home was the resistance to my continued education. Both sides of my family, Mufti's and Vati's, refused to let me enroll at the university after high school graduation. Their refusal developed into a life-changing event.

Abitur included more schooling than high school. At the time, only five percent of Germany's girls enjoyed such a high level of education. The Baccalaureate was a rigorous procedure of written tests, no multiple choices ever, and it took days to complete. To pass this exit test was to have your ticket in hand for your desired core studies. Unlike in the States, no basic courses were required at the university, because those were already earned in high school.

Proudly, I approached my father to help to ask help with the expenses of attending the university. He told me I had gone one year over his obligatory child support, and Else had no formal education, so why should I? Money shortage was the reason given more than once. Paradoxically, secondary education was free as long as the parents didn't exceed a certain income. However, proof had to be presented, and my father refused to comply. He simply made too much money and was required to pay for my secondary education. Vati avoided this and his reasoning went something like this: why waste money on a girl who has a boyfriend.

"Don't you intend to get married?" My father queried.

"Sure," I said, "Some time, but not right away.

With poor parents or only a single mother, I would have been entitled to the free tuition to Heidelberg University. My dream seemed defeated, and since I couldn't receive a degree, I considered marriage as an option.

Vati knew I wanted to be a schoolteacher. In 1958 with a shortage of teachers, it was a desirable career for a girl. Only two years of studies were required. It was the cheapest and shortest university degree in Germany. I begged.

Vati asked, "Who wants to be a spinster teacher?"

His tactics didn't impress me, and Vati read it in my face, so he bargained, "if you promise never to marry, I'll help support you with the tuition. Otherwise I suggest you make yourself pretty and attractive and marry a rich man." My boyfriend Hans didn't impress Vati.

Slap, slap. I felt spanked like a child again for not knowing my multiplication fact of 6x8. Now I had mastered a higher than average education and still didn't qualify. Mutti told me privately not to ask Papa Theo for anything.

"This is your father's obligation. He has spent a pittance compared to Papa Theo," Mutti declared. "And where would we be if it hadn't been for Papa? It isn't the worst thing to work in an office. You will probably want to marry in a couple of years anyway.

So Mutti preached like Vati. What was I supposed to do?

My mother referred to my boyfriend, Hans. He seemed happy that I didn't get my way. Since we'd met four years before he had been thinking of marriage, which made me nervous. Meanwhile, Mutti told him what the limits of our friendship and possible romance would be. He complied with her demands like an obedient little boy. But he was getting restless, and I was frustrated as well, but for different reason.

Shortly after I had moved to Mannheim, Helga's life changed. First, she dropped out of *Gymnasium* and wrote me that an academic future wouldn't be for her. Besides, she missed studying with me. Mama enrolled her in a vocational school where she learned to type, take shorthand, and acquire other office skills. We stayed in contact, and when Papa Theo drove to Stuttgart to see his mother, sister, and brother-in-law, he was willing to drop me off at Helga's for an afternoon visit and this every time he drove to Stuttgart. At 20, Helga got married while I was still in the Gymnasium waiting to take all my exit exams.

I remember this weekend with Hans when we attended Helga's wedding. We traveled by train to attend the wedding. I held a pale yellow lace dress and gave Hans adoring looks. He was good looking, tall, and blond with a few upturned curly strands that he hated. I thought he was cute, and loved introducing him to Helga's future husband and his friends who showed more interest in me than Hans.

"Are you the Mani we heard about? Mr. Schneefuß's little racehorse?" One fellow asked me.

"What did my trainer call me, racehorse?" I wondered out loud.

Albert Feuerstein, the groom, was a water polo player in the other swim club, the Police Swim Club, and was familiar with members of my previous *Schwimm Verein*. He turned to his brother, another Hans, and asked him if he remembered Helga's old girlfriend.

"Barely. All I can say is she's incredibly beautiful now. Wow." I must have blushed, for I never heard compliments at home.

"Definitely no race horse anymore," Hans mused. "I predict she will never live in a stable." My Hans didn't think that this fellow was too clever.

"She won't, if I can help it." With this statement, Hans pulled me away from Albert's brother, Hans and looked for another group to mingle with.

Graduation Time

1958, around the time of my graduation from high school, Mutti and Papa Theo moved out to the country to their new house in a small town away from Industrial Street. I was squeezed between two sets of parents who had their own agendas, and a boyfriend who wanted to become engaged. My main drive was to avoid isolation. In my struggles, Hans was convinced I would choose him, thus solving all the arguments.

It was also during this time that Vati and his new family moved to Düsseldorf, close to Köln (Cologne). He had lost his directorship at the large company and complained again about money shortage and moving expenses. In a letter to me, he felt it necessary to write about his financial problems, yet they prepared to buy another big house in a high-income neighborhood.

In the end, I was convinced I had to enter the workforce to buy time. My first job was with an insurance company in Mannheim. I commuted every day one hour each way. Trains, streetcars, and buses in succession brought me to my work place. For a year, I was entertained by new demands, and learned many helpful new skills. This initial interest quickly waned into an unbearable boredom. I had mastered what I needed to know, but I failed to see a promising future.

Hans watched me with jealous eyes. He saw me only on weekends and he told me how to act while away from him. His job training with the Siemens Company kept him out of town for months at a time. I grew lonely without him and my former school friends now studying away from Mannheim.

I had no vehicle available, never enough money to spend, and Mutti asked for DM 100 each month as my household contribution. That was more than one third of my salary, but Mutti said it was educational to learn how to handle finances. I needed transportation money and new clothes to upgrade my wardrobe as a working girl. Without a little help from either parent, I barely made it through each month. In addition, I felt an overwhelming sadness. I had no future, and hope was fading fast. On top of it, I was stuck in a small town.

Occasionally, I went back to Düsseldorf to see my father and his family. It was a four-hour train ride from Mannheim's *Bahnhof.*   Nothing much changed in our relationship, though I tried to get closer acquainted with Vati on an adult level. But a barrier remained. Vati seemed guarded. I blamed it on his wife, Else. I couldn't spend time alone with him, because Else was ever present with her antenna up.

On a rare occasion and I heard him saying, "I cannot afford another shipwreck." It was the closest he came to regretting many of his actions. But in order to stay true to himself, he masked his responsibility with the word *fate.* In other words, *fate* excused Vati once more from having done anything wrong.

As the saga continued, my brother didn't experience much happier results with his university plans either. He seemed lucky when both Papa Theo and Vati shared in his tuitions. Achim went for two years, living at home, and commuting by *Vespa.* The burdensome reports and spending accounts he was required to give Vati eventually caused reprimands and constant unpleasant discussions. This eroded until it killed their relationship. Vati made Achim's life miserable.

His girlfriend, Ute, added more aggravation. Nobody but my brother liked her, and he had himself bound to her. The arguments with Papa Theo and Vati, plus the additional comments from Mutti and Else, culminated in forcing a university transfer from Mannheim to Berlin. Both Vati and Papa Theo thought one semester away from Miss Ute would cool their love.

Wrong move. Ute moved as well. She went against the family wishes and found a bookkeeper's job in Berlin. Imagine this, two fathers cut my brother's financial support, and the young couple replied in kind. They got married without anybody's consent. Ute claimed she would support Achim's education. And she did.

Hurtful words were hurled about, and I became a witness to a hostile family war. I was equally unhappy and plotted my own getaway. The ages of 21 through 22 were the saddest time in my life. Hopelessness caused me to make rash decisions, some better than others.

The Prince That Never Was

Omi, Opa, our aunts, and the Dietz's were far away, we had no immediate communications. Telephone services were non-existent for the common citizen. Many letters remained undelivered and those which reached us had been censored. Official stamps and brown tape reclosing the envelope gave us clues and made us aware of the new ways. News traveled slowly and was as reliable as homing pigeons.

Many years had passed since Communism in the East had wiped out all riches. My grandparents became the new declared evildoers as members of the previous manufacturing class. The Communists stripped them of house and factory.

The farm in Silesia lay inside the new borders of Poland. An occasional dream reminded me of my special childhood's prince. But those dreams took flight and joined others of wishful thinking.

About twelve years later, I had forgotten all about my handsome neighbor Walter Dietz. Maybe five years earlier I would have dreamed about a prince in a romantic movie. I was definitely no Grace Kelly, just an ordinary German young woman and Walter, my former prince, didn't seem to fit my circumstance at the age of 19. What a shock, when one day my mother declared she had a big surprise for me. Not in a 100 years would I guess who.

What a miracle. I failed to remember how Walter found us. The last time we saw him was in 1945, and in 1958 we lived in Viernheim. We had moved into a new comfortable two-story house right at Easter time and after my high school graduation.

Walter had a story to tell. His parents had recently passed away. He had studied medicine in the East but interrupted his studies when his war injury became permanent and resulted in a totally paralyzed right hand.

Walter's dream faded, and he was devastated. His father had encouraged him to flee to West Germany and pursue a law degree instead. Thus, he wound up in München, Bavaria to study law. He was financially supported by the *Bundesrepublik* who financed gifted students, veterans, and war invalids. He met all three qualifications.

Here was the prince of my secret dreams. I rushed home from work, one hour by bus, streetcar and train. My feet felt light when I ran the last twenty meters to the house. I slowed in case somebody watched and looked nonchalant. I turned the house key slowly, and took my time when I entered the house.

My heart was palpitating when I heard voices in the living room. Papa Theo apparently was home early today, as he was told he would meet a Walter. I recognized my mother's melodious voice. I listened for Walter's voice, and I felt like I was hearing Santa's voice like I had when I sat on his lap in Döbeln.

My legs wobbled as I stood in the hallway and took a deep breath. I thought about stopping at the restroom to gather myself. I went down the hall, rested a moment, and ran cool water to wash my hands, when I heard Mutti calling, "Mani, hurry up, Walter has been waiting for hours."

With regained composure I made my way into the living area. Papa Theo and Mutti sat in their leather chairs facing me as I entered ever so slowly. Both greeted me cheerfully which gave me confidence to face the third person in the room.

A man in his early 30's jumped up. My mind flooded with thoughts. Where was his ash blond, gorgeous wavy hair? Only ashy, I saw, with a receding hairline. Daring to take three steps, we overcame our hesitation and stood face to face.

"You have changed. You are bigger," I heard the familiar Santa's voice. Walter touched his little belly and said, "You are funny, Mani, you noticed right away I like the Bavarian beer and the southern food."

So right, I thought. He must have been twice the size he used to be. My prince had looked so handsome in his *Wehrmacht* uniform. And now his right hand was stiff and wooden, in a black leather glove. I hadn't pictured him like this.

I was occupied with my first impression of my long lost fairy tale prince. Walter must have noticed my slow

233

response and tried to break the ice between us. He moved one step closer to stretch out his left hand, the healthy hand, and I took it and squeezing it harder than intended.

"Mani, you have grown into an attractive young lady. Your mother…" Walter stopped abruptly.

"Thanks." I pulled a chair from the dining area.

Mutti chirped like a sparrow, relieved to hand over the conversation to me.

"I have been talking with Walter for several hours. We have had coffee and cake and talked about the old days." Mutti filled me in.

"Yes," Walter interrupted. "Your mother is tired of listening to the tales of my adventures since I left Döbeln."

I saw Papa Theo lean back in his chair and look at his liquor cabinet. I knew it was time for his evening drink.

Walter took the opportunity to fill me in with the evening plans. "I invited your parents to have dinner out tonight. They declined, but they wouldn't mind if we two," he extended his left hand and continued, "would go out and get reacquainted after all these years."

Mutti rearranged herself in her leather chair as Nicki, our Dachshund, begged for her attention. "Mani, I need to go to the kitchen and fix Papa Theo something to eat. Nicki is ready too. We and Walter are caught up." With this, Mutti got up and left with Dachshund Nicki following her out the door, wagging his tail.

Papa Theo took the cue, got up, and followed both of them out.

"Was this all arranged or what?" I questioned Walter, still uncertain about the plans for the evening.

Walter sat quietly observing my uneasiness, and I didn't know what to say.

"Tell me, Walter, where are you spending the night? And when are you taking the train back to München?"

"I will spend the night here in Viernheim. Your parents invited me. My train leaves tomorrow in Mannheim around 11 a.m."

We continued our small talk. His eyes focused on me while I talked with excited animation, waving my hands. I told him I had a steady boyfriend for almost four years, and had never been asked out on a date like this. It was a strange predicament. I pondered for a second what to do. I could go to Mannheim to show him the Mannheim Insurance Company where I worked. Then we could take a little stroll down the Planken, the main shopping area before eating a bite and having a beer.

"If we leave right now, we can be back around 10 p.m. I have to leave the house before 7 a.m. in the morning to go to work, you understand."

We both stood there. I gave him an evaluating glance. He followed my example and we both laughed. My laugh was from embarrassment, yet I remained unable to form an opinion.

"Mani, wait a minute." Walter had an important message for me. "My father told me five, six years ago, to make sure and find his little girl, Mani. I went back to Döbeln. They died one year ago and I had not seen you yet. The very last time I visited with my father, he asked me again about his girl and if she was using her good mind? And here you are, and not so little anymore." Walter seemed mellow.

I detected some trembling in his voice, but he recovered. "You were cute then, and quite smart. And now, I don't know what to say...excuse me...I'm impressed." A faint remark, but I heard him.

235

I cut him off because I was embarrassed. "Why so?" More shy than crass, I changed the subject. "Let's go."

We walked to the train station arm in arm like an older brother and little sister. It felt natural. I loved his attention and opinions combined with his astute observations about my life within a complicated family. As we strolled along, it became apparent that Walter was no longer my prince. He was more like Achilles, one of Homer's heroes who had a small but fatal weakness. I hadn't told him about my fantasies, but now he admitted he'd had a crush on my mother when he was young and she was so charming. He said he envied us; our background and privileges, and his dreams had been to be part of our family.

At the train station he bought his ticket. I had my rider's pass since I went this way daily. We stood on the train's platform very close to each other once we boarded the train. I barely hung onto the pole, bouncing each time the train followed its designed loops around the town. Walter tried to support me with his left arm around my waist while leaning awkwardly into the pole that other passengers were sharing as well.

Walter was in control of our conversation. He managed to turn, throw, and catch me like a soft ball.

"Mädchen, tell me, are you in love with this Hans fellow?" Walter asked me, his words coming out of nowhere. I realized that Mutti must have told him all about my boyfriend.

"So Mutti told you?" I was shocked. "What else did she reveal?"

"One thing about your mother, she cannot lie. She may be reserved, but I pried her shell open during our hours of conversation."

"Hmm," I acknowledged and waited to hear more.

"Mani, you answered my question with another question. Do you love this fellow?"

Another jolt of the train, and he rearranged his arms. With his right arm around me, I felt the hard paralyzed hand for the first time. It jolted me like I had stuck a key into an electric outlet. What horrific pain he must have been in when the Russian bullet hit him.

"Yes or no?" He urged me.

"No." The word jumped out of my mouth. What had I said? Walter is an excellent interrogator. I bet he had done the same thing to Mutti all afternoon. She had obviously been glad to take refuge in the kitchen.

Walter didn't remove his arm. Instead he moved closer, held me tighter, and looked down at his little sister with misty eyes. "Mani, I see the picture of your family's situation. I got the drift about how your mother washed her hands of your failed university education, because your father Hunger is unwilling to let some of his precious money go. On the other hand, she never filled out the proper papers when you fled East Germany. There is a procedure to file for refugee status. This alone would qualify you to get state assistance for the university." He looked up for a second to read the sign on the next stop. I waved a 'not to worry' gesture.

"Listen, Mädchen, you didn't know it either. Your father is legally obligated to pay for your education up to a certain age. You could take him to court on this issue."

Some anxious feelings made me uncomfortable. This was too much information all at once. He is an attorney, but I needed time to sort out what he said. I was concerned about getting off at the right train stop, so I said, "Walter, let's talk about this later, we are to get off here."

I redirected his attention to my plans to show him Mannheim's center. There was not much we could see. Our time was short. We stood at Mannheim's landmark, the *Wasserturm,* which had been destroyed during the war. Now that it was fully restored to its turn-of-the-century style, I wanted Walter to appreciate it. I took Walter's sleeve and gave it a firm pulling.

"Look straight ahead, about one kilometer where the Autobahn is. And right before the entrance to the highway is a tall, 11-story building. That new building is the *Mannheimer Versicherungs Gesellschaft.* I work on the second floor. I do statistical work."

Walter looked politely in my pointed direction, but showed little interest. Instead, he made a 180-degree turn and directed his attention down the *Planken.* "That's where we are going tonight, I hope." He seemed pleased and gave me a long look. He grinned as I nodded and loosened my grip on his jacket. Walter had his own plans. "Show me where the *Wiener Wald* is located. We ought to have some rotisserie chicken and beer."

The restaurant was one of Germany's first chain restaurants. It had popular specialties and a cozy ambiance. I don't remember too much about our meal other than we ate by candlelight and devoured our chicken. I had one beer. I noticed in one hour's time, Walter drank three bottles, which I immediately thought as excessive. His excuse, he said, was that he worked at becoming a real Bavarian! He still carried a certain singsong Saxonian dialect like the one I had struggled with years earlier. We continued to eat in silence when suddenly he gave me a strange look, motioning with his fork. He was amused by how I maneuvered with knife and fork simultaneously, European style, eating my chicken properly.

"My little Mani, don't strain so much, for heaven sake. You've me mixed up, you know. I'm not sure what our relationship is any more." Barely aware of his emotional shift, he said, "Mani, it's time you become your own person."

I perked up. Walter got off guard once more.

I followed his suggestion and started eating with my hands. I had gooey, sticky grease all over my face. Faster than I could react, Walter cleaned it off with bunched up napkins.

"Good, isn't it?" He beamed and took a break from chewing his food.

After savoring his chicken, he changed again into his attorney persona. I still swallowed chicken, while he continued his earlier conversation and lecture.

"I trust I can speak openly with you. I played the devil's advocate this afternoon. I tell you, your mother has masterminded your life with this boyfriend of yours. By the time he comes back from his training, she will have you married, and living all under her roof." And so he trailed off. I ignored his prophetic words for a moment. When he reminded me that my insurance job was good enough to hold me over, keep me busy. "Bang, one morning, Mani, you will wake up next to a man you never loved."

I almost swallowed a wishbone. I coughed and gagged, while Walter jumped up and helped me raise my hands above my head to prevent choking. After this distressing moment, we settled down to calmer conversation. But inside, I felt nervous and couldn't comprehend my possible future with Hans being tied to this hick town.

The conversation shifted once more. He must have noticed my changed expression. I felt my cheeks heating up. God knows if I blushed. I was acting like a teenager. Then out came his life's story which I had asked him about earlier.

I learned a few important facts about Walter. First, he didn't believe in God, because He wasn't there when Walter was shot and forced into Russian captivity. Next, he resented the fact that he lost his youth, his dear parents, and had to join the Communist Party to be eligible for medical school. After he restarted his life in the West he was without money, without family, and without any remaining friends. He lamented that he was an outsider in West Germany. Lastly, he told me he felt guilty he had failed to contact us, especially me.

At this point I realized I was in control again. This was my town, and I wasn't going anywhere. Besides, I didn't totally understand his intentions. I dared to ask him point blank, "Have you ever been in love, Walter?"

Without blinking an eye, he answered, "No, never. I did have a little crush on your mother, maybe on a couple of students, and only one or two meaningless relationships. But love, no." I felt he spoke the truth.

"Now it's my turn, Mani. Be honest and tell me, did this Hans of yours ever touch you?"

"What do you mean touch me?" I wondered out loud.

"Mani, this is the second time you answer me with a question." Walter laughed out loud. "You're very clever."

"You mean, be intimate?" I looked at him and he nodded.

"No." I said honestly. He covered his mouth with a clean napkin.

"Sweetheart, I am not laughing at you. But that Hans of yours is an idiot, and your dear mother is a manipulator. Lord, the way they've got you bamboozled, and trained like their Nicki. You'll be of legal age by next year, am I correct?"

"Yes," I admitted, "late in the year."

"I remember you were born on the fourth, two days after the sixth, which was *Sankt Nickolaus Tag.*

"I remembered especially how sad you looked when you didn't find goodies in the shoes you left outside the door, because your mother figured having a birthday on the fourth was plenty, so why observe *St. Nickolaus* two days later? She thought one celebration had to be cancelled. I always wanted to sneak over to your place and hide candy in your shoe, but we didn't have anything either. How sorry I felt for you. I wanted to cry, Mani."

I consoled him as if he really had cried. "It truly doesn't matter anymore, Walter. I'm grown and I got over it."

We ended our outing as friends and traveled home, mostly in silence, in time for me to get a good rest before morning. I said good night. As we stood in the entrance of the house, he whispered to me: "I want you to come to München as soon as you can. We will figure out a way for you to go to the university. We'll find a way. If nothing else, Mani, your father can be forced to help you. I can do this for you, you understand."

I stood and thought about the fourth commandment: "honor your father and mother." My former prince talked about suing Vati. He mentioned earlier he'd get a new apartment, and I wouldn't have to worry about living expenses, that he'd take care of me until what?

He must have noticed my worried face, and pulled me into a firm bear hug. "I am not forcing you to do anything, Mani. You alone shall think about our conversation tonight, and you alone shall evaluate what you want out of life. My father predicted that you would be successful in life. I want to see you do it." His grip slowly loosened.

He hesitated and let me recuperate from an onslaught of feelings. I'm sure he could read my face and most likely knew more about life than I did. I needed time to think.

Before retiring, Walter had something else to say: "Mani, you and I have changed; we are no longer little sister and big brother. Your mother has changed so much. I don't want you to become like her. Your brother is hiding out at his girlfriend's. Doesn't that tell you something? I warn you, that Hans is creating another prison for you. My father noticed the spark you had as a little girl. It's still here. In one year, you'll be 21 and of legal age. I will not call nor write to bother you. This is your decision. But remember, it is better late than never."

For a second, Walter stood very still. I was worried and saw his head lowering, so I waited and watched, wondering if I was going to get another lecture. But then he looked up and our eyes met and held firmly. He said, "As far as I am concerned, I am struggling with my feelings as much as you are. I have watched you all evening, Mani. You cannot lie, and in this respect you are your mother's daughter. You shook me up, Sweetheart. Please, give us both a chance; don't expect your mother's support."

He kissed my forehead and added a swift goodbye. I hurried upstairs to my bedroom. Walter disappeared into our guestroom downstairs. In the morning, while fixing my breakfast in the kitchen, I didn't hear anything but the dog rousing in his basket. I never saw Walter again. Two years later, he married the daughter of the law firm's owner.

The magic was gone for good. My prince was a complex human being. In my struggles to rethink my life and future, I kept Walter's observation private. He had opened my eyes to what I'd have to do in the near future.

Walter's Influence

I couldn't imagine Hans and me as a couple. No way, I wasn't about to marry the know-it-all genius. So I broke off with him, saying I still loved Dieter. The break off was justified, but a lie. I regretted treating him that way. Though my reasons were truthful, I was unable to express or explain my feelings and aspirations. I was afraid of being told otherwise. Hans and I had been good friends, but I longed for my own space. I wanted to grow into a woman who also had a mind. An epiphany was revealed to me: I didn't love him after all. That was what I told Walter when he asked me if I loved Hans. It was serendipity, and the devil's advocate had opened my eyes.

When I turned 21, I re-evaluated my relationship with my father. I had nothing but ambivalent feelings about Vati. There was never a genuine father-daughter talk, maybe because Else wouldn't allow us the privacy. He was unable to be himself, played the role of a successful businessman who had to keep up appearances and be seen with important people. Then, I considered the fact that my parents' divorce may have distorted my image of him. I searched for all the desired attributes a father should have, and waited in vain to meet Vati as a natural, down-to-earth father who would play with us, allow himself to make mistakes. The dream to have a real father dangled in front of me like a precious Christmas ornament, too fragile to unwrap. I found that nothing about him was ever easy.

He gave me a few presents which I treasured. I remember a delicate pearl necklace on my 21st birthday. The necklace had 101 pearls. One larger center pearl, and 50 gradually decreasing on either side, to a total length of 16 inches. Pearls were very expensive in the early 1960s.

According to old German wives' tales, pearls meant tears and shouldn't be given as a present. Unfortunately, this old saying held sad truth. The necklace was banned to a satin bag for close to 20 years before I started wearing it again. I didn't care to be reminded of his lecturing and justifications why he couldn't be the caring father he probably wanted to be, I avoided wearing this reminder around my neck. Finally, after his death, I had worked through old hurts, and the pearl necklace was resurrected as a nice piece of jewelry.

I developed ideas about traveling and seeing the world. Dreams were taking shape. I envisioned glossy and inviting pictures from my first English text book. They winked at me with stunning depictions of San Francisco, The Golden Gate, Niagara Falls, and New York City. "You need to leave all this behind and see the world." They called to me.

Dr. Paul Buck

But not quite that fast, traveling and seeing the world had to wait. A year at the Mannheim Insurance Company had passed uneventfully, and no significant career was about to unfold. Instead, I met the personnel director who was also the firm's attorney on the annual company excursion via train to the Palatinate, a famous German wine region that had good restaurants and entertainment. On the way home, Dr. Buck joined the younger employees in one of the train's compartment and found immediate interest in me.

"Did you get this nice suntan today?" I asked trying to make conversation with him.

"No, I go skiing every year with my friend, Richard Bender."

"You mean Dr. Bender?" I was surprised to hear this

name.

"Yes, how did you know?"

"Well, I actually don't, but my Papa has friends at the Chamber of Commerce," I explained. "I heard his name being mentioned before."

"Yes, you're right. He's a member of the Chamber. Now, who's your Papa?" Dr. Buck was curious.

We chatted until we reached Mannheim's *Hauptbahnhof.* He walked next to me toward the exit, and as we said goodbye, he stopped with a surprise invitation.

"Miss Hunger, may I call you some time?"

He asked me point blank. I was shocked. I didn't know how to react. Did he want to meet Papa Theo, or what? Was he interested in me? The man was good looking, but maybe he was too old? Then I realized that he was the very same man who interviewed and hired me. I looked for paper and pencil to give him my phone number and he told me not to bother.

"I have all the information I need. Lovely evening and lovely talking with you. Have a good night." I was dumbfounded.

Our meeting on the train was the beginning of a courtship that lasted over three years. My parents liked him immediately, in spite of our 20-year age difference. I was shocked that they had no other concerns.

Paul and I saw each other several times a week. He lived in Mannheim, close to the company, and one hour by public transportation. But with the convenience of his company car, a short cut over the Autobahn, and he could visit me in less than half an hour. We went to swimming pools in the area, took trips to Heidelberg or drives to the Blackforest. In his fancy Ford we drove many miles and still could be home before midnight.

The freedom of getting around fast was new and wonderful to me. Paul was respectful of my parents' desires, entertained me with many outings, but at the same time we kept our relationship secret at work. I worked on the second floor, while he had his office on the tenth. An occasional encounter in the elevator resulted in only a polite acknowledgement. "Good morning, Miss Hunger." Always polite.

My 21st birthday arrived and we had a party at home. Paul held my hand and my brother and his girlfriend sat next to us. Everyone was smiling. He asked me to marry him that day, but he explained he needed to look for a nice lot to build a house in Palatinate, west of Ludwigshafen. I was happy to think about our future away from Viernheim and Mutti's domination. Having my own family sounded great, and the intellectual stimulation I felt with him replaced my earlier desire to get a degree.

The day arrived to meet his parents from North Germany, about 400 miles away. I was satisfied, not deeply in love, still hesitant, because I lacked a passionate feeling of oneness with him. I was honored that he found me lovely and intelligent, and I was willing to share life with him. I felt I would be the wife of the respected attorney, Dr. Buck.

I continued working another year at the insurance company. I never spent the night at his apartment. He'd drive me home. The relationship wasn't clear to anyone, including myself. We had great outings, cooked together, read and discussed legal opinions, as well as court presentations he was working on. In fact, I became quite efficient with parts of the German law, especially this relating to transportation, ships, and river barges.

Paul appreciated my interest and remarked how proud he was of my ability to learn and understand legal jargon. He also complimented me on my appearance, and good personality, but his touch felt vague, unsure and awkward.

On an outing in the spring, we stopped at a farm to pick strawberries. The weather was gorgeous, around 25 degrees centigrade, and we each filled a basket with ripe berries. There was no telling how many berries went into my mouth before Paul stopped me. He stood square in front of me and gawked, like he had never seen a young woman eat strawberries before.

"What's wrong? Do you think the farmer is watching me?" I asked him.

"No, my *Dirn*." He kept staring. By now I realized that it was a look of open admiration. "The red of the berries and your beautiful white teeth are breathtaking."

He didn't hold me firmly in his arms, and he touched me with stiffly extended fingers like testing a hot pot. I could not stand that stare. I wanted to know how he saw me most of the time. He didn't seem to show sexual interest.

A clue came with his parents' visit. The day I met them, I immediately understood why he wasn't able to love me as I wanted to be loved. His father was a pleasant man, normal all around. His mother, in contrast, looked at me with beady eyes and sent me waves of cold North Sea winds that made me shiver all over. It was obvious, she hated me because I was about to steal her boy.

One day, Paul decided he had to meet Vati in Düsseldorf. We drove four hours north. Our meeting at a restaurant was disastrous. Paul acted arrogant, didn't allow my father to pay for the meal, and both men shot sarcastic remarks back and forth. Paul actually forgot the purpose of

247

our visit and didn't ask Vati for my hand. We left without much to-do, no politeness of good wishes. The two men despised each other on sight.

Vati promptly wrote a letter strongly discouraging me from wasting my life on this old man.

The mutual admiration between me and Paul lasted a bit longer. I don't know who was out-waiting whom. We still talked about marriage, but the construction plans for the house hung in the air, and I didn't inquire. The crux of our mutual dissatisfaction was Paul's impotence, something I didn't comprehend at my age, and his behavior seemed totally lacking in desirable attentions. He put me on a pedestal and bought me many presents that I didn't care for or appreciate. In addition, I noticed that he liked erotic books. Then he surprised me with one of those books, Lolita. I was unfamiliar with such genre and wondered why he thought it would benefit me. "Strange," I thought, "why would he want me to read erotic books, if they didn't do him any good?"

More tension crept into our relationship. He took long trips back home to carry his dirty laundry to his mother. He mentioned that he consulted a physician, an old school friend of his, concerning his problem, as he coined it. I should have asked him if it was a psychiatrist or urologist. Why couldn't he speak openly to me? Why did he have to consult his mother on everything?

The last incident happened when he told me that he had purchased a lot together with his parents in Lübeck. He intended to take a job in Hamburg to be on the board of a large insurance company. Why did he have to surprise me with all of this at once? I couldn't understand why he hadn't consulted me earlier.

"I am through," I told him. "You're already married to

your mother. I'd rather be an old maid in South Germany than freeze my butt off in your precious, stuffy North Germany, eating fish every day." I was beside myself with anger.

Paul stood with his mouth wide open. I wasn't his sweet little *Dirn* anymore.

With trembling voice I breathed audibly, "I feel betrayed." My knees buckled. I offered one last goodbye to him: "Paul, *Auf Wiedersehen*." Then I turned around and started to run.

Behind me, I heard him call. "Mani, *Dirn*, we'll talk in a couple of weeks when you have calmed down."

But I knew that this was the end for me. I had enough.

We had another encounter months later when I repeated what I had told him earlier. However, this time my voice was calm and resolved. Under the circumstances I was through with him and I wished him well. "Besides, I met someone else at the swimming pool. I met a man, you hear me?" I wasn't sure if my smart attorney, ex-fiancé, could comprehend. I sounded mean.

One thing I didn't realize, Paul belonged to Gemany's "Silent Generation," such as Walter did. These young people had been tricked into going to war with an enthusiasm they believed in. They were brainwashed by Hitler *Jugend's* activities, the flashy uniforms, flags and hails to the chief, and they lost their footing in later years. They remained unable to see the reality of having been misled.

For example, Paul was proud of his officer's uniform. I got upset when I saw a picture of him wearing it. I told him it was inappropriate to show it after a lost war. I expressed my sorrow for our country's atrocious war crimes against humanity. I hated to be reminded of it and abhorred any sign of the Nazi regime. I felt my blood come to a boiling point.

But Paul Buck's war experiences were in the Ukraine, where he was under Russian fire, sick with Malaria. Somehow, he'd escaped, walked all the way home where his mother hid him until the official surrender. She understood him, whereas I didn't. Certainly, there was no love lost between me and his mother. In the end, I saw no way of bridging these differences.

Thirty years later, I saw Paul again. He had never married, but did keep track of his *Dirn,* Mani. He knew about my life and family. At least once a year he visited my parents and his friend, Dr. Bender. Nobody told me until a few years before his death. I made arrangements to see him in Lübeck, and was glad to reconnect as old friends. But when I saw the house where I was supposed to live with his parents, I felt overwhelming sorrow for him. He was a rich, old, and lonely man who missed both his mother and his *Dirn.*

After Paul, 1961 – 1964

I had a short relationship with a man I met on a train. His name was Gerd, and he was ten years older than I. As it turned out, he was entangled in a corruption trial with the German equivalence of an American IRS. His legal predicament seemed insurmountable. Our love for each other could only flourish with the support of both of my parents. I wasn't able to fight one parent or make a move on my own.

I had introduced Gerd to Vati and his family and I found overwhelming approval for my friend. Gerd was a good looking, charming, and intelligent man with whom I shared many interests. However, communication without access to phones during the day was difficult. And the resistance of Mutti, who controlled the mail and the house phone, meant that our love couldn't prosper. I was hurt when his letters and phone calls stopped. Out of pride, I didn't pursue him any further. And so went the love of my life. It felt like death on arrival. I was heartbroken and mourned for quite some time.

The last years I lived with my parents in Viernheim, I had more time than earlier when I commuted to work. I found a comfortable office job locally, rode my bike, or walked to work. With time, I found peace about my breakups, but still retained dreams of doing exciting things and living somewhere else. For a while, I reconnected with former classmates who were sad reminders of how I hadn't been forceful enough with my family about pursuing a degree.

Paul Buck never stopped calling me even when I told him I'd met somebody else. In fact, it was an unusual stranger whom I happened to meet at a swimming pool one Saturday afternoon. I was lonely, as I sat by the edge of the crowded pool watching people and listening to their conversations going on around me.

Maybe it was meant to be that I happened to overhear a group of Spanish-speaking girls converse with a young man. I was trying to understand what they said as I had three years of Spanish which I'd never used. How rewarding it felt to be able to put into practice what I once learned. The group of young people, I assumed, were new immigrants from Spain who worked in a small clothing factory in town. As I listened, my facial expressions must have given away that I understood them quite well.

By the end of the afternoon, I had this young man following me out of the pool area. He attached himself, and even though I came by bike, attempted to walk with me. As it turned out to be, he was not an immigrant from Spain, but was Bernard Restrepo, born and raised in Bogotá, Colombia, South America. I learned that he was educated in several private schools in the United States during most of his high school years. His stepfather apparently didn't like him, so his mother sent him back to the States after he graduated from a private Catholic school in Bogotá.

Bernard persistently wiggled himself into my life. He wasn't about to leave until he was called back to the States. When I met him, I was unaware that he didn't have American citizenship while serving the U.S. Army.

We dated, and soon he was showing up every evening, much to my parents' chagrin. Papa Theo even called him a "Snake Catcher," an image Papa made up, connecting Colombia with a jungle. The more Mutti and Papa complained, the more we attached. I thought Bernard was worldly, spoke very good English, and was interesting with stories about his deceased father who ran a farm in the Magdalena River region in Colombia, S.A. He was slender, a few inches taller than I, and had a light complexion with dark wavy hair. Nice looking. What impressed me the most was his family's background, former colonial Spanish people who seemed to have a very good reputation.

I enjoyed our outings, seeing American movies and going to the club on the base. I showed him Mannheim and Heidelberg, parts he hadn't seen before, and he merged into German civilian life, which he loved.

When the first letters from his mother arrived, I was sold. It became apparent that Bernard Restrepo was indeed from a prominent Colombian family whose ancestors influenced early Colombian history in that country. His mother, Isabel, sounded wonderful, and her sophisticated Spanish impressed me.

At about the same time, my parents had an international inquiry made about him through the Catholic

Church. They also received positive reports about the families Restrepo and Ucros. I wanted to go see where in Colombia, South America, my friend was born.

Our courtship was not effortless. But we were both young, adventuresome, and saw a bright future in the United States of America. Even though the Vietnam War was beginning and Bernard was in the military, we saw no obstacles. He promised he'd enter Officer Candidate School as soon as his citizenship went through. We planned to marry and go back to America.

Problems arose because Bernard was Catholic and I Lutheran. The priest advised Bernard against marrying me. Our first marriage application was conveniently lost, but we didn't give up. The second attempt was made, this time through a Lutheran chaplain. This time, we succeeded, and all the required paperwork was approved.

We had no qualms about starting a future together. We had no fears about an uncertain future, and it helped that I knew I could come back to visit. It was only a matter of buying airplane tickets. My main concern was Omi, who was elderly. I had to see her one more time, before I married a military man. I bought a train ticket to Zittau in East Germany behind the Iron Curtain. It was July 1961, exactly one month before the Berlin Wall went up.

The train ride was horrible, and I feared the East German police would go through the train to check passports. The threat that I could be arrested played in my mind and made me shiver with fright. I feared the thought of having to live in East Germany. Fortunately, I made it there and back without a hitch. But I avoided phone calls back to Viernheim, or God forbid to my fiancé. No telling who might be listening.

I was happy to discover my Omi was fragile but had a clear mind. I smelled the scent of lavender, which caused me to remember my wonderful childhood with these loving people. Opa was still alive, though very quiet. Tante Annemarie concerned me with her "liberal" talk. I didn't want to draw attention. In the small town of Zittau, people knew her as a harmless old, crazy lady. Well, in my book she still possessed a clear understanding of world politics. The longer I stayed, the more I wanted to leave for my new home in America. My mind was made up.

In the end, everything worked out fine. I had many conversations with Omi, most memorably on what she told me, "Do not forget," she noted, "I am a child of the nineteenth century and I enjoyed living in style. You, my child, are born into the next century, a totally different world from mine." She was serene.

Omi reached for my hand and continued, "I'd say, take advantage of all the good. You are strong and independent like your grandfather Hunger was."

I questioned her about my real paternal grandfather, Richard Hunger, who was long gone before I was born. Before now, I had never heard her mention her first husband.

"I loved both husbands, and also dreamed about traveling, meeting people and seeing places." A sigh followed, "Yes, I wanted to do many exciting things." She squeezed my hand ever so slightly and continued, "You should be free, my child. So, fly away like a bird. Go to America."

Omi paused again and wiped a tear from beneath her glasses. "Remember to be free within the limits of your beliefs. Don't hurt yourself or other people. You should to be rich and beautiful on the inside where it counts most."

254

It pained me to see Omi cry. She took off her misty glasses and her voice broke. My throat tightened, and I wondered if we would ever see each other again.

"Keep all of us in your heart, and write often. The whole world has changed – and not for the better." Omi ended her advice. "I believe, Mani, my dear child, you will manage."

I needed to hear all these encouraging words. I said, "Omi, one more thing, you may want to know." I moved the chair nearer to her. "Do you remember *Pfarrer* Lehman? He baptized Achim and me in Mannheim in 1940. You know he chose the very same Bible verse you were given on your confirmation as I received on mine."

"Omi nodded." I knew she would have liked to hear what the Army Chaplain Wood said. He had agreed to marry Bernard and I. And our pastor in Viernheim arranged for bilingual marriage vows to celebrate with my relatives and friends.

I continued talking, "He actually asked me if I had a special verse he could write in the Bible he intended to give us as a wedding gift."

Omi's eyes grew larger. "Are you telling me 'for the mountains shall depart, and the hills be removed; but my kindness shall not depart from thee, neither shall the covenant of my peace be removed …'"

"Yes, it is Isaiah 54:10."

There was nothing to cry about. It was all good. We said goodbye and hoped it would be temporary. I was starting a new life.

Omi grew old with grace. I was too far away when she passed, but I dreamed one night that she was lifted in a cloud, surrounded by angels. This premonition reached me within hours of her death. The family missed her. My mourning was mixed with a consoling message that she had entered a better home. One day I will see her again.

I regret not having kept up with Pastor Lehman and his wife. Life propelled me from Gymnasium to the Mannheim Insurance Company and from Mannheim's Industriestraße to Viernheim's newly-built family house. My only excuse was the fact I had neither a personal telephone nor a car like we all do today. The new constructed Paul Gerhardt Church was in our direct neighborhood, and Luther Church started serving another district. Due to Germany's division of church and state, we would never attend Pastor Lehman's church again. How sad.

I never thought much about it, but to an American who'd drive miles to his preferred church, the German system seems strange. However, in the 50's we had only two state churches, the Catholic and the Protestant whose administration was state-run and funds were raised through contributions and directly taken from citizens' salaries.

Going to the Promised Land

When President John F. Kennedy was murdered in 1963, Bernard Restrepo and I were newlyweds. I had married at the age of 23 and saw nothing but a bright future for us. We would grow, prosper, learn new customs and skills, have a lovely family and make the military service our way of life for the next 20 years. I was sure!

Six months later we said goodbye to my family and our friends, took a train to Bremerhaven, and went on our way. From there, we sailed through the English Channel and stopped for the night in Southampton. The next morning, we boarded the SS Upshur T-AP-198, a ship that was part of the

256

Military Sea Transportation Unit in service from 1952 until 1973.

Soon after embarking, I lost my husband from view. I knew Bernard couldn't be too far, as he loved to talk to strangers. All alone, I stood by the rail, facing the dock. Waving handkerchiefs were everywhere, the Upshur's horn sounded, and the ship pushed away from the quay. Time stood still for me. For a short moment, I felt lonely among hundreds of the parting people. My old homeland disappeared miles to the south, and mixed feelings tried to invade me. In my heart I anticipated the shores of America. "Is it really me who's going to see America, this majestic country I read about for years, whose language I studied for years, and whose great literature I read in both German and English?" I had no regrets.

The barrage of feelings subsided. A spray of water sprinkled my face and washed away anything faintly resembling tears. The Army Band started playing an unfamiliar tune, at least still unfamiliar to me. I liked it and longed to learn many more songs. And it would be only a matter of time. The American dependents and military personnel cheered as the ship sailed. I was with them all the way!

After all: Many Years Later

Modern electronic times don't allow much leisure for storytelling. My earlier intention of writing about my experiences in the school system passed in 1995 when my fourth graders asked me to talk about how it was way back then. To my surprise, one student even asked me if I lived during the Civil War. I realized that to them WWII was as remote as American history of 1861. Both my children,

Bernie and Bettina, know little about their mother's childhood. How did she become the mom and Oma they know? I also noticed they had problems with places, names, and dates that were significant to my German heritage.

I decided to correct this. My memory significantly increased as I allowed my subconscious mind to bring forth "forgotten" incidents, inaccessible names and places from my childhood. In doing so, I relived and reexamined what I thought was an ordinary life in very unusual times. The best part was that I found closure for situations that required an end.

What happened to the boy, Dieter I had a crush on in Mannheim? In 1960, two years after my graduation from the *Gymnasium*, I met Dieter by chance. We had a cup of coffee at a sidewalk café. It was close to the train station from where I commuted daily to my work place.

Did he expect somebody? Apparently not, for he jumped up waving his arm and grinning from ear to ear. After our polite preliminaries, he said, "Manu, I am in Law School. Are you surprised?" He reached for my hand and squeezed it. "Thank you, Manu. You always have been like my younger sister."

"Really?" I kept my lips sealed, because I felt my cheeks blushing and felt embarrassed. The crush hadn't left me, but I couldn't get over that inbred pride and Mutti's words sounding in my head, "Remember, a girl needs to let the boy persuade her." So I remained quiet. I had to still my heart. Instead, I checked my watch to make sure I wouldn't miss my next train.

"Are you in a hurry, Manu?" Dieter told me that two of his friends would be here in a minute or so. "In fact, you know them. Frank and his brother are about to join me here any minute. You know, we are all in Law School."

I hesitated for a moment, but felt I needed to go home immediately since I had spent too much time window shopping after work, and Mutti would be upset if I showed up after 7 p.m. and late for supper.

"Are you telling me, you are in a hurry to meet up with our class genius, Hans, the one that nobody but you liked?"

I loved his naughty teasing, he surely knew that Hans and I had broken up, but I answered, "No that's history."

While I talked, Dieter had gotten out of his chair and reached for my arms. It was a firm grip.

"Manu, why are you are *not* with us in Heidelberg studying pedagogy as you had planned?" You would make a great teacher."

I couldn't have been more truthful when I said. "You are a real refugee, Dieter, and I am *only* a fake one, if that makes sense to you. I thought that I qualified, but I was wrong. Our social government doesn't finance education for rich parents' kids. My father will not support me, much less reveal his income. That's all." I felt tears swelling and wanted to run. I forced a fast goodbye, freed myself from his hold and couldn't hear what he called after me. I was gone.

In later years, I heard, Dieter was married to a teacher and had two children. Strangely enough, he and his wife named their daughter Tina, which I also happened to name my daughter. His law office was in downtown Mannheim. From all accounts, he was successful until alcohol abuse disabled him physically and mentally. I felt sorry for his family who had to endure this tragedy.

Hans Wund had a successful career. I never saw nor heard from him personally, but while visiting Germany I'd attended class reunions and met some of his former

Gymnasium's classmates. They informed me that "old Wund" was too good to associate with his old buddies from high school. He apparently acquired a physic degree. No surprise to me.

Over the last 50 years, I crossed the Atlantic often, traveled to South America, and zigzagged through North America. But the journey into my past and writing about my young life was more thrilling. As an American citizen, I came to appreciate where I am today, compared to where I came from. I was given many opportunities such as undergraduate scholarships and state-supported graduate classes in Oklahoma to become a specialized teacher. This help, combined with hard work, enabled me to reach my goals and ultimately provided me with a secure retirement.

On reflection, I noticed how several of my relatives, friends, and teachers grew in importance as I got older. Omi always stood out, but other more challenging people including my Mutti and Vati, empowered me in the determination to follow my own dream.

One of these people was Dr. Müller. I give him well deserved kudos. As a former *Kulturminister,* he was already given much recognition as he influenced the educational system for Baden-Württemberg. Former Baden and Württemberg became one state after 1948, as did Rheinland-Westfalen.

Dr. Leonhard Müller had a distinguished career. Personally, I had a love-hate relationship with him. I didn't appreciate his rough ways, but he pushed me in my maturation process, specifically when he proposed to the class to place my name on the ballot for class speaker. Surprising to me at the time, the girls voted for me, and I developed some early leadership abilities. I also learned to accept reprimands and criticism when due. During my years of teaching, I thought often of him and imagined Dr. Müller even sitting in my class taking notes, a smirk on his face and mumbling, "That Hunger does all right." I stood with confidence when I told him, "Well, Dr. Müller, that's how we do it in the United States. I have learned a more delicate way engaging with young school children."

I felt blessed having grown up with fascinating people like Papa Theo, who taught me to laugh, mostly at myself. At some of the class reunions I attended, my broken pipes-episode in Buchklingen's school home still caused laughter and reminiscence of those crazy years.

I admired Vati's older sister, Annemarie, for many reasons. After losing Silesia and the farm, she joined my grandparents in Zittau which became East Germany from 1945 until the reunification in 1989. Annemarie took care of Omi and Opa at home. She never married, although she was engaged once and had a relationship with a country doctor in Silesia. She didn't talk much about herself, but she became our family's historian, safeguarding old letters, documents, photos, and plenty of oral history. Compared to her mother's, my Omi's feminine and sophisticated ways, Annemarie came across as a woman with masculine traits. Nobody ever mentioned the possibility that she could have been gay. To me, she was a woman ahead of her times, which worked physically very hard and was a learned person who expressed strong opinions. She was not intimidated by either the Nazis or the Communists.

How I'd love to meet her today. We old ladies would discuss history. I doubt she'd call me Zimttüte anymore. Even as a child, I knew I wasn't about to become a spoiled brat, whining and complaining. In fact, I went beyond

Annemarie's courage when I plunged into an unknown future in America. My older generation avoided making changes at all cost.

On a visit in 1954, Annemarie reflected on the Premonition Woman, our *Ahnfrau*. I was about 16 years old when I took the train into East Germany to visit. She admitted to me that the ghost was not "pure bunk." She explained how the ghost became increasingly active as the winter of 1944/45 approached. All the upstairs rooms were kept empty and unheated. Cook Suse and Annemarie lived downstairs and heated only one flat with a large hearth. Both women hunkered down for encroaching sub zero weather. During this time, almost every night, they heard strange noises upstairs. Drawers were opened. Items were dragged over the wooden floor. By then, they had given up checking its source. Every night the same thing happened. The ghost would also slide open the little wooden window to the downstairs dining room. No one was present in the house, so it had to be *Ahnfrau*.

The other revelation was that the Wagners had two war prisoners living on the estate. I was surprised and wondered how Jean and Louis, the strangers from France, came to live in Schosdorf. I neglected to ask pertinent questions, or maybe I should have taken better notes.

Russians were approaching fast by spring of 1945. Before the final order was given to leave the state of Silesia, the ghost had been excessively active in spooking the house. Aunt Annemarie came to accept the Premonition Woman's activities as a sign of horrible things ahead. She admitted that strange things existed between heaven and earth. Nobody, not even those with the smartest school knowledge, could explain. The *Ahnfrau's* warnings prepared them to get ready to leave and never turn around. She remained restless up to the last minute. So Annemarie and Suse accepted their fate and escaped Silesia alive to tell our story.

Annemarie buried my grandparents. They rested in the Wagner family burial vault in Olbersdorf. In the 1970s, the Communists bulldozed the cemetery to get closer to mining brown coal. This cheap energy source was so inferior that already Hitler had rejected it. Omi and Opa's stone-enclosed coffins were hauled to a plain grave in Zittau. Urmi's family, the Leupolds, rested there. The relocation of these stone coffins unnerved Aunt Annemarie.

Germans care about burial ceremonies and upkeep of graves. It may seem strange and overdone to foreigners. Cemeteries are oftentimes turned into small parks, one plot nicer than the next. Seasonal plants and flowers are planted, manicured and weeded. I sometimes saw people polish tombstones. Visitors could sit for hours and contemplate and admire these individual little garden spots, surrounded by shady trees and flowering Rhododendron bushes. It was no surprise to me when Annemarie planned her own death.

I hadn't seen her in 30 years. I feared the possibility of being retained by East German authorities. However, the political climate changed in 1989 with the reunification of Germany. I decided to see Annemarie one more time.

When I announced my visit in 1994, Annemarie let me know that she didn't receive visitors. She stated that she was too old, too weak, and too ugly. I was told to remember our good times together.

Of course, I didn't believe her and insisted on making my trip to former East Germany, now part of a reunified Germany. Annemarie was ninety, and I knew she wouldn't be around much longer. I bought a train ticket to Zittau, took a taxi to Olbersdorf, and looked for the Wagner villa. An old village woman pointed me to the house and she couldn't believe that I was Mr. and Mrs. Wagner's granddaughter. In turn, I was shocked when I looked at one of Brother Grimm's castles, totally overgrown, where *Dornröschenchen* (Sleeping Beauty) slumbered in her hundred-year-old sleep.

The whole landscape had changed. A park with ancient trees was replaced by a soccer field, and the old factory stood deserted with occasional pigeons flying in and out of broken windows. The ugliest sight of all was a newly constructed steel mill, dominating half of the property.

I rang the doorbell at the iron gate. There was no answer and no movement. I looked at the upper window, peeking through some high beech trees. I repeated my ringing. No answer. But I knew my arthritis-plagued Annemarie sat in her padded chair, wondering why Mani would not take her seriously. I looked around, didn't see anybody, then I noticed the rusty mailbox with a clothespin holding a letter with my name, "To Mani, "it said. My hands trembled. I ripped the envelope open and read:

"Dear Mani,

My caretaker is writing this letter. I surmised you wouldn't heed my words when I asked you not to come. Nevertheless, my greetings to you. I have followed your life's story through Elisabeth and your Mutti. I admired your adventurous spirit and the drive with which you achieved what you wanted.

As I'm near death, things are prepared. Achim and Joe will handle my estate or what's left of it. You don't need to drag furniture to America. Your brothers can set smaller items aside for you. If you care to visit family members at the cemetery, you can find the Leupolds and Wagners next to each other at Zittau's cemetery. It is a lovely and well kept garden.

You know of course that Elisabeth didn't want to join us, and is buried in an unmarked grave in Karlsruhe. Quite typical for my sister. In 1981, when she flew to America to see you in Oklahoma at your first school assignment, I thought she was out of her mind to go so far, disregarding her poor health. When Elisabeth returned, she never stopped telling me about your good life over there. Your Omi would have been so happy to know that.

I will see all of them soon. I do not know what happened to my religion and my beliefs. I guess they got erased under the Nazis and Communists. I gave up worrying about anything, for I'm ready to go. I fought windmills of all kinds, bureaucracy, hypocrisy, overall ignorance, and most of all, stupidity. I probably failed you as a godmother, did the best I could. We had great fun together, especially in Schosdorf. Never forget this.

Blessings,

Your decrepit old Aunt Annemarie

I replaced the letter with a package of Annemarie's favorite *Bahlsen Kekse* (butter cookies), and stuck them into the mailbox. I left no note. Feelings overwhelmed me, and I rushed off. It was the strangest goodbye ever.

Both my parents had lived in a nursing home. Achim and his wife managed their affairs. In their last years, I flew annually to Germany and saw them like flickering candles, dying of lack of oxygen. Mutti remained alert to the end with an amazing keen mind. But she had returned to her earlier depressions, and I was distressed watching them ending their lives bedridden and without being able to console each other.

In his last days, Papa had a sudden awakening while I stood at his bedside. His eyes were shut when I talked to a nurse. My familiar voice triggered a reflex. Papa suddenly opened his eyes and said, "Are you Mani?" He shocked me. Mutti had warned me earlier and indicated that going to see him in the adjacent room would be useless. Papa had neither recognized nor spoken to anybody in many months.

"Yes, Papa, I came to say hello." I heard some mumbling and lowered my head down to his face. I substituted missing words to make sense of what he was trying to convey, but I could only discern the two words, "Viernheim" and "home." It hit me: he wanted to go home to his house in Viernheim. Instead, he was about to go to his heavenly home.

During Mutti's 10-year stay in senior care, I had weekly phone conversations with her. Mostly we discussed health-related concerns and exchanged family information with occasional surprising insights and revelations. All this brought me closer to her.

"Well, Mani, you broke out and made your life in the USA. It turned out fine for you."

"True." I said wondering why now, since I was gone for decades.

Mutti continued, "But your choices of earlier boyfriends were problematic."

"True again." This strange conversation today puzzled me. "What is Mutti trying to tell me?" I thought.

"First, you let Hans go who was a promising young man. Then you got engaged with Paul Buck who still wanted you after thirty years. Every year he came to see us. Nice fellow, however too old. By the time you decided to marry Bernard, I had given up."

"Mutti, why are telling me this today?" I asked.

"I need to make a confession...I handled another boyfriend of yours...," her voice sounded faint.

"You did what?" I perked up, trying to think back and remember another boyfriend she knew.

"This man quite charming, actually interesting to talk you. He seemed in love with you, had all these complications with the *Finanzamt* (IRS). And I learned he lived not too far from your father's. This story didn't sit right with me. Why would you keep him a secret?" Mutti trailed off, or was it only my perception? My hand started to shake as I held the receiver, and I had to control my voice when I said, "No, you didn't!" I was glad she wasn't sitting next to me.

Mutti wasn't finished yet and said, "Yes, I told him to call me back in a week so I could think things over. And he did, asking for my support to see and communicate with you. I reconsidered shortly, but told the man point blank that he'd better do everybody a favor and solve his personal problems before calling again. My daughter was too proud to run after a man or even call him." A long pause followed, and she added, "And I'm so glad that I was right."

I had heard enough. I didn't say anything, got up from the hard chair I had been sitting on during our conversation. I moved over a few steps, stretching the phone line, and let myself fall into a soft chair close by.

"Hallo, hallo…Mani, are you still there?" I heard her calling me over the line.

After a deep breath I answered, "Yes, but I barely hear you, Mutti. My phone is acting up. I'll call you back tomorrow." Click went the phone. I sat in my chair for a long time, eyes closed, almost paralyzed.

Mutti's intervention had killed my short-lived love. Even after so many years, it was hard to swallow this belated news. In the final analysis, however, Mutti helped me open the door to America.

More than 40 years have passed since Vati's sudden death. Vati had been retired since he was 60 because of a defective heart valve. He seemed in denial about his illness. Vati entered a private heart clinic and was given a good prognosis for survival. However, two days after a successful surgery, Vati died from kidney failure. At this time, I lived in Lawton, Oklahoma and had only written contact with him. In 1972, I wasn't aware of the severity of Vati's procedure and didn't know how compromised his general health had been already.

I was shocked. With a baby girl, six-month old, and a boy of over three, I hoped Vati would meet his grandchildren someday soon. Instead of this wish, I received a scalding letter from Else Hunger which I suspect Joe had to write. She accused me of being a neglectful daughter who didn't bother to call or send flowers to her sick father. I couldn't remember any phone calls from Vati's house to the States ever. In 1972, over sea's phone calls were costly, and I couldn't afford those on a sergeant's salary. I found it rather painful, how Else involved Joe in her scheming, and I never saw evidence of her writing ability other than of a short grocery list. Besides, Vati's death announcement was sent so late that it even prevented Achim from attending the funeral. At the time he had lived in Brussels, a couple of hours away.

Else had reverted back to the earlier image I had of her. This time, I cried and cried what Vati had missed in life, and the grandchildren he never met. What a sad end for a gifted man who wasn't allowed to maintain an equally healthy relationship with his three children.

With Vati's death, I slowly found peace. My harbored resentments toward him got finally buried with him in October 1972. Vati was a Mason and emphasized his affiliation to the

Lutheran Church, although he very seldom stepped foot into a church. I wasn't aware if he had a Christian funeral or a memorial. I do know that Vati adored his family history which was glorified with huge oil paintings for Else, Joe, and the world to admire. Ultimately, Joe would become the keeper and protector of many oversized paintings.

Achim and I were for the most part disinherited which explained Else's letter justifying Vati's last will and testament. As a token, Vati bequeathed his old violin to Achim. I was to receive one of Tante Male Male's Schosdorf landscapes I liked so much. Achim refused his inheritance, and I followed his example. In the end, it was the right decision. Achim and I freed ourselves from Else Hunger for good.

I'm astonished to have elaborated on the first 23 years of my life in Germany. These years pale in comparison to those over 50 years lived in the United States which truly became my number one homeland. But without my previous life, contrasting events, searches through ruins of places, broken families, and relationships, my new life in the United States of America couldn't have become more precious.

EPILOGUE

I entrusted my book for revision with four friends from our RCI-writers group. Meanwhile, I took off with my husband on a European river cruise that included several side trips. Rickie and I finished riding the Elbe River coming from Magdeburg, over Dresden upwards to Prague. Our Bavarian friends awaited us in the Czech Republic and took us on an adventure tour to Poland, in search of – what turned out to be like searching for the Holy Grail. I looked for the remnants of my childhood paradise - the estate outside Schosdorf – which had fallen into a noxious dream, totally destroyed and held tight by century old trees and thick shrubbery. 69 years passed since I last saw the place. During this time, jungle-like growth created a new paradise for strange and uninvited wild life.

In August 1944, when I was six years old, I remembered our estate in Silesia. In old German records, still existing today in Polish records, my grandparents' land was referred to as a *Rittergut* (Knights estates). We saw the very same land. Missing were the haystacks from the 40's, and no modern machinery anywhere. Maybe the heavy rains had kept farmers from taking their machines out into the fields. I recalled the pure melted gold of another rich harvest. *Was it already more than half a century ago? Remember 69 years back.* The red poppies and blue corn flowers were gone, now replaced with overgrown weeds. The landscape was unchanged, rolling fields of barley and wheat stretched over a wide area, interrupted here and there with patches of forest and groves of trees.

Over its lifetime, how often did this house greet visitors and whisper stories of splendid summer vacations? During my generation, our personal world was still a whole one: love, peace, and a comfortable security embraced my childhood.

Aunt Annemarie passed away at a very ripe age. She loved her years in Schosdorf as the family's farm administer. When I lived in Germany, I frequently talked with her about this area of Lower Silesia east of the Oder/Neisse/Line as it was referred to after WWII. Of course, Germany lost this land to Poland. But my aunt knew my inquisitive nature and warned me repeatedly never to return to see the estate.

Three generations later, the village's name changed from Schosdorf to Ubosce. I recalled Annemarie's robust voice fainting with age into a whimpering when she spoke of her lost land.

"Mani, they burned down the place and left the fields fallow for years - actually decades." Annemarie's impossible dream to be buried in Schosdorf remained a wish.

My life turned out differently from hers and far removed from my origins. I honored Aunt Annemarie's memory, but my yearning to return one day stayed alive.

An earlier attempt to go to Poland in summer 1994 failed. At that time, I rented a car in Germany and waited on the German-Polish border. But my attempts were in vain, for certain rules kept me from crossing over. German rentals were prohibited from crossing the border. Besides, there was a convoy of mile-long trucks lined up to have their papers cleared. I concluded that my trip back into history wasn't meant to be after all, and I heard Annemarie's warning ring in my ears. In fact, border personnel informed me of an eight-hour wait. "Mani I told you so, are you ever going to learn?" Annemarie's raspy laugh felt like she wanted to call me once more *Zimttüte*. She realized that I had become an adult.

But in 2013, my vision to return took on a new meaning. My book longed for closure. Pure serendipity changed this luck. I do believe that a forgotten prayer was answered. It was timely, indeed.

A cousin of a German friend of ours came to New Braunfels. The famous Wurstfest was in full swing. We hosted both Hans and Cousin Karl-Heinz. During the cousins' stay I mentioned my book. Karl-Heinz showed immediate interest and wanted to know details. So he helped me with a Google search to locate my family's estate in Poland. Karl-Heinz, well aware of my excitement, was caught up in my story. He inquired about specific war experiences of my family.

Spontaneously, Karl-Heinz offered to drive us the next summer to Schosdorf. With Internet pictures in hand, he and his wife met us at the end of July 2013. We set out from Prague, where our Viking Elbe River cruise had ended.

I was prepared with maps and old family shots reaching back as far as the year 1924. Among the photos, I found views of the original exterior and interior of the house including one with uniformed coachman Jan holding the reins. Mutti wore a foxy straw hat and my brother and I sat next to her, ready to get off at the estate's entrance. Another picture showed Omi, taken in 1926, sitting with kitty, Putzi, in the "garden room." For a modern observer, the setting was too fancy to match the image of a winter garden. But I saw glimpses of the nineteenth century.

Reminiscing about my happy childhood years in Schosdorf, I couldn't hold back tears when I considered the possibility that Karl-Heinz was willing to take us there.

"Honestly, that's no problem." As we got closer to our overseas travel, he reassured me various times. "I'll make a short vacation with my wife and meet you in Prague. Besides, we have a van from our wine business that will comfortably travel and carry four people's luggage." He sounded convincing and confident.

It came to pass. Up to the very moment we connected in the Czech Republic, I was in doubt. "Why would Karl-Heinz and his wife, Gerlinde care about our old homestead?" But they did, and their patience was incredible as we drove north through the Czech Republic and entered Poland – no checkpoint this time – into a much poorer country than its neighbors, the Czech Republic and Germany. At least, that's what I observed in the rural and border areas of Poland.

The roads were windy and deserted. We drove through the *Isergebirge*, part of the *Riesengebirge* (Giant Mountains) with elevations not higher than 5,256 ft. Growing up, I heard and sang folks songs about the friendly giant, *Rübezahl* who lived there and protected good people. It touched me as incredible that I'd visit the original places. My childhood's fantasies calmly presented themselves in a vast and lonely landscape – with only dots of human habitations, sleeping away their century-old existence.

Not far past the mountains, we drove through rolling hills of meadows, fields of wheat and strips of forest. On the narrow road, well suited for one-way traffic, Karl-Heinz hugged the shoulders skillfully and maneuvered around many turns and through several isolated villages. "Where are the people on a hot summer's day?" I thought.

The first small town on our GPS was Gryfice, formerly Greiffenberg.

"That's it!" I cried out.

Karl-Heinz seemed surprised. "You said it was Schosdorf."

"Sorry – you are correct. But this is the next little town where we used to buy supplies."

Karl-Heinz slowed the van and spoke into his rear-view-mirror to make eye contact with me. "Would you care to see the center of the town?"

I had to control myself and not shout out for joy. "I was here 100 years ago." Shaken to my bones, I felt the buggy rattling over the town's square, just as it felt then. "How unreal. All the houses used to look grey...and look now...the town is painted over with colors of magical pastels. Just like a Hollywood scene."

"Do you recognize the town?" Karl-Heinz checked with his mirror. He had the biggest smile of satisfaction on his face. I must have given him a transfixed expression of happiness. It was contagious.

"Hey, here's the train station, Manuela." Karl-Heinz stopped a moment and offered to let me look around. But I declined and assured him that I was searching for a different train station, the one of Schosdorf. Back to the 40's – I recalled - we left the train – only a whistle stop – and it couldn't have been Schosdorf since the village was so small.

My idea became my friend's command. Karl-Heinz drove off, following the signs to Hirschberg, Jelenia Gora. We left the village of Schosdorf behind as nothing seemed familiar to me. Instead, our attention was directed to roadwork and various detours on account of previous flooding. Usually the creek was held in a low canal-like bed a good six feet below the street's surface, but during June the water had risen and caused an awful flood. Miniature machinery did road work, and men in long rubber boots swung their shuffles.

It was past lunch time. Rick and I nibbled on fruits and dry bread. Our friends with different eating habits felt okay driving until late that day. It was Thursday, August 1, 2013. The adventure's suspense held me by the neck. But growing anxiousness crept into my body as we headed toward Jelenia Gora. 20 kilometers down the same road, I concluded that we had to turn around.

"I am afraid that's too far out." I told Karl-Heinz. "Our place belonged to the community of Schosdorf. But I'm confused as to the railroad which ran on a dam above the town."

"*Macht nichts,*" and with this, Karl-Heinz made the most elegant U-turn, possibly only done by a European male. "*Kopf hoch* (heads up). We'll find it."

Gosh, I was glad that our friend was confident. I had a dreadful sinking feeling. I had definitely taken my friends on a wild goose chase.

Along the way and back to Schosdorf, I regained my composure. Karl-Heinz stopped a few times along the way to ask people for information. All I could observe was shoulder shrugging, head shaking and a person mouthing a long Nooooo. Suddenly a bicyclist came along, swiftly passing on the opposite side. Karl-Heinz screeched to a halt, and so did the young man on his bike.

We encountered the first human being that actually spoke English. Yes, he motioned, straight ahead, turn at the monastery…bad road…maybe walk…way out there.

"Do you know by any chance an Internet café?" I heard Karl-Heinz ask the man.

"No. Only library open for three hours." And he pointed in yet another direction.

"Thanks, dankeschön und aufwiedersehn."

Another exploration to the mentioned monastery brought us nowhere. I looked for the old gravel road leading away from the railroad stop. Instead, I saw Schosdorf from all sides, up and down every little hill. The picture needed one more puzzle piece.

As we returned to the center of the village, I spotted a long plain yellow building with a sign not larger than a computer screen. I read, *"Bibliotece."*

"Karl-Heinz, stop. Back up. I believe this long building is the library."

And it was. We waited outside as our friend disappeared inside the house, two steps up, into the "library."

I sat in the car with frosty hands in spite of it being 90 degrees Fahrenheit and climbing. The van's air conditioner had quit. My head was spinning, thinking about my diabetic husband in a hot vehicle and friends who had driven five hours to Prague and two, maybe three hours to Poland. And this crazy writer had her apparition and was trying to pinpoint a forsaken spot in a vast landscape after almost 70 years had passed. The search was nothing short of the proverbial needle in a hay stack. "God give me grace to get out of this predicament. It involves three other people, a lot of good will, several tanks of expensive gas, and lodging expenses"

God did answer. The house's door opened and a cherry-red-haired female waved us in. We were like long lost family who came to visit. Gerlinde, Karl's wife, Rick, and I climbed stiffly out of the van and followed our invitation.

"*Guten Tag, ich bin Joanna.*" The librarian stretched out her hand and greeted one after another with a firm shake.

Everybody smiled, as we turned around and looked, observing our surroundings, part school house, and part library, and also temporary workshop for an upcoming wedding.

My travel companions faded in the background as I conversed in German with my new-found friend, Joanna. I tried to speak very slowly and in a very basic German to make Joanna understand what brought me all the way from Texas. Then I showed her faded black-white pictures and an Internet printout depicting the old family estate in its glory days.

"*Ja, ja, ja, ja, ich rufe Freundin.*" Animated and happy to indulge me, she spoke in pantomime style. Then she took her cell phone out of her Capri pants and called several friends to help us find the estate.

"*Warte bitte*" (Wait a minute). With this, she ran to the library room, part of the room, to retrieve typed pages in document covers.

"We had three palaces around Shosdorf. Is this one of them?"

I noticed that she said Schosdorf and not Ubosce. I appreciated her sensibility as I spoke and remembered pre-war conditions from my childhood. Joanna studied the old pictures with people out of the 1920s, an ornate house, almost 300 years old with interior furniture to match.

"No, this is not our palace," I told her. The description palace surprised me a bit. But Joanna, who was around 40 years old, obviously of Polish and Slavic decent, was far removed from my German ancestry of a middle-upper-money class, early manufacturing people in Saxony.

Joanna and I exchanged e-mail addresses. Since she showed interest, I promised to send her a history of the estate with names of the people who used to own the place. But I had yet to see the ancient house. I used my waiting time to bond with the librarian and teacher of first, second, and third graders, and then I took pictures and told her that I had taught as well. Her students had left for the day, and we caught her during her three-hour duty as a librarian. Perfect timing. In reality, she was working on wedding decorations for her son, Gregory.

I was confused and very emotional. It overwhelmed me to consider all the people involved in work on my behalf and in three different languages. In fact, they all dropped everything to help me locate an old estate. At this moment it hit me like a lightning strike.

"This is my forgotten prayer that I'd come back one day. And this day was here." I was showered with happiness, and this was the second perfect timing of the day.

Joanna's girlfriend turned out to be a man. Well, just a language difference between male and female. Farmer "Joe" in blue bibs had dropped his lawn mower and rushed to meet us. I honestly didn't know; he may have been after all a professor on vacation. He looked clean, hands washed, big smile on his sun-burned, reddish face as he greeted us in Polish. His name could have easily been Josef.

Two pairs of hands were flying. Joanna and Josef communicated with each other. I understood she conveyed my story, and he told her he knew the location. His mother used to live there right after the war. Nodding heads, broad smiles from him and her, and I was told once more to wait to see if Irena, an over 80-year-old woman, could be located. After some additional calls from Josef and Joanna, I knew

Josef would take us to Miss Irena.

Thus we bid goodbye to Joanna. We hugged and smiled, and I promised pictures for her missing third "palace." Outside the building, the lovely teacher/librarian waved us on. I noticed her white pants, stylish wedge sandals and a brightly yellow T-shirt and her red hair catching the summer's sunshine. What a godsend she was! I loved her generosity and sensitivity about past wars that had changed landscapes, erased original settlers, and transplanted another people who themselves had become uprooted.

Joe jumped together with us into the van. Slender Gerlinde climbed into the van's back, barely accommodating her among the entire luggage. Apparently we were on our way to pick up the old lady, Irena, to come with us to the farm. After some turns, Joe motioned to make a left turn into a small farm with a smaller brick building in front of an elongated house with rows of small windows, decorated with pink hanging geraniums. Pretty. A small dog of unknown genetics barked at our car. He backed off when Joe got out to see if Irena was available.

Miss Irena apparently heard her dog barking and came running from her house. We couldn't follow their Polish conversation, but she gave a broad toothless smile toward the car and looked at our German license plate. Then she wiped her wet hands on a wrap-around apron, probably her summer wardrobe, and glanced at her shoes - plastic kind of house slippers – and seemed to find them in order. Miss Irena called her little dog, chasing him into the house. Three minute's preparation and Irena was ready to go. She never locked the house and was willing to go for a ride and show strange German folk the old, dilapidated place.

"*Alles kaputt,*" she surprised me with her broken,

childlike German. *"Ja, ja ich spreche Deutsch."* I was told that she came from Posen in 1945, former West Prussia when she was twelve years old. "We live out there and I learn German with children for long, long time."

Meanwhile, we all settled into the van. Six people total, six bags of luggage stowed away in a German van which, of course, is a miniature version of an American van. Gerlinde, a quiet woman, smiled as I checked on her. "It's okay for a short trip," she assured me.

Irena's constant chatter distracted me from trying to orient myself. I still wasn't quite sure where we would cross the railroad. And when we did, I turned around toward Schosdorf and saw the familiar film in my head. It was running in slow motion, and yes, there was the ancient train station – all deserted – but standing as if left from the last Hitchcock movie set. Strangely, it was suddenly on the wrong side of the road. Did my child's mind play a dirty trick on me, or what? But on second thought, had the crossing been moved over about 200 yards?

"Alles kaputt," I heard Irena once more. "People take all. Table, chair, picture, and carry away."

"Yes, I can imagine…a deserted place and displaced folks with nothing." I added. "I wasn't blaming everybody, just paying a visit after 69 years, you know," I told her truthfully.

"Irena, who does it belong to now?" I was curious to know.

"Poland."

It wasn't the answer I wanted to hear, but dropped it.

"Nobody seems to take care of the land like it used to be. Even the gravel road is covered by mud and knee-high grass," I thought.

The van came to a sudden stop as Joe called out "halt." He jumped out and examined the path step by step. Then he raised one hand and indicated the end of our little trip. We all got out and fought our way through mud and sticks, and Irena chirped optimistically.

"*Schon hier,*" (Already here). But I couldn't see anything but a grove of century-old trees, oaks and lime trees. So we walked on for fifteen more minutes and I didn't mind the mud around me, nor ticks descending upon us, bees buzzing, and critters scurrying through the grass. I looked around and saw expanding fields. I was able to "see" the old sight of golden wheat, rolling with the land, only interrupted by intermittent forest and groves. The smell of harvest time intermingled with the sounds chirping birds. Up ahead, I saw pieces of a structure peaking through greenery.

I knew we had found the Wagner estate.

My heart jumped like it did earlier in Greiffenberg's town square. My happiness was a mixture of bittersweet homecoming. Suddenly, a scream interrupted my contemplations and I heard somebody in our party holler "snake." From a dreamlike state I jumped into the stark reality of time and place.

"We never had snakes," I assured everybody.

"But you do now. Watch as you pass! It's a black snake, probably harmless," Karl-Heinz said.

Coming closer to the stone structure, I recognized the former gate. My imagination added immediately the missing fancy wrought-ironed gate of an eight-foot-high door with a matching fence sitting on top of a three-foot rock base that originally demarked some of the estate's property. The gate's post still had its shingled top, matching the house's pointed roof. It fascinated me that this post had stood guard for centuries and exposed the added electricity lines. Its cut wires stuck out from two remaining porcelain insulators. To me it was a symbol of a cut lifeline.

Still hearing Irena's "*alles kaput*," I tried to have my quiet reflections. I stayed with my group for five more minutes as we saw the first signs of abuse and neglect. Bottles, both plastic and glass mingled with rusty cans, and a previously deserted campfire spoke of parties unknown to its original owners. I felt numb, but unemotional. It looked like a crime scene without its staked yellow ribbons. But who would find fault after three generations of decay and youngsters partying, totally ignorant about the site they defiled? No blame.

Irena took me by the hand and pulled me toward the house. Bony hands with a strong-willed purpose, I thought. One picture depicting my grandmother in one of the rooms excited Irena's memory. "I remember the furniture – all gone – all taken –*alles kaput.*" She parroted once more. But I allowed her to lead me to the room where the furniture stood in 1944.

Three walls of the house were standing. The empty windows of the remaining first floor stared at us like blind people begging for charity. I indulged Irena – and she did find the correct room. No wonder, she had lived out here in one of the servants' quarters after her family had come from East Prussia in the summer of 1945. She probably knew who took the furniture, but I didn't care to know for my purpose in coming here was not to bemoan political changes.

At last, I was alone with the old estate. My friends and chattering Irena stayed on safer ground. I crawled around the wet ruins and made my way to the back of the house where the kitchen was located. I could see the staircase inside. It was hanging on an imaginary silk thread. I crawled, climbed, slipped on mossy stones and chased away disturbed bees and wasps to claim my spot next to the window and a door. The temptation to step inside was overwhelming, but my earlier fall convinced me that the exposed rotten floorboard probably couldn't hold me. Possible rats in the house's cellar didn't excite me the least. What horror. I knew that my searching in ruins had ended for good.

For a moment I gathered myself. "Premonition Woman, do you recognize the granddaughter of Ilse Wagner? I came to greet you." With those thoughts, I climbed on yet another rock which had settled near the kitchen's window and stuck my head inside as far as I possibly could do.

The unusual summer's heat was oppressive that day. But here, I felt a cool, eerie draft coming from a tomb. I was neither sad nor scared, but alert to perceive even the slightest scurrying of an insect. War and its after effects had erased our personal paradise. But I was calm to the point of being sedated. Any message – if ever possible – could reach me now. The message came instantly:

"It is peace now – Rest your mind."

After returning to New Braunfels, Texas, I researched on the Internet, "German influence in Poland." In my surfing attempts I found a site with a man who spoke both German and Polish and who cited passages from a large book. With paper and pen in hand, I copied what caught my interest. Thus I formed the following verse into an English rendition without being able to credit the author.

"Instability leaves its tracks.
Nature plays with sadness and joy.
Laws of this life – I play with nature,
And I take its light and darkness."

And so my search ended. Three precious items from the destroyed house made it home with me. A five inch heavy nail, a piece of white kitchen tile, and a splinter of the slate roof traveled to Texas. Another tempting sliver of weathered, curled up wallpaper caught my attention. I left it untouched. The reach from the hollow window's perch was too precarious. Just in time, the *Pemonition Woman* exerted her warning power one more time. I felt an arm pulling me back. Indeed, it was another remarkable timing to keep me from bodily harm. "The search of ruins is over." I was made to understand.

My forgotten prayer was answered, leaving me happy and satisfied. This last excursion into an adventure-filled past filled my heart with gladness and gratefulness. My homecoming to Texas and New Braunfels was accompanied by a renewed feeling of peace. No more ruins for me, for new life has replaced the old. A new chapter has just opened for me to explore.

THE END

Acknowledgement

Barbara O'Connor invited me to join their group; otherwise my sketchy writing would have lain around unfinished. Many heartfelt thanks to *River City Ink* in New Braunfels, Texas who helped me immensely. My other writer friends are: Stefanie Daily, Joy Elkins, Frank Kavanaugh, Alexandra Marbach and Naomi Patterson. Their suggestions sharpened my writing. I thank my Dallas editor, Julie Richie, who read with special attention to details. My dear friend, Maria Roberson corrected my computer glitches and calmed me down when I was about to pull my hair. Once again, Barbara O'Connor gave me the technical support to finish the job.

I like to mention another writer, my daughter, Bettina Restrepo-Williford who suggested for years that Mom should take up writing. Since then, we have used each other as sounding board for creative ideas and literary know-how. In addition, I gratefully acknowledge scholarships received from Cameron University in Lawton, Oklahoma and from the State of Oklahoma and my professors who encouraged me along the way.

My husband, Rick, soul mate, dance partner and German singing buddy, cheered me on and never complained even when sometime I was late serving supper.

GLOSSARY

Abitur	Baccalaureate, diploma for entering a university
Achim	Short form for Joachim, author's brother
Albert	Albert Wagner (Opa), Omi's second husband
Alle hinsetzen	You'all sit down (Texas jargon)
Alles ist gut	All is well
Annemarie	Aunt Annemarie, author's aunt, Vati's sister
Arbeitsamt	Employment office
Aschi	Nickname for author's brother, Achim
Auf der Heide blühlt ein kleines Blümelein, und das heißt Erika …	Soldiers marching song. (On the heather blooms a little flower
Auf Wiedersehen	Goodbye
Autobahn	German Interstate
Baccalaureate	Proof of baccalaureate to enter a university in Germany
Baden-Württemberg	Southern German state w. capital: Stuttgart
Bahnhof	Train station
Betreten verboten	No trespassing
Bienel	Nickname for grand-uncle Eberhard
Bettfedernfabrik	Featherbed Factory
bitte	please
Bitte festhalten	Please hang on
BDM	Bund Deutscher Mädchen, organization for girls during Third Reich under Hitler
Bundesrepublik	Federal Republic of Germany
Carl Teichmann	Author's paternal great-great-grandfather, father of Frida Leupold (Urmi)

Danke	Thank you
Danke schön	Thank you
Das Dritte Reich	The Third Reich (Hitler's Germany)
DDR	German Democratic Republic (Former Communist East Germany)
Deutsche Fahne(n)	German Flag(s)
Deutscher Gruß	German Salute (*Heil Hitler*)
Die Schwaben	People from the state Württemberg (Stuttgart area)
Dirn	Plattdeutsch word for Mädchen (girl)
Dirndl	Bavarian, Austrian custom dress
Doktor	Doctor (medical) or title
drüben	Over there, on the other side
Einwanderer	immigrant
Dr. Richard Bender	Paul Buck's friend
Dr. Paul Buck	The man the author didn't marry
Brüssel	Brussels
Dr. Joe Hunger	Author's half-brother, born in 1950
Dr. Joachim Hunger	Author's brother, born in 1940
Dr. Leonhard Müller	High school teacher in Mannheim
Elefant(en)	Elephant(s)
Elisabeth Wagner-Goerner	Daughter of Albert Wagner, my step-grandfather
Else Hunger	Author's stepmother, second wife of her father
enteignet	Disowned
Gerlinde Schafberger	German friends in München ,Germany
Frau	Woman or Mrs.
Frau Mutter	Formal: "Mrs. Mother"
Fräulein	Miss or Ms.
Frida	First name of author's great-grandmother, nickname: Urmi
Führer	Leader
Fußball	Soccer
Gesellschaft	Company

Searching the Ruins

Gestapo	Geheime Staats Polizei (Secret Service during Hitler's regime)
Johann Wolfgang von Goethe	German writer, poet, artist, and politician, 1749
Gosse	Gutter
Glocke	"Bell", referred to famous German poem, written by Schiller
Guten Morgen	Good Morning
Grüß Gott	Hello, how are you, used in Southern Germany
Handarbeit	Handwork such as needle work, crocheting and knitting
Hauptbahnhof	Main train station
Hedi	Short form of Hedwig, Author's mother(Mutti)
Hans Wund	Author's first boyfriend in Mannheim
Helga Knosp-Feuerstein	Author's life-long girlfriend in Stuttgart
Herr	Mister
Hesslach	One of Stuttgart's neighborhoods
Hitler Jugend	Hitler Youth, an organization
Hitlergruß	"Heil Hitler"
Hochdeutsch	High German, standardized German for official use
Hund	Dog
Ilse	First name of author's paternal grandmother(Omi)
Jahresaufsatz	Large essay assignment during one school year
Joachim	Male name, short form Achim or Jochen
Kachelofen	Hearth
Kaiserin	Empress
Karl-Heinz Schafberger	German friends from München
Katzentisch	"Cats Table" – small table for children
Klassiker	Classical writers such as Goethe and

	Schiller etc.
Klauer	Thief
Kleid(er)	Dress(es)
Klein(adj.)	Small, little
Kleine(n)	Little one
Kleine Kinder	Small children
Kristallnacht	Crystal Night, Nov.1938 Nazi regime attacked Jewish businesses and synagogues
Kultur Minister	Cultural Minister in Germany
Lausitz	Lusatia, a region in the Saxony, Germany
Leiterwagen	Wooden hand pulled cart to haul household goods
Leitz	Brand name for office folders
Leute	People
Male Male	A child's created name for a painter
Mama	Name for Mutter (mother)
Mani	Manuela's nickname
Marie(chen)	Great Aunt in Dresden, married to Felix Teichmann (son of Author's great-great-grandfather's Carl Teichmann's first marriage)
Marine	The German Navy
Mark	Name of German paper money prior to the Euro
Meine Lieben	My dear (plural)
Militär Lazarett Betten	Surplus army hospital beds (folding cots)
Misthaufen	Heap of manure
Mutter	Mother
Möricke, Eduard	Swabian poet, writer, and pastor, 1804-1875
Müller, Dr. Leonhard	Author's high school teacher, became a state minister for Baden-Württemberg
Mutterkreuz	"Mother Cross"- Nazi medal for mothers with four or more children
Mutti	Name for mother (Mutter)
Nazi	National Socialist German Workers Party

Oberschule (Gymnasium)	High school
Oma	Name for grandmother, Author mentions Oma Bauer, mother of Theo Bauer and 2. wife of Opa Körber, maternal grandfather of author
Oma-Kleidung	Vintage clothes, old fashioned
Omi	Author called her grandmother Omi
Onkel	Uncle
Opa	Name for grandfather, author called Albert Wagner and Heinrich Körber Opa
Pferdeäpfel	Droppings of horses
Papa Theo	Name for stepfather
Paß auf	Pay attention
Planken	Major shopping area of Mannheim
Plattdeutsch	Low German dialect
Po	Derriere
Professor	Title
Reich (noun)	Empire, but reich (adj.)means rich
Rhein	Rhine
Richard	Grandfather Richard, Omi's 1. husband
Rittergut	Knight's manor and landholdings
Riesengebirge and Isergebirge	Giant Mountains (now in Czech Republic)
Ruhe	Silence
Saft	Juice
Sauber(le)	Clean, (le added is dialect)
Sauerei , Schweinerei	Big mess, pigsty
Sauere Nieren	Sweet-sour kidneys
Schieber	Eating utensils for little children to push food
Schinken	Ham, in story used as colloquialism
Sachsen	Saxony, a German state
Schiller, Johann von	German poet, philosopher, historian, and playwright, around Stuttgart, 1759-1805
Schneefuß, Mr.	Author's swim coach in Stuttgart

Schwäbisch	Swabian (adj.) dialect around Stuttgart
Schwimmerbund Schwaben	Name of swim club
schön	Pretty, beautiful
Schlesien	Silesia, pre-WWII German state, now in Poland
Schlitterbah n	Sled ride
Schuhe	Shoes
Schultüte	Traditional sugar cone for first-graders
Schwabe(n)	Swabian(s), a person from the Stuttgart area
Seelsorger	Person working in the ministry (administration)
Sehr gut	Very good
Seifenhandel	Compound word, made up from soap and trade, used as a German metaphor for contraband goods
St. Nikolaus Tag	Dec. 6th is Germany's St. Nick's Day
Straße	Street
Swastika	Nazi symbol like a Greek cross with the four ends of the arms bent in a clockwise direction
Tante	Aunt
Trümmerfrauen	Women cleaning bricks out of ruins for recycling
Überraschung	Surprise
Uhr(en)	Watch(es), or clock(s)
und	and
Urmi	Nickname for Author's great-grandmother
Ute	Wife of author's brother Achim
Vater	Father
Vati	Name for author's birth father
verboten	Forbidden
Versicherung	Insurance
verstanden	Understood
Volksschule	Elementary school
Willkommen	Welcome

Wirtschaftswunder	Economic Wonder, a German concept
Wund	Family name of first boyfriend
wunderbar	Wonderful
Zimttüte	Made up family word, translated: bag of cinnamon
Zuckertüte	Same as Schultüte, a cone filled with candy
Zuwanderer	Immigrant, another German word: Einwanderer

Made in the USA
San Bernardino, CA
10 March 2015